THE SWASTIKA AND THE EDELWEISS

by

Rabbit Warren

Text and Cover Design:
copyright©2025 Ian Roger Burton
All Rights Reserved

Books by Rabbit Warren

Historic Novels:

Let Sleeping Nazis Lie

The Swastika and the Edelweiss

Short Stories of the Supernatural and Sinister:

The Madman and other Tales with a Chilling Twist

Tragic and Twisted Tales of Unexpected Death

Autobiographic:

My Dreams and Travels

My Dreams in the Alps

Children´s Fantasies:

The Fantastic World of BOZ

Charming Stinkers

The Gremlin of Nogoland

Gogonuts

Big Bloke and the Nightmare Aliens

The Curse of Griffin George

Escape to the Dream King

The Pixie´s Magic Christmas

This book is dedicated to the memory of the 110,000 Austrian Resistance fighters between 1938 and 1945, including the 2,700 who were executed by the Nazis

Picture: Liberation Arch, Innsbruck, Austria

Contents

Author´s Notes on the Facts behind the Story 7

Map of the Gletschberg Mountains and Valleys ...14

Map of Gletschberg am Brenner............................15

Plan of the Schillings´ Chalet 16

1: Flash-forward: The Battle of Hitler´s Birthday .18

2: The Man with one Testicle 30

3: Brothers at War...43

4: Silent Night, Nazi Night 56

5: The Worst Bully in the Village...........................66

6: Spying on the Nazis 76

7: Revenge of the Nazis 84

8: The Nazi Boxing Tournament 97

9: The Unexpected Hero of the Day 109

10: Treason in our Family.....................................119

11: The Mystery of the Star of David 138

12: A Test of Courage...150

13: The Summer of the Long Knives...................158

14: A Little Piece of History.................................168

15: The Death of Austria 178

16: The Terror of Franz Hofer 192

17: The Secret Sign of "Oh-Five"	207
18: Wild Passions of the Heart	218
19: A Day of Tragedy	234
20: In the Jaws of Hell	248
21: Enemies of the People	261
22: The Darkest Nights	274
23: Ten Little Nazis	288
24: Truth and Torture	306
25: Don´t Look Behind	328
26: Ghosts on the Mountain	345
27: The Spirit of Adventure	356
28: Living with God	369
29: The Edelweiss Blooms Again	381
Timeline of National Events	394
Glossary with Editorial Notes	399
Bibliography	434
About the Author	436
Also by Rabbit Warren	437
Children´s Fantasies by Rabbit Warren	439

Author's Notes on the Facts behind the Story

This is a work of fiction that is based on true events and incidents that occurred in the Austrian Tyrol during the two eras of Austro-Fascism and Nazi Austria. The national events that are mentioned really did play out as described.

Nazi intimidation and acts of terrorism such as are described really did occur in many of the villages and especially Innsbruck after Hitler came to power in Germany in January, 1933. Also, in spite of the fact that the Austro-Fascist dictator Dollfuss outlawed the Nazis that same June, the Nazis continued to thrive, sometimes secretly, sometimes openly.

The descriptions of huge swastikas being lit on the mountain sides, firecrackers being thrown at unsuspecting people, swastikas and Stars of David being painted on people's property and other forms of harassment are all true, just as some of the victims of these harassments, especially Jews, did indeed commit suicide. It is likewise true that a Tyrolean was shot because he refused to divorce his Jewish wife.

Gletschberg is, however, an entirely fictional village, as are the names and layout of the mountains in its vicinity, as well as the Devil's

Bridge. On the other hand, the village of Ehrwald is entirely real, being a ski and alpine resort on the Austrian side of the Zugspitz mountain.

Castle Jitter is, however, fictional, although its name derives from Castle Itter near Kufstein, which was where the "last and strangest battle" of World War Two was fought on the Fifth of May, 1945. This was because it was one of only two battles in the War where a rebel German force helped an American force to fight the German enemy.

The other battle had been "Operation Cowboy" in Bohemia just a week before, when the famous Lipizzaner horses of the Vienna Spanish Riding School were rescued from the battle-front. This became the subject of an unusual 1963 Walt Disney movie, "Miracle of the White Stallions".

Although Franz Hofer had already surrendered Innsbruck just two days before on the Third of May, an over-zealous S.S. Tank Grenadier division decided to attack the castle. This had served as a prison for notable French prisoners and was now occupied by a small American force, as well as two German forces who had just joined up with the Resistance.

However, this unique combination of forces would not have been able to hold the castle for more than a day and only won the battle when a large U.S. force later appeared that afternoon. In true Wild West movie style one of the castle´s handymen (a Yugoslav communist Resistance fighter) had been able to sneak out and alarm the equivalent of the relief U.S. Cavalry.

There are many "Klosters" (that is, monasteries and nunneries) to be found in Tyrol and the Inn Valley, with Kloster Stams probably being the most impressive to be found in the countryside (although it is in fact a "Stift" or collegial church). The Double Kloster of Saint Jerome and the village of Sachs are, however, entirely fictional.

The charismatic personality of Father Gabriel is inspired by a wonderful trade school teacher who once taught me in Bavaria. By co-incidence, the resistance fighter Heinrich Maier was also a very charismatic priest who ran a cell in Vienna. As a "legitimist", his cell not only wanted to free Austria from Nazi Germany but also wanted to restore the monarchy with the Habsburgs back on the throne. Maier was caught in February, 1944 and was endlessly tortured until he was finally executed a year later.

The Battle of Hitler´s Birthday is inspired by the so-called "Hoetting Hall Battle" that occurred in the Gemeinde (Borough) of Hoetting (now part of Innsbruck) in May, 1932. 150 Social Democrats tried to disrupt a meeting of 120 Nazis that was taking place in the "Golden Bear" guest-house, even though the Nazis had been given permission by the authorities to hold it. In spite of the police tying to intervene, violence was inevitable, with one Nazi dying from a knife through his heart and thirty-eight other people being injured. Although the Social

Democrats then tried to blame the Nazis for provoking them by holding such a meeting in a Socialist Gemeinde, most people agreed with the Nazis when they blamed the Socialists for infiltrating their meeting, especially as many of the Socialists had at first masqueraded as being Nazis.

The Heimwehr was a general name for the paramilitary wings of several right-wing groups throughout Austria and which occasionally even supported the Nazis. The Heimatwehr was a specific Tyrolean force that was originally formed by Richard Steidle in 1920. All these groups were vehemently opposed to the Social Democrats and Communists, as were the Nazis.

Franz Hickl and Franz Hofer were real people and are described as such, even though they never actually visited the fictional Gletschberg. Other historic figures include the national leaders Adolf Hitler, Engelbert Dollfuss and Kurt Schuschnigg.

The building that housed the police headquarters where Franz Hickl was shot dead on its door-step still exists today as Herrengasse 1. It was later used by the Gestapo as their own headquarters and today houses the State Building Projects Directorate of Tyrol. A memorial plaque to Robert Moser, a Resistance fighter who was tortured to death there in 1945, was placed next to its entrance in the 1990s.

The concentration camp in Rossau in Innsbruck was also real, although it wasn´t in fact opened until August, 1941. 8,500 prisoners were interred here during the Second World War. At least 130 of these died from either deliberate murder, brutal mistreatment or disease, even though the camp was supposed to only be a "labor camp" and was often used as a stop-over to other camps. A recycling station now stands on the site of the camp and has a large memorial plaque at its entrance.

The Heil and Pflege Klinik ("Cure and Care Clinic") in the town of Hall just to the east of Innsbruck is now the Psychiatric Hall of the Landkrankenhaus (State Hospital). It was indeed one of the hospitals where the "Aktion T4" euthanasian program on the intellectually disabled was followed through, with 360 patients being transported to two clinics in Upper Austria, where they were murdered with a drug overdose. The graves of 228 of these victims were discovered in the hospital grounds in 2011, with this site now being a memorial.

A huge liberation arch was built by the French occupying forces of Tyrol between 1946 and 1948 in Innsbruck to commemorate the Austrian Resistance victims of the Nazis. Altogether 107 names were originally listed on the walls of the arch, with another sixteen being added in 2015. This stands in the middle of the Eduard-Wallnoefer-Platz, which was until 1994 officially called the Landhausplatz and is still popularly known as such, since it lies directly before the so-called New Landhaus (that is, Tyrol´s state government house).

Hitler was obsessed with grandiose state buildings and huge parade grounds. As such, he not only wanted Berlin to have these amenities but also each of the capitals of the so-called Gaus (counties) of Germany and Greater Germany. The Nazis therefore immediately built the New Landhaus in 1938-9, with the so-called "Old" Landhaus having been built in the eighteenth century in the city center close by. The Nazis´ plans for the parade square, however, had to be put on hold when the War broke out. It was finished after the War with the building of the Liberation Arch, with part of it today being used as a skate-boarding park.

A small memorial commemorating Innsbruck´s Jewish victims of the Pogrom murders of the Ninth of November, 1938 was erected on the Eduard-Wallnoefer-Platz in 1997. After the Pogrom most of the 700 Jews and part-Jews who had lived in Innsbruck managed to then flee the city. Those who didn´t would be rounded up during the following year and sent to Vienna for transportation to concentration and extermination camps in the East. At least sixty-eight of them died in the Holocaust.

This book is a reminder of how easily far-right radicalism can escalate into terrorism, war and genocide and that it should in no way be tolerated or appeased. The reason why so many far-right radicals are called "Nazis" by so many people today is not only because they are using the same play-book as the Nazis but are also opening the door to such extremists.

A **Glossary wth Editorial Notes** can be found at the end of this book. All words that are typed in **bold print** in the text of the novel can be found in it.

Rabbit Warren,
Innsbruck, Tyrol,
February, 2025

Map of the Gletschberg Mountains and Valleys

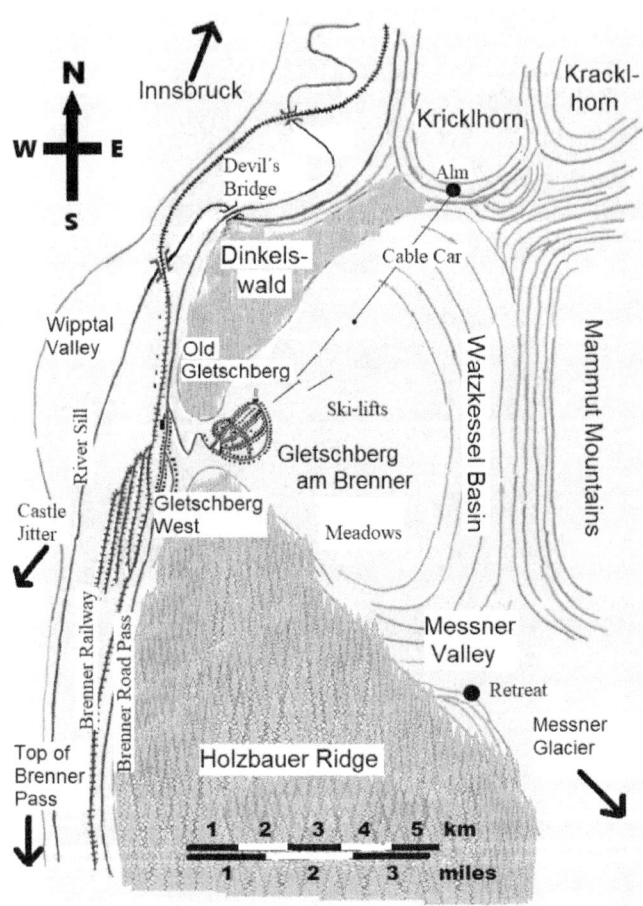

Map of Gletschberg am Brenner

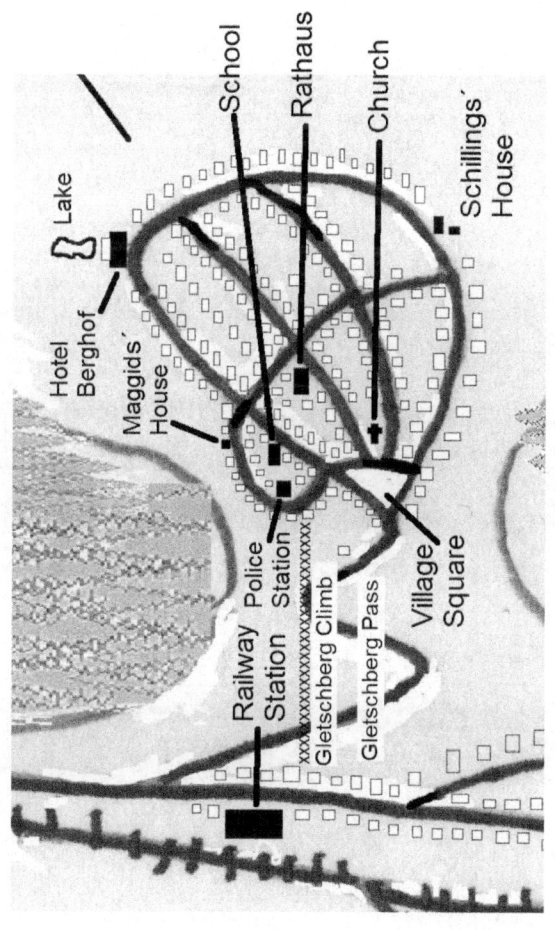

Plan of the Schillings´ Chalet

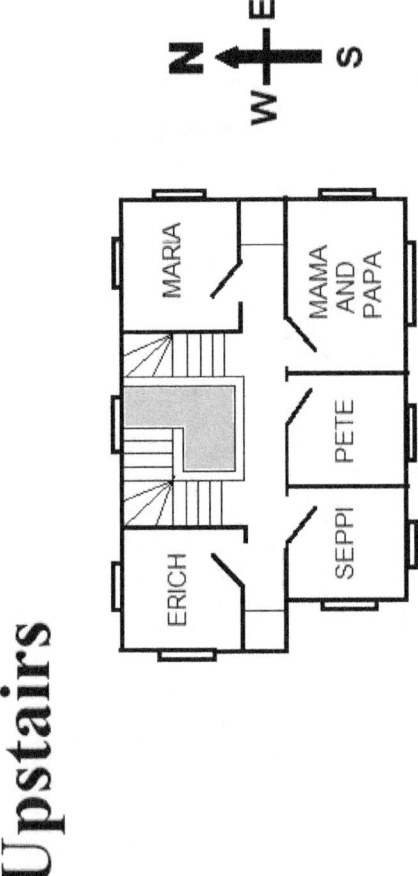

Downstairs

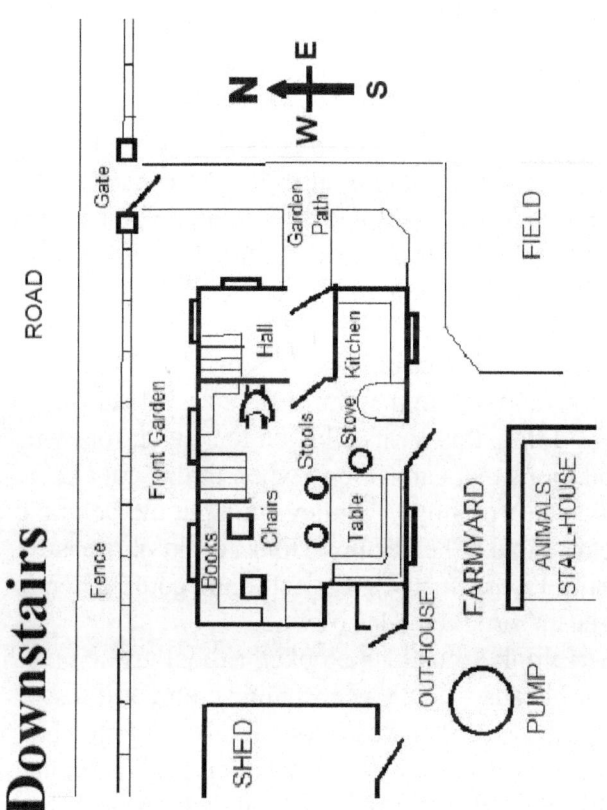

1: Flash-forward: The Battle of Hitler's Birthday

The first time that I ever saw Nazis in actual uniforms was a month after I had turned eleven years of age. It was just after I had helped Slimey Stefan out at his parents' hotel – the only one in our village of Gletschberg – the "Berghof" over the April Easter weekend of 1933. I had already worked during the **Fasching** holidays that late February as an errand boy in the mornings and had had such a good time that I was allowed to stay on for extra odd jobs that came along when things got extra busy. Surprisingly, Slimey soon put me behind the bar to make the "Happy Hour" cocktails because, he said, I was "such a great actor and could listen to guests' drunken tales of woe."

I think I must have looked ridiculous behind the bar because, being a short and stumpy kid just turning eleven, I wasn't much taller than the bar itself. However, with a natural knack for mixing drinks (although I never tasted them myself) I soon got the hang of things and made a ton of tips on the side, except for when I kept having to pull beers until my wrists nearly broke whenever a party was going on. With the extra money that I saved up I managed to buy my Mama a leg of lamb for our Easter Sunday dinner.

That had been the last big week at the "Berghof" for that winter, with the snow already having disappeared on the meadows and the miniature lake directly before the hotel no longer being frozen. Slimey´s parents, the Kratzkopfs, took off in their brand-new **380 Mercedes-Benz Cabriolet "C"** on the Tuesday after Easter to spend a few relaxing days of their own over the mountains at Lake Garda in Italy.

It was just two days later, on Thursday the Twentieth of April, that the church bells began loudly ringing just as we were leaving school.

"Hallo," said my best friend Dani, "it sounds as if Father Murrsea fears that Armageddon is fast approaching."

The sound of bells, however, was soon competing with the sound of marvellous band music and it seemed as if the music was winning. Before very long we could see the cause of this spectacle: a three breasted column of young men in brown uniforms and kepi hats came marching through the village square. Some of them were playing instruments, such as the clarinet, the flute, the trombone, the cornet, the euphonium and, of course, the snare drums and even a glockenspiel, whilst the rest of them were singing a stirring song.

However, whilst the melody on the instruments sounded like an impressive hymn, its actual lines – such as "A million are looking at the Swastika full of hope" and "Soon the Hitler flags will be flattering all over the streets" – were frightening and disgusting.

"I didn´t know that we had any soldiers around here," my older brother Seppi said to Dani as we ran alongside the marching men, with my sister Maria tagging on behind us.

"Don´t you know anything?" Dani replied with surprise. "That isn´t the army: those are Nazi boot boys: the paramilitary force of the Nazi party."

Up till then I didn´t know what paramilitary forces were either – but I could see that these guys were Nazis because of the swastika arm-bands that they were all wearing, as well as the Nazi swastika flag that they were carrying at the front. As well as this, most of them were dressed in brown shirts like **desert rats**, although many other paramilitary forces in Germany and Austria also dressed in military brown.

Following the **Great War**, all the political parties in both Germany and Austria began forming paramilitary groups in order to supposedly help the police keep order, at least when it suited them, or to "protect" themselves: which usually meant trying to knock merry hell out of other paramilitary forces, as well as citizens if they got too close to them.

These included the S.A. (short for "Sturmabteilung" or "Storm Division") of the Nazis (who were the worst of the lot) the Heimwehr and the (Tyrolean) Heimatwehr of conservative parties like the Christian Socialists, and the Republican Schutzbund of the Social Democrats.

Seppi, however, couldn´t have cared less if anyone had bothered explaining that to him. Indeed, although he was two years older than me he could sometimes act like a six year old, as he was certainly doing now: being thrilled and totally captivated by the music and its excitement and not for a moment thinking about what it might really mean.

The magnitude of the occasion was made even more apparent by the fact that it was drawing huge crowds from the village, with the curious thing being that they showed various different reactions to the Nazi boys marching through them. On the one hand there were all sorts of people, especially older women, who were shouting and swearing and sometimes even spitting at the boot boys, whilst there were also plenty of others who were actually encouraging them with shouts of "Heil Hitler!" and "Sieg Heil!" whilst cheering them and waving their hats in the air. There was also a third group who just watched dumbfounded and in negative amazement but said nothing.

Although I didn´t realize it at the time, this tumultuous scene made a deep and lasting impression on myself. Indeed, it was not long afterwards that I began to wonder that if our village could be equally divided over the Nazi Question (that is, a third for them, a third against them and a third don´t know) then so too could the whole of Austria also be so divided. By extension, although my Papa claimed that all of the Kratzkopfs´ guests and their servants must be Nazis, the Germans could also be so divided.

But what most perplexed me was wondering where these village Nazis had also come from. I had often heard my Papa and my Uncle Max talking about village politics and so I knew that there wasn't a single Nazi yet sitting in the **Gemeinderat**. Even so, I quickly realized that this must have been quietly brewing for some time now.

Almost as if following a traveling circus that had just arrived in a new town, the crowds and we children followed the parade to no less than the terrace of the Hotel Berghof. Slimey Stefan was also standing on the terrace, sticking out like a sore penis, with his legs spread out and also now dressed in Nazi brown shirt uniform. I fully expected the huge crowd to stop in front of the steps up to the terrace, which was already full of hotel guests sipping their afternoon coffee, and let the Nazis boots boys inside. It was therefore to my astonishment that, for the first time ever, I now watched dozens of the village men walking up the steps themselves and onto the terrace as if they had as much right to be there as anyone else.

"They can't fit all those people into the hotel," Dani said to me. "There's going to be absolute pandemonium."

"They must be having a Nazi Party meeting," I said, feeling as if we were witnessing the mindless walking of damned souls into the Pits of Hell.

"But they would have to have permission for that," Dani said. "You know how funny the

Gemeinderat is about political meetings being too large."

I didn´t – but I did know that Dani´s own Papa had a seat on the Gemeinderat and that Dani took a lot more interest in politics, our village or indeed anything else than I did at the time.

"Maybe old Kratzkopf, being the Buergermeister, gave his son permission," I suggested.

"No way," said Dani. "Slimey Stefan is definitely trying to pull a fast one behind his Papi´s back whilst his away with Mamikins. Mark my words, there´s going to be hell to pay when Kratzkopf finds out that all this has been going on."

It was at that moment that I saw that Slimey Stefan was trying to catch my eye by briskly gesticulating at me.

"ERICH!" he tried to cry as loudly as he could above the noise of the Nazi throng. "Can you please help me for a couple of hours? I NEED you to help serve the drinks! Half of the staff seems to have disappeared for the day!"

Whilst I couldn´t help noticing that Dani was laughing at all this I also wondered if I should, for the first time yet, refuse Slimey´s bidding – as working in such pandemonium would more than likely freak me out with unnecessary stress. On the other hand, I was also dead curious to know what was going on inside the hotel, so that I soon agreed, in spite of what they say about curiosity killing the cat.

"No, Erich, DON´T GO!" I heard Maria crying behind me as I climbed the steps onto the terrace. "There´s only going to be terrible trouble tonight!"

As kids are prone to be, I wasn´t particularly fond of my sister at that time but I did appreciate that she had a wonderful sense for judging situations to a tee – a rare talent which other people might call clairvoyance. Nevertheless, I decided to follow my curiosity instead of her instincts.

Indeed, I had hardly got into the lounge where the main drinks bar was situated then I saw a massive portrait of Adolf Hitler that Father Murrsea had once privately claimed to have seen. Since it was also the first time that I had seen it myself in spite of the fact that I had now been working part-time at the hotel for several weeks, I couldn´t help wondering if Slimey had dug it out from storage somewhere in the hotel and hung it up for the party.

The portrait was certainly larger than life – and indeed seemingly larger than the mountains outside the windows – with the Fuehrer dossed up in what looked for all the world like a brown colored, baby-boy-scout uniform, including huge, baggy pants that's looked like over-sized diapers.

"Of course, you do realize," Slimey told me, casually catching a moment from his dozens and dozens of guests to speak to me, "that it is Herr Hitler´s Birthday today. That´s why we are all here today: to wish him all the Best."

I thought that that would be a bit difficult unless the Toothbrush Dictator were also coming in person, before suddenly catching on that a political party that was staged as a birthday party might not be considered to need permission to be held.

To my great surprise, no one seemed to be worried if they got their drinks or not, so long as they kept shouting all sorts of obscenities at one another. However, when they started getting cranky about having to cough the lolly up for their drinks each time that I placed them on the bar, I decided on a new strategy: that is, to make them pay for their drinks before I even started making them.

At first, most of the Nazi buggers were cranky about that as well but when they saw that others were getting their drinks lickety-split when they forked out in advance, they all jumped onto the band-wagon. Fortunately for me, many of them were already so far sozzled that they forgot to collect their drinks so that I just gave them to others, whilst reaping a tidy side-profit in forgotten payments for myself.

Indeed, it was by the time that I began to feel like a Rockefeller in the making that both the village police and the local Heimatwehr suddenly and unexpectedly surrounded the entire jam-packed hotel, as if trying to quash an orgy of forbidden delights. It actually took me quite a while to realize what had happened as it took the Old Kaiser (who was the village Chief of Police) an awful lot of blasting on his police whistle to finally manage to stop everyone babbling at once.

As such, I just carried on merrily pouring out drinks as if I were a saloon keeper in the Wild West who couldn´t care less what shoot-outs were escalating between the Sheriff´s posse and the cowboy bandits, just so long as I kept making money. Until, that is, I suddenly heard the Old Kaiser yelling through a megaphone that someone seemed to have found for his convenience:

"This is the POLICE. All visiting guests are now ORDERED because of the non-compliance with the 1932 Registration of Political Meetings Act to leave these hotel premises at ONCE!"

When I heard these words I knew that Trouble was about to be served big-time. I therefore moved up towards the windows that looked onto the busy terrace and managed to squeeze my small self through the mass of browns-shirts that were also goggling through them. To my horror I saw that both the police and the Heimatwehr were armed to the teeth with bayonets.

The Old Kaiser meanwhile stood solidly on his ground like his namesake, Franz Josef the Emperor of Austria, with his medals glistening in the spring sunshine, just as his magnificent cotton-wool sun-burns were blown about by the subtle wind. I looked for my Papa (who was the Second Chief of Police) amongst the ranks but couldn´t find him, little knowing that he was now standing on the other side of the hotel with his own batch of men, ready to charge the front lobby on command.

"Go and suck your grand-daddy´s eggs!" one of the Nazis suddenly shouted back in a way that I refuse to properly translate here.

Needless to say that the fight between the Goodies and the Baddies – the Sheriff´s posse and the cowboy bandits – soon got under way. Whilst I made the speedy decision of expediently removing myself from the premises whilst taking any money that didn´t rightly belong in the till along with me, the fur and guts really began to fly. Bottles, beer-mugs, ash-trays, pictures and anything else that wasn´t nailed or riveted to a surface was picked up and thrown at the enemy, to say nothing of knives being drawn and plunged into places that one wouldn´t expect.

Plenty of prize furniture also began to see the light of day for the first time in years after sailing through what was left of the windows, so that Herr Kabinett the furniture maker would later happily discover that he had just been set up for life in the repairs department. Expensive tapestries also got torn down from the walls for goodness only knows what purpose, whilst even the Boesendorfer grand piano went for a burton with a tremendous chorus of musical notes when it was hit by a human missile that went straight through the middle of it. In fact the only object that didn´t seem to have bitten the dust that fateful day was the gigantic portrait of baby-boy Hitler in his diapers.

It was just as I was deliberating on if I should dive out of the window that I suddenly saw none other than Kratzkopf and his lady wife (who was widely ridiculed as the "Queen of Sheba") about to enter the room through the terrace doors. Just as Kratzkopf looked like a pantomime rooster because of his just as widely ridiculed wild comb of hair, his aristocratic wife looked like a cross between a polar bear and an ostrich on account of her being all dressed up in white furs and white feathers. It was just at that precise moment that tragedy struck the Kratzkopf family as some goon now came on the bright idea of throwing a knife at Kratzkopf's chest circus-style.

Unfortunately for the wannabe assassin, Kratzkopf had also decided to push his wife through the doorway at that exact same moment, so that the said knife missed him completely and instead went straight through her heart, as if a dart had suddenly scored an accidental bull's eye.

The Queen's blood suddenly splattered everywhere whilst her gleaming white clothes gradually soaked up the blood from her bleeding heart. As I watched on in horror at this terrifying image, I could not help thinking that the dying queen now looked like a white rose slowly changing into a red one, as the bloody color gradually radiated outwards from its center pistil and towards the edges of its outer petals.

"You must have been INSANE to have invited your brown shirt buddies around whilst we were away!!!" I later heard Herr Kratzkopf roar at his dopey son. "What the hell were you thinking?"

Dozens of people were taken to a hospital in a much larger village nearby, with some of the injuries being so serious that they had to stay a week. It also turned out that many of the men who walked into the hotel were in fact from other parties pretending to be Nazis. As such the Nazis were soon seen as the victim by many of the villagers whilst the police and Heimatwehr were regarded as the bad ass trouble-makers.

2: The Man with one Testicle

It had only been four months BEFORE what soon became known in village legend as "The Battle of Hitler's Birthday" that I had even heard the word "Nazis" for the first time. It had been almost dusk on the day before Christmas Eve – Friday the Twenty-Third of December, 1932 to be exact – and my Uncle Max had been taking me along with him up the mountain slope behind my Papa's chalet to cut down a Christmas tree for the family festivities the next day. There had been an unusually heavy snow-fall that December so that it was rum hard work trudging uphill and knee-deep through the snow, even though I loved the snow and even now, as I grown man, never get tired of seeing it each winter.

"Max: why are we getting our Christmas tree today and not tomorrow morning, as we usually do?" I asked.

"Because of all the jolly new hotel guests that will be arriving tomorrow!" Max brightly answered. "With Christmas Eve falling on the Saturday this year there's going to be a mountain of extra work to do tomorrow!"

I never called my uncle "Uncle" but always just Max. Although he was my Papa's younger (and only) brother, he was more like a much older brother to me than an uncle. He had realized his dream of becoming one of the village´s handful of ski instructors and mountain guides and would often also take me along with him into the mountains for ski tours in the winter and long hikes in the summer whenever he had some time off.

Max also taught me how to fish in the streams and remote lakes so that I can still remember my first attempts as a toddler trying to catch trout in the streams with my bare hands. Needless to say that, by the time that I was eight, I was both as fleet and as self-sufficient as an **ibex mountain goat**. The funny thing was that, although ibex are pretty stumpy as goats go, Max and I were even more so – as well as being quite short – so that we probably looked more like a couple of alpine kobolds.

My Papa, on the other hand, only ever had one reason to go into the mountains that were literally at our back-door and that was for hunting. In fact, it was said, my Mama had only married my Papa in 1919 because he was a war hero who had made quite a name for himself for being a hell of a shot with a rifle whilst earning himself the rank of major. It was even said that he could shoot a plum off someone´s head from five hundred yards without blowing their brains to smithereens as well – although I was damned if I would ever let him prove that with me William-Tell-style.

As a young junior policeman my Papa had also started the local village boxing club and still ran it, in spite of the fact that he now had a heck of a lot more work to do as Second Chief of the village force.

Like Max, however, I couldn't see the point of punching the crap out of my fellow human beings or shooting defenceless animals. Yes, one might argue that it was okay if one were hunting them for their meat and fur or even to cull the herds so that they didn't become too many and destroy the countryside, but some of these hunter fellows seemed to positively enjoy blood sports and killing for the sake of killing. Of course Papa would argue that Max and I going fishing together was the same thing but we always claimed that it wasn't.

It was my older brother, Seppi, who liked boxing, although he wasn't much good at it. In fact, although he frequently visited the boxing club he just as often returned home from it with a black eye or a bloody nose, many of which were the handiwork of younger and smaller kids than himself. He was, as they say, a true glutton for punishment.

Seppi had been born a couple of years before myself in 1920 and, as my older brother, seemed to think that he should be better at me in everything. Fat chance of that because he was a lazy little monkey who was easily bored by apparently everything except being a vicious little sod – and then only if he didn't have to put any hard work into being so.

Indeed, Seppi should have loved hunting because he delighted in the idea of blowing off innocent animals´ heads off from afar. However, apart from being a lousy shot, he couldn´t even be arsed to make the steep trek up the Messner Valley behind us whenever Papa made one of his all too few hunting excursions whilst we were growing up.

Whilst Papa would have preferred that I had taken an interest in both boxing and hunting instead of skiing and climbing he did insist that I learn to use both a rifle and a gun, as if he had been fully expecting a second Great War to come along from the very beginning. Like Seppi, he took me along to a firing range that was near a neighboring village and – as I just mentioned – Seppi was totally crap at shooting whilst I was pretty good at it.

In fact, realizing that there wasn´t anything that he was better at than me, Seppi got so riled up that he really began getting vicious at home whenever he could, attacking me from behind and even trying to bite me whenever he couldn´t land any punches on me. In fact, I got so annoyed by his repeatedly doing this, even though he always came off worse, that I really thought that I would have to take a boxing lesson myself so that I could deliver him a once-and-for-all knock-out punch – or just stick a pitch-fork through him some day.

Seppi became even sillier still with jealousy when Papa also began taking my best friend Dani along with us on our firing range expeditions, with Dani turning out to be an ace with the rifle, even though he had never had a lesson before in his life.

Dani´s own Papa was Jewish and the only tailor in the village. With his surname being Maggid he was also known as Mad Maggid because he was always trying to pump himself up as having been some kind of war hero in the demolitions corps of the army during the War. Dani told me that "Maggid" actually means a scholar, teacher or preacher in Hebrew and that his Papa had actually taught him lots that he had already been able to put to good use. I could easily believe this because Dani was always inventing all sorts of gadgets, such as home-made roller-skates and a pair of walkie-talkie telephones that we used in the mountains until I accidentally dropped one of them down a ravine.

Like a true Renaissance Action Man, Dani seemed to have an insatiable curiosity for everything under the moon whilst having a whirl (as well as excelling) at just about everything that presented itself to him, including the aforementioned shooting and boxing with my own Papa, as well as hiking and ski-touring with myself and Max in the mountains.

Dani also had a particular hankering for the Brenner Pass railway on the other side of our village in the **Wipptal** Valley and the locomotives that ran up and down it with their huge hauls. He also decided very early on that he wanted to work on the railways when he left school because he wanted to see "far-away places".

At that time I didn´t care for far-away places, least of all Innsbruck, which lies at the bottom of the long chain of valleys north of the Brenner Pass and is the capital of Tyrol. I had plenty enough to do in the mountains to the east of our village, Gletschberg am Brenner. I even felt that I could live a hundred years in that magical corner of the Alps and I still wouldn´t know every crook and cranny and mountain rock.

Gletschberg had grown out of a small saddle-like opening between the forest-covered Dinkelswald and Holzbauer Ridge hills as they run to the east of the Wipptal Valley that is now famous for its Brenner Pass. Hidden behind this opening is our village and its valley: which looks like an enormous cyst that has been carved out of the mountains by glaciers ten thousand years ago. This is the magnificent half-bowl of the Watzkessel, surrounded in the north and east by the steeps walls of two mountain ranges, with idyllic grassy meadows gently rolling below them. The mountains are the towering Kricklhorn to the north-east and its just as mighty twin brother the Kracklhorn just behind it, as well as the even taller Mammut bulwark of peaks to the east.

It was in the Watzkessel that the tourists then almost always found their mountain pursuits: from comfortable hiking trails and relatively easy climbing walls at the bottom of the Kricklhorn to the four brand-new ski-lifts of Gletschberg and a couple of country roads that were ideal for sleigh-rides in winter. Indeed, I always thought that the Watzkessel looked particularly fantastic in winter when all the meadows were blanketed in a coat of sparkling white whilst the mountain walls were peppered with gleaming, glinting powder.

Indeed, it is only from the village itself that one can see the huge, almighty slabs of ice that hang permanently over many parts of the cold, western rock faces of the Mammut peaks as if they had been hacked out of a ginormous giants´ wedding cake. On the other hand, it is only when one is standing directly below these magnificent brutes of mountains that one fully appreciates the naked rock faces in them, with their devil-may-care ledges and precipices, as well as multi-colored slates that have through time been vertically compressed together like the pipes of an organ.

Gletschberg am Brenner had meanwhile only just begun to make a name for itself as a ski and mountain resort for the tourists. As well as the four brand-new ski-lifts in the north-east there was a tiny cable-car that went part way up the Kricklhorn, with a small alm next to the top station – and which you could ski back down to the village in un-pisted snow in winter or walk down in summer.

The ski-lifts and the alm – but not the cable-car – were owned by the same owners as the only hotel in the village – the Kratzkopfs of the Hotel Berghof. The hotel stood on the edge of the meadows in the north-east of the village, directly in front of a miniature lake that, for some weird reason, had no name. The Kratzkopfs were also Max´s employer.

It may have been because I didn´t like rich tourists or because the back of our chalet stood on the edge of the large expanse of meadows to the south-east, but my favorite corner of our mountains was always the **steep hanging Messner Valley** directly behind us above those meadows. The valley lay between the southern reach of the Mammut Mountains to the east (that is, to our left as we climbed upwards) and the Holzbauer Ridge (on our right) that also lay to the immediate south of the center of the village.

The mountain sides that stretched all over my corner for miles uphill and into the skies were full of lonely alpine pastures, streams, hidden gorges, screes, boulders and peaks, whilst being occasionally dotted with both **chamois** antelopes and ibex mountain goats. Further below in the meadows nearer the village, there was constantly chiming of the bells of the farmers´ own goats and cows (as well as my Mama´s own little herd) that gave a musical harmony to the heaven-like vista.

Climbing up the ever steeper slopes of the Messner Valley one eventually comes to the almighty Messner Glacier, jagged with frozen white teeth like the bones of a Jurassic plesiosaur that had just been turned inside-out.

This was therefore my backyard. Each year Max and I would climb up the slopes of those lower meadows and into the lowest forest of the Holzbauer Ridge to find our next Christmas tree and chop it down. It was from up there that we could just see the opening between the Dinkelswald and Holzbauer Ridge hills to the Wipptal Valley beyond.

This was a whole different world for us, with both the Brenner railway and the Brenner Pass road slowly curling and looping their way up the steep Wipptal Valley all the way from Innsbruck in the north and towards the final saddle across the mountains in the south that also marks the border to the South Tyrol in Italy.

As I said, it was almost dusk when Max and I left the forest with the Christmas tree that we had just chopped down. It had been a pretty glum day of miserable cold and cloudy weather – and none of the kind of magical scenery that you would want to photograph for your jolly ski-holiday memories album. Indeed, the alpine skiers often call this kind of weather as being "Flat Light", with all the heaped up snow having no contours and thus looking two-dimensional, so that it´s difficult to gage distances to other skiers ahead of one´s self.

Max had already noticed a strange rumbling as we stepped into the forest, with snow tumbling down from the branches above us and merrily spraying us whilst we stepped on snapping twigs hidden in the snow. We both thought that it might be an avalanche, even though it was a bit too early in the winter for those. Coming back out of the forest, however, we could slightly hear voices coming from far, far away and, looking up at the alm at the top of the lower icy walls of the

Kricklhorn, could dimly see the flickering of lights, even though the alm appeared to be closed.

"Surely one of those idiot tourists hasn´t already got lost on the mountain this early in the new winter season?" Max asked himself rather than me. "You wouldn´t believe what silly notions some of them have about our mountains."

I could. Only a year before four tourists had died after deciding to go skiing on the high mountain in spite of avalanche warnings, whilst two wannabe climbers were drowned in a ravine by a flash flood during the summer after refusing to take storm warnings seriously. It was clear that whilst they were right in seeing the Alps as a playground of sorts, they had no idea just how damned dangerous the buggers could become.

"LOOK!" I suddenly shouted as a huge spider-like cross suddenly lit up on the side of the mountain whilst I was sure that, even from across the massive valley, I could distinctly hear a crowd roaring with delight.

"My God!" Max also cried. "It´s a swastika! Don´t tell me that those bastards are now here as well?!"

"What bastards?" I asked.

"Oh, excuse my unholy language, Erich – although that´s exactly what those damned Nazis are!"

"Nazis?" I asked. By the sound of their name, which sounded incredibly like "Nasties", I thought that he was talking about imaginary mountain creatures and other monsters, such as goblins and morlocks.

"Yes, short for Nationalist Socialists – although they are about as much socialist as a bunch of boot boys at a boot camp – which is in fact just what they are!"

"Socialists?" I also asked, although I hardly needed to. I had already heard Max and Papa use the word many times and come to the conclusion that it either meant everyone sharing everything for the benefit of everyone or simply stealing from the better off, depending on which of them was using it.

"Yes," Max quickly answered with open hatred and disgust. "The Nazis used to be a vicious little nut-job party in Germany but now it's a monster party of thorough-bred psychopaths. Their idea of running a country is beating everybody who disagrees with them to a pulp whilst also stealing everything that they've got! I thought that these vile Nazis had been permanently hammered in last month's elections in Germany – and lost all chance of coming to power – but now it seems as if we've got the buggers in our own backyard!"

As I keep saying, I had no idea what any of this Nazi stuff was about – but now I do. The Nazis had already won thirty-seven per cent of the vote for the seats in the German Reichstag in July of that year and so became the biggest party in a system of proportional representation. However, because the other parties couldn't form a working coalition against them, they called another election that same

November – and this time the Nazis "only" got thirty-three per cent of the vote. As such, it had indeed looked for all the world as if they had been hammered permanently.

"But you know what is even worse about this damnable party?" Max now asked me, even though he knew full well that I didn´t have a clue what the answer might be.

I shook my head whilst being unsure if I were particularly interested or not.

"It´s their leader. He´s a madman, a liar, a cheat, a fraud, a charlatan, a bully and a blackguard who even shot his own niece dead in a fit of jealousy. He´s also got a ridiculous toothbrush moustache and just one testicle."

I couldn´t help laughing out loud at this but my uncle was in no joking mood. In fact, he was so deadly serious that he was also on the brink of descending into an insane fit of fury himself.

"But worst of all," Max ranted on, "this raving nut-job is also a bloody Austrian – one of us! He´s also a bally traitor because, whilst he couldn´t be bothered to fight for our Kaiser during the Great War, he instead went off to fight for the German Kaiser! He wants Austria to be a part of Germany, of all damned things!"

Had none of this happened, Max and I would have jumped on the sled that that we had brought along with us and begun cheerfully crying out and wailing Christmasy things as we sled back home with our new tree under our arms. Instead, Max practically ordered me to jump sharpish on the sled with the tree and began crying out, "Damned Nazis! Nazis here, Nazis there, Nazis every bloody where!" as we roared downhill and back home like an out-of-control missile-propelled tiger tank.

3: Brothers at War

"I don´t understand you, Max!" Papa shouted at my uncle during our Christmas Eve dinner the following evening. "You claim that you are a Social Democrat and that you hate Nazis and yet you work as a ski instructor and climbing guide for the richest tourists in the village, most of whom are Nazi Germans!"

Papa may have had a point there – even if everyone knew that the Hotel Berghof had the only ski school in the village, as well as being the only place that employed hiking and climbing guides in the summer. Apparently not wishing to get bogged down in details, however, Max instead decided on a new line of defense. Leaning forward over his Christmas Eve dinner of poached carp, root vegetables and parsley potatoes, he menacingly told Papa:

"Well, does it ever occur to you that you Christian Socialists and **Dollfuss** are no better than the Nazis?"

"How dare you!" Papa suddenly cried, slamming down his fist on the table so hard that the carp´s eye-ball literally leapt off his plate and up his nose. "The Nazis are nothing but bully boys – as you well know! I demand that you take that back IMMEDIATELY!"

"Whatever for?" Max asked, suddenly beaming as he realized that he had got Papa where it hurt. "Ever since Dollfuss managed to get to be Kanzler this May he´s been modelling his politics on **Mussolini´s fascism** – just the same as Adolf Hitler. It´s all the same stuff."

"No it´s not."

"Yes it is. Mark my words, big brother Josef: next year Dollfuss and his boot boys will also be marching about in uniforms all over the parade grounds and turning Austria into a full-blown fascist country."

Papa now looked as if he were about to jettison the carp´s remaining eyeball towards Max´s own nose when my Mama suddenly slapped the table with her napkin and cried:

"BOYS! Can´t you two supposedly grown-up men set an example to our own children on the eve of the Lord´s Birthday, instead of acting like a couple of fighting cockerels throughout the entire dinner? It´s an absolute disgrace! Behave yourselves before I send you both out of the house!"

My Mama didn´t often snap like this – and when she did, it rarely lasted long. Instead of throwing a temper tantrum like Papa or Max she would just as quickly return to being her warm-hearted and good-natured self. As such, just as she tried to love almost everyone under the moon with a Christian fervour, almost everyone seemed to love her back. I also particularly loved her in my own way and would often bring her **Edelweiss** from the highest alps and secluded corners of the mountains to show it. Mama was also damned hard working, whilst expecting little reward or recreational time for herself, which was an attribute that was still very common in those days.

"Is there going to be a FIGHT?" my older brother Seppi asked, clearly hoping that the situation would soon escalate into a round of fisticuffs, whilst suddenly and unnecessarily punching me in the ribs as if to prove a point.

"FIGHT! FIGHT! FIGHT!" my younger Pete suddenly cried with wild gesticulations, whilst throwing food all about the place. Poor, poor and most dear, little Pete had been born what we then called "silly" but which others, especially from the outside world, had been calling **"mentally handicapped"** for half a century.

At that time I was still quite shy and so hated quarrelling. As such, I would have much preferred for Papa and Max to have simply got along, especially on Christmas Eve, and for Seppi to have simply not existed. Seppi of course had the most ridiculous and obnoxious notion that older brothers were duty-bound to terrorize their next younger brother, just as I regarded him as being nothing more than a natural-born shit-stirrer who never missed an opportunity to pour oil on a fire or rub salt into old wounds.

"Can´t we just sell Seppi off as a slave?" I suggested, speaking for the first time during that dinner.

"Can´t be done," said my younger sister Maria, looking up for the first time from her book, which she discreetly held just under the edge of the table whilst eating her dinner. "Emperor Joseph the Second got rid of serfdom in Austria in 1781 as part of his enlightenment program."

Whilst being a whole year younger than myself, Maria could not only read and understand grown-up history books at the age of nine but was the only person that I ever knew who could both read a book and listen to a conversation at the same time.

"Of course, you know what the real source of all this is," Seppi carried on, still hoping to stick the needle in and sew even more division within the family. "It's because Uncle Max wasn't old enough to prove himself in the War like Papa but had to stay in the village like a school-boy instead. He's been griping about that ever since."

"Oh, I'm not sure about that," Mama said briskly. "Max joined the air cadets in Innsbruck whilst the War was still on and learnt how to fly."

"Really?" I excitedly asked as my ears suddenly pricked up like a rabbit's. "I didn't know that."

"On top of that," Seppi rudely went on before Max had a chance to tell his version of his own story, "Papa is still waiting for the Old Kaiser to retire or just plain snuff it so that he can finally have the old goat's job. Of course all this endless waiting must really rattle him, so that's why he also gets so touchy when Max comes to dinner and starts annoying him."

The village Chief of Police had earned his nickname "The Old Kaiser" on account of the fact that only was his actual surname Kaiser but his giant lamb-chop sideburns even made him look like the ancient **Kaiser Franz-Josef** of the Kaiser and King Era from before the War, whilst already looking just as old. He was also a so-called "legitimist": that is, someone who believed that the only legitimate government for Austria was a return to the Habsburg monarchy.

For some reason Mama and Papa never seemed to be able to control Seppi, whereas they were constantly ticking Maria and myself off and putting us back into line. Perhaps they thought that Seppi was too stupid to be constantly disciplined, although they had no problem in disciplining Pete if he decided to be naughty. On the other hand, Maria and I were certainly Papa´s favorites because, as he kept saying, we were so "smart", although we had to work hard for this praise.

In a rather cruel way, Papa didn´t think that Seppi and Pete were even bothering about. At that insensitive age I also didn´t think that Seppi was worth anyone´s bothering about. Unlike Papa, however, I didn´t believe that, with unfortunate exceptions like Pete, people are born stupid but become stupid as they grow up because they are just too darn lazy to learn anything. As such, Seppi was a classic case of this "If you don´t use it then you lose it" syndrome, since he not only refused to switch his brain on but wouldn´t even let his imagination or sense of curiosity take fly either.

As for poor Pete, it was only Mama, Maria and I who took a proper interest him. However, as much as we tried to encourage him to do to simple tasks on his own, such as eating his food without making a mess or going to the toilet, we hadn´t enough experience with the mentally handicapped to know how to treat him properly. Indeed, these were still the days when handicapped people – both mentally and physically – were shunned as undesirable freaks and failures by Society and treated as something to be ashamed of.

Thank God, therefore, there were people like my mother who lived by her heart and not by what stupid Society told her to think. Then there was our village priest, Father Murrsea, who applauded us for everything that we did for poor Pete. He even said to Mama:

"Pete will always remain a child and be in need of your help for the rest of his life, Frau Schilling, even when he has physically grown into a man. However, he will also never grow out of rewarding you with that unlimited love that children always have for those that care for them."

In the meantime, there was a long and deadly silence after Seppi had made his grievous comment, with Papa finally laying his hands down on the edge of the table and staring at Uncle Max between the eyes as if he were indeed about to pass the Death Sentence on him.

"For once the boy is right," Papa said. "Max is just jealous of me because I have always been waaaaay more successful than he has because I have a proper career. It may be all very jolly good fun to be skiing and playing in the mountains all day long but it hardly counts as a REAL job that brings in REAL money. Mark my words, Erich: you don´t want to follow your mad uncle´s foot-steps when you grow up."

My Papa stared at me particularly hard when he said this last sentence to me, much as if he already knew full well that my dreams were also to become a ski instructor and hiking and climbing guide like Max.

"Oh, I don´t know about that," Mama replied. "Max still manages to pay his own way in life."

"Yes – but he still doesn´t have a house of his own, nor even a wife and a family as I do!" Papa retorted. "Instead he has to live in a tiny staff room in the attic of the Berghof – "

"You know perfectly well that Father left the entire house to you whilst leaving me without so much as a **Schilling** because he didn´t want us fighting over this house when he was dead!" Max shouted back. "What´s more, everyone knows that even the Chief of Police hardly earns a fortune when compared to what some climbing guides manage to make."

Papa took a deadly stab at one of his potatoes before responding:

"That´s only the case in other villages where there are so many rich guests and flashy hotels that well-heeled mountain guides can set themselves up privately."

Max now paused whilst looking for all the world as if he were about to boil over and completely snap, which is basically what he then did.

"That´s RIGHT!" he suddenly shouted back as he shot up from his chair and back onto his legs. "All that you ever do is ridicule other people´s dreams whilst grumbling and griping the whole time about your own dull, flat-footed life."

"What do you mean by that?" Papa demanded whilst remaining seated as if it were a sign of being the Big Boss. "I´ve never grumbled or griped or done any kind of complaining in my entire life!"

"NO-O-O???" Max cried, with the steam clearly now whistling out of his ears as he heard this supreme irony of a statement. "Grumbling and griping is all that you ever do! This Christmas Eve it´s all about my dreams and beliefs – and last year it was all about the dinner itself, in spite of the fact that Lilly had spent hours and days preparing it for you!"

"I NEVER complained about that," Papa said, like a four year old who had just eaten all the cookies.

This was so ridiculously untrue since we could all remember the last Christmas dinner performance perfectly well. Indeed, it was so ludicrous that we all let out a gasp of surprise, with even Pete getting in on the act. He had meanwhile spent the entire dinner making all sorts of alternating happy and frustrating noises in half-delight and half-annoyance at the adults´ performance, whilst my mother kept trying to encourage him to eat properly whilst eating her own Christmas Eve dinner.

"Of course you did," Max stated, beginning his Case for the Prosecution, with none of the witnesses wanting to defend Papa. "For starters, you went on and on about our eating poached carp every year whilst also constantly telling us that all the guests at the Berghof get goose for their Christmas Eve."

"And so they do and so they should!" Papa demanded. "Christians have always eaten goose for Christmas – no doubt because it is much tastier than this rubbery water-creature."

"Yes," Max quickly replied, "but Christmas Eve is not part of Christmas but part of Advent: which used to be a time of fasting like Lent, according to the Church. That's why we eat fish on Christmas Eve."

"That was in the Middle Ages, little brother. Since then – "

"But goose is SO expensive, Josef," Mama quickly interrupted her husband. "And have you any idea how long it takes to cook? Besides, those birds are so big that I wouldn't even be able to fit one in the oven."

"Where there's a way, there's a will," Papa sagely noted.

"Only if you are rich folk like the Kratzkopfs and their guests and can afford all this fancy stuff," Max observed.

"Well, what's good for the Kratzkopfs is good enough for us," said Papa.

It was a very interesting statement, like a kindergarten teacher putting himself on the same level as a university professor.

"He's also a very rich Buergermeister," added Mama, "although it's clear as daylight that it's that horrid hussy of his that is the source of all his riches."

"Sausages," I suddenly intervened, deciding to perk things up with my own limited knowledge of the world around me. "If we were traditional Tyrolean folk we would be eating sausages on Christmas Eve."

"PORK," Papa retorted, as if trying to put one over me. "During **Saturnalia** the Romans used to feast on roast pork. Why don't we just eat that pig of yours, Lilly? You've had it these last three years and we still haven't eaten it."

"PORK! PORK! PORK!" Pete suddenly blurted out whilst making grunting noises like a pig.

"Is that the one that Herr Kratzkopf gave Mama as a tenth wedding anniversary present to you and Mama?" Maria asked.

"Of course it is," said Papa. "Is there any other pig?"

"What I've never been able to work out," said Max, "was why old Kratzkopf wanted to give Lilly a tenth wedding anniversary present at all."

"You would clearly never make a detective, Max," Papa answered with a conceited smirk. "Isn't it obvious? Kratzkopf felt guilty that he had never given Lilly a present when she married me when she left the Berghof ten years before then."

"I thought Herr Kratzkopf gave Mama a chicken when she left the Berghof," said Maria. "That's how she got her brood of chickens started."

"You keep out of this," Papa suddenly told Maria, almost losing his cool altogether as if he didn't like her being smarter than he was. "This has nothing to do with you."

"Wow!" I quietly said to Maria. "How did you know that?"

"I pay attention, dummy!" Maria answered, reminding me that she was just as much a listener as a reader.

Mama had in fact built up quite a menagerie over the years. As well as the pig (who she called Franz) and her brood of chickens, she also had a small herd of continuously bleating goats and a very old cow who she called Edelkraut. If the chickens kicked up a fuss every time that we invaded their privacy in the hen-house, then it was nothing to the cacophony that the goats were continuously creating. As if their bleating wasn't enough to keep one wide awake at night, Papa also insisted that they also wear goats' bells ALL of the time.

Indeed, these bells may not have been very large but their continuously ringing and dinging seemed to be everywhere. This would have been great if we had ever managed to take them to the higher pastures in summer but they simply refused to budge out of our own field around our chalet. They therefore remained like a tireless symphonic orchestra that simply never grew bored of practicing, even though they couldn´t play for toffee.

Just as the chickens gave us a regular supply of fresh eggs – at least in the summer when there was plenty of daylight – the goats gave us milk, which we also turned into cheese and sold. Poor old Edelkraut, however, was so old that she spent most of her "retirement" years just wandering around our field with moo-cow eyes, as if wondering when she would finally be given the chop by being sent to Fleischklops the butcher for the Last Rites. However, it was clear that the reason why Mama didn´t get Fleischklops the butcher to slaughter either Edelkraut or Franz was because she was much too fond of them for that. I even wondered if it would have been much more useful, as well as a lot more fun, if the Buergermeister had given Mama a dog instead of a pig as a tenth wedding anniversary present.

"Fun fact," Seppi suddenly said, which meant that we all knew that he was about to say something completely daft, if not thoroughly disgusting. "Did you know that cockerels don´t have penises even though they can mate up to thirteen times a day with fifteen other chickens?"

"Seppi, PLEASE!" Mama cried at my older brother. "Not in front of Maria!"

"PENIS! PENIS! PENIS!" Pete now also blurted out, whilst flapping his arms about as if he were indeed a cockerel trying to mount a hen and mate with her.

"But how does he manage to do it, then?" Maria asked, full of curiosity.

4: Silent Night, Nazi Night

"He instead has a hole in his front and he simply pushes this own hole against the hen´s and Bob´s-your-uncle!" Seppi nevertheless shouted as his answer.

Even Max began laughing at this riotous fact-of-life, whilst Mama and Papa simply sat in stony silence and with red faces. But Seppi still wasn´t finished as he added his punch-line:

"It certainly takes the cock out of the cockerel!"

"COCK! COCK! COCK!" Pete then shouted, having no idea that he was being cheerleader to a star performer.

Whilst my parents glowered at Seppi everyone else began almost choking on their laughter, with Pete also feeling that he should join in on the act. It was therefore after a while of mixed disgust and embarrassment on the one side and merry mirth on the other, that Mama finally threw down her napkin and left the table whilst saying:

"I just don´t know where these children come from."

Papa promptly answered: "You should know: they came out of you."

I was damned sure that Seppi was about to say, "Yes, but who put them there in the first place?" but Papa slapped him around the ear-hole before he could.

Maria then helped Mama clear up the dishes before returning from the kitchen recess with a whole load of various Christmas cookies that the two of them had baked over the last few days. They had also made a large Stollen – a soft but heavy bread-loaf brimming with currants, candied fruit, almond slivers and marzipan – which Papa was particularly fond of having with his prized French Cognac.

It seemed that, like domestic house work, Christmas was especially a woman's thing, for it was again Maria and Mama who decorated the Christmas tree in the early afternoon of each Christmas Eve. In a time and a place when commercially made ornaments were still unheard of (unless you visited the Berghof) all our tree decorations were hand-made. Indeed, most of them came from Maria's delicate and creative hands, who was always as excited at making a "fresh batch" of decorations each year as she was of helping Mama to bake the cookies.

In fact, Maria's excitement was so bright and intense that it would always soon brush off onto Pete's own good nature and lighten up his spirits. Unfortunately, being mentally handicapped, the poor boy was never invited to join in. Instead, without any proper professional medical advice and guidance, he would spend most of his life just sitting on his stool and flapping his arms about like a cockerel mounting a hen.

Sometime after dusk had fallen and Papa had returned from work, we children were shooed out of the kitchen-cum-dining-cum-living room that we always called the "main room" and into our rooms upstairs for at least a couple of hours. Unlike countries like America and England, Christmas in Austria and Germany is celebrated on Christmas Eve rather than on Christmas Day.

Indeed, instead of a jolly **"Christmas Man"** coming down the chimney sometime during the night, an angelic-like child called the **Christkind** is supposed to somehow come down from the Heavens during the afternoon of Christmas Eve and distribute not only the presents around the tree but also decorate it as well. We knew, of course, as we entered the now-sacred room again, that all the presents had been either purchased or made by Mama and Papa, just as they had also decorated the tree themselves, as well as lighting all the extra candles that now made our home look like a **Lourdes pilgrim sanctum**.

Only Pete would be allowed to stay inside the room all this time because, apart from kicking up an horrendous fuss every time anyone suggested he should leave his beloved stool, he still couldn´t figure out what this thing called "CHRISTMAS! CHRISTMAS! CHRISTMAS!" was all about.

Also, unlike the American and English Christmases, Austrian Christmases are a lot more solemn and religious. Papa was also the picture of solemnity once the Christkind had been and gone so that we could come down stairs again to find our surprises – and would have made a great Saint Nicholas on the Sixth of December. This was the day when the serious, old headmaster-like saint would give out presents to the children – but only if they had been good little boys and girls. Indeed, looking back all these decades with hindsight, I now realize that, for all his faults, Papa took his Christmas duties very seriously indeed – no doubt because he had been brought up that way at the end of the Kaiser and King era.

Papa was also meticulously careful that all the extra candles didn´t set anything alight because our chalet was built entirely out of wood and could have easily gone up like a tinder-box, as had happened to many an entire alpine village on a windy night when someone had careless dropped a match. Needless to say that once the present-unpacking was over and Mama had begun bringing out the Christmas Eve dinner, Papa dutifully snuffed out all the unnecessary candles, except those around the table.

It was sometime around then that Max would show up, depending on when the Hotel Berghof released him from his duties. Max would bring presents of his own for us kids – usually toys that he had made himself, having once been apprenticed to Kabinett the furniture maker´s father as a carpenter – but after that the Christmas mood would go to pot. Papa and Max were like two dogs: keep them apart and they would be fairly well-behaved for most of the time BUT put them together and they would be at each others´ throats like a pair of fighting cockerels in next to no time. I often wondered why Papa allowed Max to come at all until Maria reminded me that Christmas is a time for family get-togethers and that it would have therefore been very uncharitable and very un-Christian for Papa not to have allowed Max to come.

Meanwhile, back to that Christmas Eve of 1932. After the Stollen and Cognac had managed to calm Papa down a bit and Max had begun telling jokes to Seppi and I whilst Maria and Mama washed the dishes, we all went off for the Christmas Eve Mass at the village Catholic church. The church, although quite plain on the outside, was very ornate on the inside, with countless paintings and sculptures having been donated by the federal railways, as well as the baptismal font and the glorious eastern stained-glass window above the altar.

I normally didn´t like the idea of going to church. I hated being forced to belong to a community and hated even more being preached by Father Murrsea about what I could and couldn´t do and think. Worse still, his sermons were so devastatingly long that it was literal torture trying to stay awake during them and not fall into a refreshing doze of snoring bliss. Besides, Father Murrsea was also my teacher in our three class village school so that I had already had quite enough of his laborious lessons during the rest of the week.

However, Christmas Eve Mass was always different, what with all the fresh snow lying around everywhere outside and the sheer magic of the night. There was also the annual singing of our own Austrian carol, "**Stille Nacht**", to look forward to, which was always particularly moving and poignant when played only on a single guitar, as it originally was when it was first composed more than a hundred years before.

The only thing that I still didn´t like was that – believe it or not – all the pews were marked with the names of every single man, woman and child who regularly attended the church services, family by family, row by row, according to their prestige in the church community (ie. how much they donated to it). This meant in my wild imagination that, once any children became old enough to have their own pew to kneel, sit down and stand up again, they were as good as marked down there for the rest of their lives. It was as if the only way out of this enclosed community was to hurry up and die – or just leave the village altogether whilst everyone else shouted out "Shame on you!" as if one were some kind of traitor.

On the other hand, the advantage of this physical form of a register was that one could instantly see who was and who was not attending church, which put the fire into gossip and gave one plenty of ammunition to play with if one wasn´t the missing person. It also meant that a lot of people took a long time in getting to sit down as they waited for everyone else to sit down so that they could properly see from their higher positions who was and who was not there.

The one person who I was always looking out for was of course Slimey Stefan: that twenty-one year old son of the Kratzkopfs of the Hotel Berghof and who I mentioned at the very beginning of this memoir. Whilst Slimey was tall, dark and ugly like his mother (until her untimely demise the following Easter) Herr Kratzkopf was a large and jolly fellow who had a haircut like a chicken's comb.

Kratzkopf was also the "Buergermeister" or mayor and, as such, always the best-dressed man in the village: which also meant that he was always instantly recognizable, even from a long distance. His wife was also an eyeball-catcher but that was because she was like a strutting peacock who loved feather hats, mink coats and glistening pearls galore: which was no doubt a major factor in her being nick-named the "Queen of Sheba".

Frau Kratzkopf was in fact a German of aristocratic Brandenburg stock, whilst Herr Kratzkopf's father had just been a simple local farmer. His mother had also run an even simpler guest-house where the Berghof now stood and which she had called the "Edelweiss". It was therefore as clear as the loudest church-bell that Kratzkopf had married the old bird primarily for her oodles and boodles of money.

In the meantime, just how Kratzkopf had managed to find his Prussian Queen of Sheba and woo her all the way to Gletschberg am Brenner was anyone's guess, just as whose idea (that is, his or hers) it was to sell his father's farm and turn his mother's simple guesthouse into the only hotel in the village was also anyone's guess. Fact was that they quickly rebuilt and kept renovating his parents´ simple guest-house whilst re-naming it the "Berghof" so that it soon became completely modern, grand and totally unrecognizable. It was even said that Frau Kratzkopf actually kicked his husband´s parents out of their guest-house, wheelchairs and all, to go and live in a mushroom nearby.

It also wasn´t long afterwards that Kratzkopf then had his alm built on the side of the Kricklhorn and the first of the four ski-lifts installed on the slopes below it, whilst also persuading the **Gemeinde** to cough up the money for the cable-car to the alm. Needless to say that the Kratzkopfs became the leading pillars of our village society and that Kratzkopf seemed to have bagged the job of Buergermeister for Life, like some Giant Goblin King of Sheba. Meanwhile, while some of the villagers (like Max) thought that the idea of bringing the rich tourists to the village was a great idea, others (like Papa) thought that tourism would be just as grotesque as the railway industry that was supposed to have already improved life in the village.

One thing that no-one doubted was that, as a Buergermeister with considerable sway, Kratzkopf was now calling all the big shots for the future of the village, whether one liked it or not. As such, Kratzkopf and the Queen of Sheba were always to be seen in the front row of the congregation, although the same couldn´t be said of their one and only son.

Slimey Stefan (that is, "Schleimiger Stefan" in German or just plain "S.S.") was meanwhile renowned as being the worst bully in the entire village – although I surprisingly didn´t have much trouble with him when I began working at the hotel a couple of months later. He had spent years terrorizing the three classes of the village school during his time there until he had left it some years before now to work full-time at his parents´ alm on the Kricklhorn.

I was meanwhile surprised yet also glad not to see the unsavoury know-it-all standing at the front with his parents on this night when absolutely everybody was expected to show up for the service. Papa had clearly also noticed that Slimey Stefan was missing when he spoke to Uncle Max as we finally left the church together after the service:

"I´m not surprised that that ghastly creature has decided not to soil this sacred place with his wicked presence: not after you said that it was the German guests who were responsible for that idiotic swastika on the mountain yesterday evening. You know how well he gets on with some of those guests so let´s just hope that he makes a permanent habit of staying away from church services from now on."

It was a brisk, cold and bracing night: the sort of night that actually makes you enjoying panting in the air just to watch your breath steaming up before yourself. For the first time ever there were lights on all around the church, having just that year been connected to electricity, thanks to the "generous" help of Kratzkopf, whose own hotel was likewise so powered. Yet as we looked up at the twinkling stars in the otherwise pitch-dark night's sky, with the mountain peaks covered in coats of distant white so that they looked like models of papier-maché, we could all now see another swastika brightly lit up on the Krickhorn mountainside, no doubt having just been lit during the church service.

"My God!" Uncle Max angrily muttered under his breath. "They've got a nerve doing that evil trick again on this night of all nights. It's nothing but blasphemy!"

"It seems as if it's going to take a lot more than just a handful of policemen and paltry fines to put a stop to this maniac's antics," Papa added.

It was then that I noticed with a terrific jolt that Slimey Stefan was now actually standing directly behind myself, grinning away like a madman who had just completed his day's dirty deed. Bending over my shoulder like a creepy vampire, he now whispered into my ear:

"Happy Nazi Christmas, Erich! May there be many more to come."

5: The Worst Bully in the Village

If the night of Christmas Eve at the church had been quiet and enchanting until we saw the fiery swastika again on the mountain, then the night of the following Thirtieth of January was noisy and spectacular. Hearing fireworks galore being suddenly shot off from the direction of the Berghof in the north, Seppi and I ran out of our family chalet and towards the hotel, whilst wondering what on Earth had seemingly possessed them to again celebrate the New Year barely a month later.

Sure enough the fireworks were being let off from beside the frozen miniature lake just before the hotel, as they always were. We also found Dani standing at the wooden fence that divided the frozen lake from the hotel´s terrace above it, along with a number of other village children and even some of the grown-ups, including the butcher, the baker and the furniture maker.

"They must be celebrating the fact that Hitler was made Kanzler today," Fleischklops the butcher said.

"It´s all over the news," said Datschikoenig the baker. "The city centres are alive with Nazi torch-light parades. I´m telling you: these people are devil worshipers."

"What scares me," said Kabinett the furniture maker, "is if this Hitler bloke will be able to get his claws into **Dollfuss**."

"No chance," answered Fleischklops. "Dollfuss is a Christian man and wants Austria to remain its own Fatherland, which is what Mussolini also wants so that it remains a puffer state to Germany."

"My goodness," commented Kabinett, "these fireworks are going on a heck of a long time. They must have at least three times as many of them as they had for their New Year celebration."

"They must have expected Hitler really would be Kanzler and had the fireworks stored well in advance," said Datschikoenig.

Hitler had already demanded that he be made Kanzler (Chancellor) of Germany when his Nazis won the most seats in the July, 1932 Reichstag elections – and did so again when they remained the largest party in the November elections, in spite of a four per cent drop in votes. However, the German President, Paul von Hindenburg was having none of it, being a celebrated old war horse who had been brought out of retirement in 1925 whilst having his medals freshly dusted. Beginning his presidency at the grand age of seventy-seven, it was hoped that he would be able to bring an aura of sanity to a chain of ever more chaotic and indecisive democratic governments, many of which had lasted only a few months.

Hindenburg positively hated Hitler, with Dani later claiming that Hindenburg had said that Hitler treated Germany like a toilet in that he just wanted to sit his big, fat arse on it and do his business in it. The then German Kanzler had been Franz von Papen, leader of the also far-right but minority Deutschnational Volkspartei, having only won six and then eight percent of the vote in the two elections.

However, since Papen also managed to make a proper hash-brown of his job like his predecessors, particularly with his ongoing austerity programme, Hindenburg decided to instead make the conservative and wannabe "strong man" Kurt von Schleicher the next Kanzler that December. Surprise, surprise: **Schleicher** made an even worse job than Papen, so that Hindenburg was finally forced to bend to public pressure and make Hitler Kanzler on the Thirtieth of January: the very same fateful day I´m talking about it.

As Vice-Kanzler, Papen and other such conservatives still thought that they could "control" Hitler when Papen helped to form a supposed coalition of right-wingers in the government – but, boy, were they wrong. **Papen**´s own party was soon forced to integrate with the Nazis, with Hitler calling another Reichstag election that March and their winning a massive forty-four per cent majority. It would be the last democratic election until the Nazis lost the War, as Hitler then managed to ban all other parties, so that all future elections were a scam.

Meanwhile: back to Gletschberg am Brenner. Once the fireworks were over – which took an awful long time – most of the other children and all the grown-ups began leaving, to return to their winter fire-hearths and various household chores. I stayed on with Seppi and Dani, leaning on the neat, little fence at the front of the wooden terrace of the hotel, which was where its wealthy guests often sat on expensive chairs at tables decked with fancy white table-cloths for their lunches and refreshment breaks.

In fact, it was perfectly common for (especially on busy Sunday afternoons) there to be more villagers (including grown-ups and sometimes even entire families) standing at the terrace fence and gawping at the Upper Echelons of Society enjoying their holidays (which was a thing that few of us ever had in those days) than there to be locals actually skating on the lake or even just standing around it.

Now, as the smoke from the bright sparklers began to disappear so that we could finally gawp at the posh hotel guests still standing around on the terrace, we were astounded to see that they were no longer dressed in their flashy and fancy ski outfits of the day. Instead, the men were trussed up to the hilt in dinner-suits and tuxedos, whilst the women wore the flimsiest of glittery dancing dresses under their mink coats.

"Those men look like constipated penguins in all that garb," said Seppi.

"And the women look like skeletons dressed up as polar bears," noted Dani.

"OOIIIY!" a voice suddenly cried at us. "What do you three pieces of turd want around here!"

"Oh-oh," Dani said. "Here comes Stinky Sneaking Slimey Stefan himself."

A clumsy figure suddenly appeared on the terrace just above us, also dressed in a tuxedo and looking for all the world liked an escaped ape that was still dressed in its circus costume.

"Nothing wrong with us standing here," I told Slimey Stefan: who, in spite of his very expensive, spoilt rich boy´s outfit, was still as tall, dark and ugly as ever. "You know perfectly well that the miniature lake belongs to the Gemeinde for the use of everyone and that this footpath here is a public right of way."

"Yes, but just in case you have forgotten (or, more likely, never even knew) it is my Papa (that is, Herr Kratzkopf to you lot) who is the Buergermeister of the Gemeinde."

"It still doesn´t mean that he owns the lake," I said. "Not unless he manages to persuade the Gemeinderat to somehow sell it to him, which I would deem to be extremely unlikely."

Dani now looked at me with a smile, clearly fascinated that, although I wasn´t an academic like him but just a simple mountain lad, I too could speak like a posh grown-up whenever the mood suited me. I had certainly taken the wind out of Slimey Stefan´s sails, who now looked at me with startled befuddlement before eventually changing his tact and saying:

"I say, you three look as if you could make up a whole brain when put together: I wonder if any of you rascals would like to make a few Schillings on the side. With the Fasching rush and school holidays coming along soon, we could do with an errand boy in the early mornings to collect all the goodies from the butcher, the baker and the furniture maker."

We three boys must have looked like the three moneys who could see no evil, hear no evil and therefore also spoke no evil because Slimey then said:

"Come on, we will make it well worth your while – and it´s only in the early mornings."

There was another silence before Slimey suggested "Dani?"

"Nothing doing," Dani answered. "My old man always needs me during these holidays to help with the Fasching costumes."

"Seppi?" Slimey then asked.

"Sorry, Stefan," Seppi answered. "My old man needs me to help out at the police station."

I knew that Seppi was of course lying and that the real reason was that Seppi was just too darn lazy to want to do anything, even for money. It was a terrible lie – as if anyone could use a child to do police work other than spying – but Slimey was himself daft enough to buy it.

"Erich?" Slimey now asked me.

"I also can't," I also lied, not wishing to give up any of my winter ski-touring holiday time. "My Mama needs me in the kitchen and to look after the animals because Maria – "

"The money will do you good," Slimey excitedly told me, somehow reading my mind even though it was a perfectly plausible lie. "You'll be able to buy some brand new equipment for your skiing!"

"Yes, but if I've got to work in the mornings I won't have time for ski-touring afterwards," I answered, before suddenly realizing my slip of the tongue and that I had now exposed my lie.

Slimey gave me his usual dark smile for whenever anyone made a mistake and before also telling me:

"You won't have to go ski-touring: I'll give you a free pass for all of the lifts for the entire winter and then you can use them to your heart's content for the rest of the day as soon as you've finished working."

The fact was that the ski-lifts were mighty darn expensive so that about the only people that used these were the Kratzkopfs, their friends and the Berghof guests – and the occasional rich eccentric from some other village or town who showed up in some flash motor car that they had just driven up the somewhat in-need-of-repairs Brenner Pass.

As such, ordinary folk like myself would spend their ski recreation time trudging up the mountain either on their skis or with their skis on their backs (some also used snow-shoes to get up) and then skied down once they had decided that they had trudged up high enough. Since this could easily be more laborious than fun as one trudged up and skied down the same meadow all day long, I would often go on a long ski-tour with a packed lunch and flask of herb tea and explore the higher grounds instead. On the other hand, I couldn´t but jump at the chance of skiing all day long without having to do any more trudging, so I readily agreed.

My Papa, however, wasn´t at all happy about the deal when I nonchalantly told him this little bit of news on my arrival back home, least of all because I hadn´t even asked him first.

"WHAT? Are you crazy?!" he almost roared. "Don´t you realize that those Kratzkopfs are NAZIS? Do you really think that they just happened to bring all those fireworks along with them on the train as if they were just a few packets of sparklers? All this must have been organized weeks or even months ago, especially with that skinny minx of his being a Brandenburg Prussian. Who knows what tricks her rich, aristocratic family and friends are up to."

"I didn´t know that Hitler was even well-liked by the aristocracy," said Mama, whilst repairing Papa´s police uniform for the next day. "Hindenburg and those two other Kanzlers don´t seem to have liked him much either."

For a country woman about the house in those days my Mama was unusually well-informed in German and Austrian politics – but then, as Maria would have put it, she also LISTENED whenever Papa had the radio on.

"Hitler´s in with everyone," Papa said, "be they aristocrat, industrialist, businessman, tradesman, shopkeeper, school teacher or just local bully boy. The only people he´s not in with are the socialists, the communists, the Church and the Jews. For everyone else he´s got a different face and the only one that is true is the bully boy one."

"Well," Mama answered her husband, "maybe it will be good for you to have someone in the Berghof so then we might be able to find out if Kratzkopf has any more plans up his sleeve for Gletschberg. As the second chief of police, you might be able to profit from that."

"You mean like a kind of spy?" Papa asked, with a slight gleam in his eye as if he were already warming to the idea of being able to get one over Kratzkopf in the future.

"More like a kind of domestic eavesdropper," Mama replied.

"But what about Max?" I asked. "Isn´t he already a spy as he also works at the Berghof?"

"Like heck he is!" Papa almost shouted, crumpling his paper as if he were wringing his brother´s neck. "Everyone knows that he is a Socialist – and the only one in the entire village. People avoid him like the plague when talking politics."

I much preferred the name of "Spy" to "eavesdropper" as it immediately filled my imagination with images of adventure and mystery, whilst also giving another very good reason for taking on the job. I therefore had some difficulty trying not to grin my silly face off the next time that I met Slimey when I started my part-time job at the beginning of the school holidays a couple of weeks later. I kept thinking to myself, "I´m a spy! I´m a spy!" in much the same way as if poor Pete had been frantically shouting those words from his stool.

6: Spying on the Nazis

I was also surprised that Slimey Stefan didn´t treat me like a little shit as he was wont to do with most children. Instead, he was actually quite kind to me: as he was with all the guests and even their (usually German) man-servants and maids.

Being a mere errand boy I wasn´t allowed anywhere near the guests or even in any of the recreational salons (like the dining and drawing rooms) except very early in the morning when no one but other staff were there. However, even when I stood beside the man-servants and maids I felt like a rag-doll whilst dressed in my everyday village clothes. I had therefore expected the man-servants and maids to be very snobbish and stuck-up whenever I had to speak to them, so that I even began to wear my Sunday best for the job. However, whilst some of the man-servants just smiled at my choice of attire for the most menial of menial jobs after dish-washer, no one ever put me down for it. In fact, everyone was incredibly polite and pleasant towards me.

"You know what," Slimey presently also said to me whilst giving me a packed snack for my skiing after work, "you´re very smart for your age. You´re quick to learn and everyone likes you. It seems that you have a knack for getting on with everyone."

I felt like saying that it was a pity that he didn´t take a page out of my book and stop bullying people that he didn´t like.

As to my Mama, she thought that it was all a charade when I told her how well I was treated at the Berghof, especially by the guests.

"They may treat you like their favourite pet dog," she replied, "but they treat all us other village mortals like the very cow muck that they frequently have to negotiate on their various country excursions."

I could tell by the emotion that my Mama was putting into her words that she was thinking of her own experience of working at the Berghof. She clearly still had a gripe about something.

"But that was donkey´s years ago: before I was even born," I replied. "The hotel must have changed vastly since then, which means that the type of guests that it attracts has also probably changed."

"They´re may be more refined and polite but they´re still ALL Nazis these days!" Papa suddenly interjected. "Guests, man-servants, maids: the lot of them. Our old friend Father Murrsea also says as much. He told us that, rich as the masters and mistresses are and poor as the man-servants and maids are in spite of their sumptuous costumes, they have all made the Brown Cult their demagogue. In fact, none of them have any more use for any religious services if someone suddenly snuffs it – or any number of other circumstances for wanting a priest. On the one occasion when he did turn up when one of the guests suddenly keeled over from too much brandy, he was quickly and most disrespectfully shooed off – but not before first noticing that the old Catholic crucifix that had once graced the main dining-room whilst Grandpa and Grandma Kratzkopf were still alive had now been replaced by a full-size portrait of Adolf Hitler."

I had, however, seen no such picture – nor even a smaller one – on the couple of rare occasions that I had been inside the main dining-room first thing in the morning. Then again, neither had I seen any Catholic crucifixes hanging about the hotel, as was usual in both public buildings and people´s private homes.

In fact, there was nothing to suggest that the Kratzkopfs´ guests and their servants were Nazis, apart from the fireworks when Hitler became Kanzler and the fact that the mood in the hotel suddenly became almost euphoric. Whereas the guests had been just plain jolly before, as if they were simply glad to catch an alpine winter break, they were now partying every day, morning, afternoon and night as if there were no tomorrow.

Kratzkopf even had a band playing every afternoon, rolling out all kinds of oompah-oompah music that got one´s blood stirring. Whilst he clearly intended it to be for the benefit of his rich guests, it also meant that the frozen lake was soon choc-a-bloc full with local skaters, not to mention almost legions of villagers who simply stood in the snow before the terrace listening to the wonderful music.

"Why don´t we open the terrace up to the public on Sunday afternoons?" I once heard Slimey Stefan ask his Papa during one of my numerous eavesdropping moments – for I seemed to have the uncanny ability of the natural-born spy to always be in the right place at the right moment.

"Are you insane?" Kratzkopf almost shouted back at his son. "Have you no idea what cheap rubbish these peasants drink? The real money has always been and always will be in the luxury guest."

"But couldn´t you build a temporary station on the lake and have that open to the public?" Slimey then asked.

"Ah," answered Kratzkopf. "Now there you are starting to use your noodle, boy! I thought of that myself but unfortunately the Gemeinderat won´t give me permission to do so. On the other hand, we can open up the alm to everyone whilst I think that I might be able to get the Gemeindeamt to offer cheap family tickets on the cable-car."

It was a brilliant idea because, if nothing else, the alm offered fantastic aerial views of the valley. As such, families were soon spending their meagre recreational savings riding up the cable car to the alm and then skiing back down to the village afterwards.

From the alm you could see just how much Gletschberg had grown since the advent of the railways up the Brenner Pass. The original and traditional "Old" part of the village was on the ledge that led into the Watzkessel, with the church seemingly guarding it as it proudly stood before the large village square at the top of the little windy road that rose from the Wipptal Valley immediately below in the west. Surrounded only by empty fields for growing hay, this mostly deserted and primitive road nevertheless afforded a grand view of the Wipptal Valley and was affectionately known as the Gletschberg Pass.

The much less picturesque "West" side of Gletschberg had meanwhile grown to the immediate south of where the railway station now stood in the Wipptal Valley, with most of this "new" part of the village being the houses in which the federal railway's many employers and associated traders lived. Meanwhile, many farmers still lived in remote homesteads in both the meadows of our Watzkessel and in the Wipptal Valley.

Since I was running so many errands to the butcher, the baker, the furniture maker and so on in the traditional village, I soon got to know many of the people in that main part of the village – people I had previously known by sight but never really talked to. Indeed, it wasn't long before Dani was telling me that more people in the village now personally knew me than they did my Papa.

I also got to know the hotel staff – the receptionists, the waiters, the chefs and the chamber maids – who would often visit the local bars during their afternoon breaks (as they usually worked in the evenings instead). It was always just a coffee or an apple juice or the like because, in those days, if you were caught drinking alcohol during any breaks you could be sacked on the spot.

I never bothered spending any of my valuable Groschens at any bars but I was often invited there by the man-servants, who always offered to pay me for my drinks because I was still just a school-kid and basically just earned pocket money. It was at the bars that the man-servants would mix and gossip with the villagers and tell them all about the latest goings on in Germany.

It was also at these bars that I learnt how to listen to what others said and ask sympathetic questions at only the right moments. Nobody regarded me as being anything more than a nice, intelligent young kid turning eleven and, for some of them, that also meant perhaps one day joining their cause. And what was that cause, you may well ask? The answer surprised me as nothing else could have surprised me for, to hear my Papa talking about politics whenever Max at home, Dollfuss and his Christian Socialists pretty much had Austria in the bag. Some of the youngsters, however, were all raring to go and join the Nazis.

Hitler and his German Nazis, they said, were a thousand times better than Dollfuss and his own boot boys. Dollfuss wanted to keep Austria as a tiny alpine land, which was something that kept, as I have mentioned before, Mussolini happy as it was a useful puffer state against Nazi Germany. Hitler, however, wanted to bring Austria into the **German Reich**, which was an idea that had been floating around since 1848 as Austria had once played a major leading role in the Holy Roman Empire.

On top of all this was the belief that Hitler was a strong man who, unlike Dollfuss, could work economic miracles, especially as Europe was still only slowly recovering from the Great Depression. Some of the youngsters in the village therefore looked at the rich guests staying at the Berghof and wondered why they too couldn´t have some extra money for holidays and luxuries, instead of surviving on only the basics day after day, year after year, decade after decade.

"The Nazis are just a bunch of cruel pirates who steal from and murder minorities whilst stoking fear about them," Papa told me when I told him, Mama and Max one evening about what I had heard from my "acquaintances".

"They are a wicked and uncontrollable virus that just keeps getting worse and worse," said Max.

"As such, Erich," Mama added, "you must be very careful that you don´t believe a word that they tell you."

It was then that I noticed Seppi hiding in the shadows at the top of the stairs, whilst grinning stupidly away. However, instead of snitching on him I merely asked Papa:

"What minorities?"

"Mainly Jews – but also Roma and Sinti gypsies, Jehova Witnesses, disabled people, **negroes**, homosexuals and, of course, socialists and communists," Papa answered, whilst carefully turning his eye towards Max. "In fact, anyone who dares to disagree with them or has a different culture."

"Jews?" I said, no doubt looking puzzled whilst forgetting the rest.

"Yes," Papa said, clearly reading my thoughts. "Dani and his parents may be the only Jews living in our village and therefore won't seem to be a threat to anyone but the looniest of nut-jobs. On the other hand, the cities sometimes have huge communities of Jews, many of whom have contributed massively to society, as well as having fought in the War alongside everyone else."

"But why should they be a threat to anyone if they are such a big help to the country?" I asked, more baffled than ever.

"Because," Max sharply replied, "some people are just pesky little wimps who are scared of everything that is different to them and their monotonous lives."

It was then that I again noticed Seppi hiding in the shadows as Max said this, except that this time Seppi's stupid grin suddenly evaporated from his idiot face as if he thought Max were talking about him.

7: Revenge of the Nazis

Herr Kratzkopf immediately traveled all the way to Brandenburg with his wife's coffin after the so-called "Battle of Hitler's Birthday" that April. Frau Kratzkopf was then buried in her own ancestral graveyard in Germany, whilst Kratzkopf insisted that Murrsea held a memorial service for his late wife back in his own home village of Gletschberg.

Once again the church bells began ringing as if Armageddon were fast approaching, whilst I expected almost no one to turn up at the service as the old bird had been very unpopular in the village because of her airs and graces and Queen of Sheba vanity. I was therefore surprised when a few hundred of our population of not even a couple of thousand turned up for the service.

Like other important officials in the village, Papa was expected to pay his last respects for the Nazi bird, with his wife and kids trailing behind him like ducklings, even though none of us could stand the old bird whilst she had been alive. Max, as a senior member of Kratzkopf's staff, had also been expected to make a showing.

On occasions like this it was interesting to see how many of the men not only wore their medals from the Great War but also military uniforms of one sort or another. As Second Chief of Police, however, Papa wore his ceremonial police officer's uniform, which included the insignia of his final rank of major from his army years. Max, however, didn´t wear a uniform at all, although he did have two medals, although he never told me what they had been for.

"I´m damned if they´re not all Nazi sympathizers," I then heard Papa say to Max after the service in the churchyard.

"It still intrigues me just how long Kratzkopf is going to remain a closet Nazi," Max answered Papa back. "It can´t be long before he has to come out and show his true colors."

"If he does do so the folks may demand a new Buergermeister election as he was voted into the job as a Christian Socialist, not as a Nazi," Papa said.

"Well then, let´s just hope that the village doesn´t start voting for Nazis as they did in Innsbruck only this week," Max replied. "From having no seats in the city´s Gemeinderat they now hold almost a quarter of them."

"I only wish that I could stand as the next Christian Socialist Buergermeister," said Papa, "but, of course, as a state employee I´m not allowed to seek any kind of political office."

The Battle of Hitler´s Birthday had meanwhile bitterly divided the village. I, for my part, refused to go back to the Berghof with its gigantic picture of Adolf Hitler on the wall, glaring at everyone with his burnt blackcurrant eyes as they passed through.

Gone were the happy days of winter when everyone had seemed to be jolly and united. The police even asked the Heimatwehr for further support so that they could patrol the roads and keep the Nazis out of any more mischief. Seeing the Heimatwehr troops standing around the road corners, with their bucket-wagons and mini-trucks beside them, one couldn't help feeling that civil war were about to break out in the village.

However, this seemed to do the trick of calming things down for a bit, at least on the surface. The Nazis simply returned to complaining in bars and behind closed doors, although they now did so much more bitterly as they milked their victimization for all that it was worth.

Soon enough it was May, with warm sunshine everywhere and the Heimatwehr patrols enjoying what had seemingly turned out to just be a holiday of basking in the sun's friendly rays. The Berghof was also closed for what were much-needed repairs and renovations, so that there wasn't a single tourist to be seen anywhere.

When the hotel did open again in June and the tourists began arriving once more, this time for a season of hiking and climbing for the more adventurous, everything seemed to have returned to normal. The Heimatwehr therefore decided to pull up sticks and let us look after our own selves again. Big mistake: for the Heimatwehr had hardly gone when the first visible signs of Nazism began to show up on a daily basis.

It began with thousands of flyers being stuffed in unceremoniously ways into people's letter-boxes, cat-flaps, empty milk-churns, delivery boxes and even out-houses (although they no doubt soon went down the johnny). Nothing particularly illegal about that, you might say, although one might have wondered who had the time to print such rubbish.

Then came the portraits of Adolf Bally Bonkers Hitler, suddenly appearing first thing in the mornings as they stared at you from lamp-posts, sign-posts, road-signs, telegraph-poles, post-boxes and even public buildings, not to mention the back of one person´s dog-kennel. They were even stuck onto the front-doors of the homes of people who didn´t even support the little devil. A huge sign with the words "Wake up, Austria!" (as well as a cartoon of Dollfuss as the Devil and Hitler as an angel) suddenly turned up on the door of the **Rathaus** whilst the Gemeinderat was actually sitting inside and deliberating on how to put a stop to all of this.

"Can´t you do anything about this?" I asked Papa one evening at dinner. "Surely it´s against the law."

"Political campaigning is never a crime: it´s called democracy and the right of free speech," Papa answered sagely, as if he were the village judge and not the second police chief. "However, when it becomes a nuisance then it´s a different matter."

"So what are you going to do about it?" I went on.

"There´s nothing that we can do about it until we KNOW who´s doing it," Papa suddenly sharply said. "We can´t stay up all night and every night just on the off-chance that we catch one of the culprits, any more than we can bang up or fine any of the

Nazis who we do know without any evidence of actual crimes."

"And as long as this keeps going on like this," Mama said, as she helped Pete with the last of his dinner, "the Nazis here will only get cheekier."

"CHEEKY! CHEEKY! CHEEKY!" Pete cried out whilst Seppi grinned mischievously from ear to ear.

It was not long after that that the Nazis did indeed get cheeky, assembling a brass band and playing the **"Horst Wessel Lied"** directly in front of the Rathaus during another one of the Gemeinderat meetings within. This time the police did decide to do something, as they came marching up to them with the Old Kaiser at their head. However, as there were only a handful of them compared to the twenty or so Nazi brass band players, who were each as big as block-houses, the Old Kaiser ran off to the elderly Gemeinderat to get their physical support.

For a moment it looked as if there would be another battle but Papa managed to calm things down whilst carefully noting in his head who was there. You can therefore imagine the shock that all these Nazis got when the Heimatwehr suddenly came knocking on each of their doors the next day and demanded that they all immediately went to the village magistrate for a summons.

To their unexpected surprise and horror they were each given the choice between a hefty fine or a fortnight´s stint in the jail-cage in the cellar of the police station. Needless to say that twenty village Nazis suddenly found themselves a lot poorer – except for one, whose Papi refused to throw good money away just because his son was the village clown. This was none other than the ring-leader – who in turn was none other than Slimey Stefan himself. Landing in the village clink, of course, made Slimey very sore for a long time about not only his Papi not supporting him but also about my own Papa, as if he had had any choice in the matter.

However, if the police, the magistrate (a funny little fellow called Schnabel) and the Gemeinderat thought that that was an end to all this Nazi mischief then they were solely mistaken. The Nazis simply became more sneaky when they decided to exact their revenge on the village boffins. Thus, when the Chief of Police for Innsbruck, Franz Hickl, arrived one morning on a ceremonial visit (but most likely to find out what the hell was going on in the village) the village band suddenly realized that all their music scores had been nicked. The Old Kaiser was so furious about being made to look a dummy that, without a shred of evidence, he instantly had Slimey Stefan locked up in the underground slammer for another two weeks.

Kratzkopf, meanwhile, was being surprisingly coy about the situation.

"I'm telling you, Kratzkopf is the real brains behind all this chaos," Papa said to Max one Saturday evening when Max came for dinner with us.

"I would have thought that he′d be trying to calm things down," Max replied. "The German guests may be used to seeing Nazi flags and portraits of Hitler hanging around everywhere now, not to mention the S.A. flying around all over the place, whereas here it′s the Heimatwehr, but they can still sense when a village is on the brink of civil war and so want to stay away."

"It′s that damned fool the Old Kaiser who is doing all the escalating, not Kratzkopf," said Papa. "He′s making the Nazis look like victims by taking too drastic actions too quickly. Softly, softly is what I say."

The worst, of course, was yet to come. Swastikas were soon found painted on people′s houses, fences and walls and even on public buildings. What′s more, there were swastikas made of straw that were set alight in fields for people to see for miles around. Apart from looking like some hideous Halloween joke, these fire swastikas posed a tremendous fire hazard, especially when they started also being lit in the village: a village that was made up of scores of wooden chalets and which could burn down in a jiffy. This time, however, the Nazis didn′t have it so easy.

The Heimatwehr was therefore called on to raid suspected Nazis′ homes, garages and work-shops to look for condemning paint or, even better, yet un-used straw swastikas. Some of the Heimatwehr troops even got dressed up like tourists and hung around in the shadows in the hope that they might catch the culprits red-handed. Once convicted, the offending Nazis were then ordered by Magistrate Schnabel to take part in a "Putzscharren", which was when they had had to go about as a group cleaning the damned paint off with turpentine.

They were of course under a police escort, with the Old Kaiser making sure that they did their penal duties at the busiest times of the day so as to attract the largest crowds. They used to get a lot of verbal abuse from the villagers, especially the old ladies, whilst known Nazi sympathizers rarely showed up at such scenes. I was at first quite surprised by that until Papa said: "Well, what do you expect from a bunch of cowards who only show any kind of courage when they´re in a large group?"

However, whilst finding Nazi graffiti, posters and flyers everywhere was ugly enough, it was the firecrackers that really put the wind up everyone. Firecrackers are, of course, hand-held fireworks that were, in those days, freely bandied about with little thought given to just how damned dangerous they were if handled incorrectly. As a form of propaganda they were a complete waste of time but many of the younger Nazis just didn´t care less because they weren´t so much interested in the power of politics as in just plain terrorizing everyone else in order to give their moronic brains a sense of their own feeble power.

Most of these wallies cowardly hid in crowds, especially in the cinema and at the local weekly market, so as to frighten the living crap out of normal people. However, some of them even dared to run around in small groups whilst throwing firecrackers under innocent bystanders. One such person was a pregnant woman who had an instant miscarriage after such a gang of Nazis let a firecracker off behind her. As the Nazis would run away before the firecrackers went off and left people in shock, it was rare that any of them were recognized, let alone physically stopped and held down by a strong and quick-witted passer-by.

Of course we all knew who the main culprits would be but, once again, without firm evidence not a lot could be done, especially as the Old Kaiser had already gotten himself into an awful lot of trouble with Magistrate Schnabel for convicting and imprisoning without evidence – and had even nearly lost his job because of it.

As I just mentioned, the supreme rabble-rouser of all these thugs was, of course, none other than the great village bully himself: Slimey Stefan. I had been avoiding Slimey like the plague ever since the Battle of Hitler´s Birthday, which was said to have then sent him full-blown whacko and ready for mortal revenge for his late mother´s untimely demise. And then an incident occurred that really shocked the entire village.

It was now the middle of June, as well as being a **school-free Saturday afternoon**. Dani was also throwing a birthday party that afternoon since he had also turned eleven that week. As such, Maria and I had decided to take Pete along, who was thoroughly enjoying himself as we held him between us by his hands so that he could swing up and down in the air like a small kid.

My stomach, however, suddenly turned as I saw Slimey and a gang of other youths coming towards us, laughing and cajoling and being only too eager for creating trouble. A year before he would have been up on the mountain and running the alm with its extra Saturday business: but his Papa had got rid of him when he became totally unreliable and erratically rude to just about everybody after his mother´s sudden death.

Having no more imagination than a slug he was therefore now roaming the streets with his gang of equally stupid and slimey buddies. With there being no avoiding them without running back where we had just come from, which would have looked very unheroic, we simply had to brass it out.

"Hey, Erich!" Slimey suddenly shouted at me, whilst looking as if he couldn´t decide whether to behave seriously or just bally stupidly towards me. "Why are you no longer coming to the Berghof to do your bit with us? We´ve always got a ton of work to do, you know."

I would have loved to have told him that, judging by the way that he and his mates were loafing about the streets, that that didn´t seem likely – but knew better than to provoke trouble whilst Slimey had his band of thugs with him.

"I mean," Slimey carried on, starting to get mischievous, "it´s not as if I should now hold a grudge towards you, even if it is your old man who keeps banging me up behind bars for having just a bit of fun."

"That's got nothing to do with my Papa," I tried to tell him diplomatically, whilst trying to think of an expedient way of making a quick but face-saving departure with everyone else. "That's all on the Old Kaiser. He's the one who keeps over-reacting, not my Papa."

"Like hell it's all the Old Kaiser's fault!" Slimey shouted back with sudden anger. "It's your Papikins and all his pig cronies who keep snooping after us and faking evidence everywhere that we go!"

I was about to suggest that he stopped causing trouble in the first place when Maria suddenly sprang to my defense.

"Stop playing the bully the whole time!" she suddenly cried. "Can't you be nice for once in your worthless, spoilt and rotten life?"

"Ooooh, so now we have to all be nice and coochy-woochy-boochy," said Slimey, suddenly rolling his shoulders about in such a ridiculously effeminate way that all his flunkeys began boisterously laughing.

"You and your bird-brain mates don't frighten me," Maria suddenly shouted as loudly as she could – although, unfortunately, this was still not much louder than a mouse. "You just disgust me!"

"Oooh, so now we're all disgusting, are we?" Slimey said with another effeminate roll of his shoulders. "Such high spirits for such a tiny, weeny, little baby girl!"

Maria was about to shout something back when Slimey suddenly threw a lit fire-cracker at her from apparently out of nowhere. However, Maria was as quick as lightening for, seeing that the cracker was about to go off in her face, suddenly batted it away from herself and into the side of the road.

Pete, on the other hand , wasn´t so lucky when Slimey suddenly also threw a fire-cracker towards him whilst crying out, "Here, catch this Pete!" I have no doubt that Slimey expected that Pete would merely jump away in fright whilst flapping his arms around like a castrated chicken and that it never occurred to him that Maria and I had actually managed to teach Pete to catch ball over the years. Thus, it was a hell of a surprise to Slimey and his friends when they saw Pete suddenly catch the cracker in the air and then began holding it for all that it was worth as if it were a much-loved toy.

"NO-OOO!!!" Maria cried as she desperately tried to grab the cracker from her younger brother and throw it away. However, Pete was having none of it.

"CRACKER! CRACKER! CRACKER!" Pete therefore kept crying, as happy as a sandman and as innocent as a lamb.

Yet the worst still hadn´t come as Pete now began holding the fire-cracker close to his eyes as if trying to figure out whether it were animal, vegetable or mineral.

All of a sudden there was a terrific bang and blood shot out everywhere.

Pete was permanently blinded in one eye. We took some relief in the fact that it had been just the one eye. However, Fate refused to show any mercy for Pete because it was his strong eye that had been blinded, which meant that his weak eye soon "went out in sympathy", so that he finished up being completely blind in both eyes.

Not only that but the shock had upset Pete so badly that he spent the rest of his days at our house simply sitting on his stool in the main room whilst flapping his arms about like a scared bird, with it taking endless coaxing to get him off the stool to just go to the toilet outside or even to bed.

Slimey Stefan. was really unpopular when the incident became known, with half the villagers demanding en masse that justice be done. However, Magistrate Schnabel wouldn´t issue a warrant for Slimey´s arrest, claiming that without any witnesses other than ourselves anybody could have done it.

However, as if the Austrian government had itself begun to take an interest in the incident, it was only a couple of days later that Dollfuss officially banned the Nazi Party. As a mark of revenge, Hitler then introduced the so-called "Thousand Mark Barrier" just two weeks later: a ban which would have immediate catastrophic effects on Austria´s tourism and economy and, of course, our village. Ironically, it would also send Kratzkopf and his Nazi hotel business flying down the toilet.

8: The Nazi Boxing Tournament

At the same time that Hitler had been consolidating his power in the new Nazi Germany during the first half of 1933, Engelbert Dollfuss had also kept himself busy in what was rapidly also becoming fascist Austria. It began with the so-called "self-elimination" of the democratically elected lower house of Parliament, the Nationalrat, in March, 1933.

This was triggered off when its president resigned his seat so that he could take part in a tightly-fought vote in the house. The two vice-presidents then also resigned their positions in order to counter-balance the votes, with Dollfuss immediately seizing on the opportunity to shut the pesky house down altogether on the technicality that, without any leaders of their own, they had effectively snuffed out their own powers.

Dollfuss even did this physically, sending in his boot boys to stop any of the delegates getting back inside the house after they had all gone out for a quick sausage sandwich. Max therefore turned out to be all too right about Dollfuss turning Austria into a full-blown fascist country, even if historians have since argued that it was only an authoritarian one like Mussolini´s Italy and not a totalitarian one like Hitler´s Germany, where every single walk of life was tightly controlled by the Nazi regime.

However, just like Hitler, Dollfuss now used the emergency powers that his country´s post-War democratic constitution invested in his office to ban other political parties, even though these powers had ironically been devised to protect the constitution and not destroy it. Although Dollfuss didn´t ban the Social Democrats until the following year, he did ban their para-military wing, the Republican Schutzbund, as soon as he had got rid of the Nationalrat. A couple of months later, in May, he banned the Communists and now, just as summer was beginning, he also banned the Nazis.

Hitler immediately flew into one of his famous huffs and ordered the so-called "Thousand Mark Barrier". This meant that any Germans wishing to visit or even just travel through Austria had to pay a whopping amount of money (namely, a thousand Reichsmarks) to the Third Reich just for the pleasure of doing so. Austria suddenly found itself cut off from its main source of foreign trade and tourism so that, needless to say, the bottom suddenly fell out of the small alpine land´s economy. Hitler would not repeal the catastrophic "Thousand Mark Barrier" until just after the Berlin Olympics of August, 1936, some three years later.

As Papa said, however, the only good thing about the "Barrier" was that it had also wiped the all-too smug face off Herr Kratzkopf´s face. Kratzkopf had now been having his hotel permanently booked out for both the summer and winter seasons for what seemed to be donkey´s years, only to find that his expected bookings for the entire coming summer suddenly dropped down to a mere handful.

"I´m telling you," Papa would often say to Max, "the only Germans who can now afford to take their holidays in Austria are high-ranking Nazi officials, some of whom may even have a pass for exemption from the Thousand Mark Barrier."

"Until now I had thought that only a few of the German guests were real Nazis," Max would reply, "but now I´m beginning to think that you are right and that the guests that we get really all do belong to the Nazi Party. I just hope that they are just treating the **Berghof as a holiday home** and aren´t planning anything big for Gletschberg."

With fewer guests Kratzkopf had had to let many of his staff go, as well as the afternoon oompah-oompah band. Max was lucky to be one of the few to be able to keep his job, although he was no longer happy about the fact that the hotels German guests who he now took on hikes and climbing expeditions were all without doubt high-ranking Nazis. Indeed, Max later told me, he often thought about ways of getting his punters to do something foolish and so break their own necks – although he never put his whimsical fantasies into actual practice.

Those staff who lost their jobs immediately found themselves in a raw pickle as hotel and tourist staff all across Austria were given their leaving papers. What´s more, related trades like the butcher, the baker and the furniture maker were also suffering from the lack of tourism, as well as many industries that simply lost their German business overnight.

Needless to say that the unemployment rate sky-rocketed throughout the country, with Dollfuss often being blamed for unnecessarily upsetting Hitler. On top of this, many of the unemployed now took to the streets and joined the Nazis, who were clearly now enjoying a better life in Germany. As with many other foreign leaders during the next few years, Hitler had played Dollfuss like a fiddle and straight into his own hands.

It was then, during the height of summer, that Kratzkopf and his son jointly had a brilliant idea that was both a sheer stroke of genius and a rare moment when they actually agreed on something. Ironically, it all began when Kratzkopf managed to get himself into trouble with the Old Kaiser by flying a Nazi flag next to the Austrian flag at the front of the Berghof hotel. My Papa was also there in uniform at the time so I got to hear all about it when he later told Max all about it at the dinner table.

"You need to take down that Nazi flag right now, Herr Kratzkopf!" the Old Kaiser had apparently thundered whilst several of the German guests stood watching with mingled disbelief and amusement. "You know as well as I do that the Nazi Party is now VERBOTEN, which means that any such displays of its insignias or logos are also no longer tolerated!"

"But this is no longer just a political flag but the new official national flag of the German Reich, my dear Hauptmann Kaiser," Kratzkopf apparently answered with a mischievous grin. "It would be an insult to my German guests if I were to still fly the old flag."

"Since when?" the Old Kaiser demanded, not believing a word that Kratzkopf was telling him.

"Since the Ninth of July," Kratzkopf answered, without mentioning that the old German tricolor flag of black, red and gold could still officially be flown for another two years.

Looking thoroughly red in the face, the Old Kaiser then asked my Papa if this were true.

"It was mentioned in the newspaper," my Papa answered, whilst all the German guests nodded in accord.

The Old Kaiser then decided to turn tail and hop it instead of continuing to look a fool whilst the German guests giggled behind his back. This giggling, however, really riled him up so that he was on the point of exploding when one of the German guests suddenly gave him the Hitler salute.

Whilst almost choking himself to death with fury, the Old Kaiser then ordered my Papa to arrest the unsuspecting German tourist and throw him in the jail-cage for twenty-four hours. This time it was the German guests who got all riled up as they vehemently told the Old Kaiser that this was not the last that he had heard of this whilst furiously shaking their fists at him to show that they bally well meant it.

Kratzkopf was just as furious as his guests and told the Old Kaiser in no uncertain terms that he had no business arresting foreign tourists for breaking a law that they might very well not even know existed in Austria. Of course, in reality, this was about as likely as not knowing that bears and wolves are dangerous animals that shouldn´t be approached for a good cuddle.

True or not, Kratzkopf therefore decided to challenge the Old Kaiser to a duel of fisticuffs. This would have normally been highly irregular – if not downright criminal – but since the Old Kaiser and Kratzkopf had once not only been a member of Papa´s police boxing club but also one year even won its championship, it was a challenge that the Old Kaiser simply couldn´t resist.

On the other hand, since the Old Kaiser was no longer so sprightly on his knees, it was suggested that my Papa take his place. Well, a boxing match between Kratzkopf and my very own Papa really fired people´s imaginations, not the least Seppi´s. However, it was then that Slimey Stefan was supposed to have suggested that he instead bring in his (unofficial) S.A. boys in from the village to smash the boys from Papa´s police boxing club.

The boxing tournament consisted of different matches, with like being fairly pitted against like, and was set to take place on a summer Saturday afternoon on the terrace of the Berghof hotel – which Kratzkopf had meanwhile had to finally open to the public as he now had so few guests of his own. The boxing club usually met in the cellar of the police station (yes, next to the ominous jail-cage) so that most people never got to see the blood and gore of the actual matches, only the consequences. This time, however, the entire spectacle was on full display for everyone to see, with Kratzkopf making a tidy profit for the first time that summer on the drinks that all the new visitors began buying whilst satisfying their curiosity and lust for violence.

The weather, however, turned out to be severely ominous on that fateful afternoon, with heavy thunder clouds constantly threatening the tournament as they let the sunshine in one moment but then blocked just about all daylight out the next. Indeed, ever since the bright and sunny spring the summer months had been a saga of constantly changing sun, cloud and rain, not to mention the occasional thunderstorm and wash-out.

I was amazed by the size of the crowds that Kratzkopf had managed to bring in, in spite of the crazy weather, not just from our own village but from all the villages around. As I just said, Kratzkopf certainly made a killing that day, with the lines before the drinks bars being several men deep, with many of these visitors still having to go dry.

Sport has the amazing attribute of being able to either unite or divide people, depending on how it is presented. Kratzkopf certainly managed to unite the villages, presenting the S.A. boxers not as the thugs that they actually were but just as honourable amateurs fighting another team of honourable amateurs, which just so happened to be the police.

No doubt, of course, Slimey Stefan would have much preferred it if the police and their friends had been showcased as the sucker losers who were just there for the sake of the star team but it was clear that it was his Papikins who was running the show from behind the scenes and pulling the shots. Slimey did, however, have a big say in choosing his team of S.A. buddies from the other villages and even one from Innsbruck, whilst Papa bolstered up his club regulars (many of whom had just left school) with a bunch of large, strapping young Heimatwehr men.

In those days fisticuffs – that is, boxing without gloves – was a popular sport that was still seen as being an honourable way of settling scores when fragile egos were injured. Whilst punching under the belt was definitely not allowed, punching in the face and even the kidneys were still regarded as fair play and a great way for learning how to toughen up. Indeed, many schools encouraged fisticuffs as a respectable alternative to what otherwise invariably escalated into a universal brawl, where everyone finishes up being beaten to a pulp and everything smashed to smithereens, as we had already painfully witnessed with "The Battle of Hitler´s Birthday".

I, myself, still thought that it was a bloody stupid way of entertaining one´s self and more or less had to be dragged away from my afternoon in the mountains to witness the event with just about everyone else from miles around. Seppi, on the other hand, was all rearing to have a fight himself and had to be kept being told by our Papa, the police coach, that he was still too young for real matches.

Max of all people – a pacifist if ever there was – was given the job of Show Master and Referee, even though he knew little more about boxing than my own self. However, for such a quiet man as he usually was, he turned out to have a terrific flare for animation, as he managed to unwittingly whip an already excited crowd into a huge frenzy.

In fact, many men in the crowd – young and older ones alike and even aged grandpas – were soon openly baying for blood as they kept shaking their fists wildly in the air whilst shouting out obscenities like "Give it to him, you wanker!" "Tear his heart and liver out!" and "Punch him in the bollocks, you shit-for-brains!" The oddest thing, I noticed, was that these foul expletives were directed at whoever was winning (regardless of which team he was on) and not (as I had fully expected) just the S.A. men as they finally got a chance to beat their arch enemies to a pulp.

No one seemed to be more enthusiastic about the tournament than Seppi, as he kept jumping about, shaking his fists and generally dancing about in much the same fashion as Pete had used to before he had been blinded. Of course, Seppi still kept badgering our Papa about letting him have a fight of his own and Papa of course kept telling him, "Not on your nelly, son." This was hardly surprising: considering the many gruesome, gory and bloody injuries that were the frightening outcomes of many of these same fights.

In the meantime, Max followed to a tee the principle that the boxers from each team be paired off "like for like": that is, according to their size, weight and age. Naturally Max began the tournament with the youngest and smallest boxers who had been allowed to fight and then worked his way up to the very largest, with the crowd growing wilder and wilder as the violence grew more and more vicious and bloodier than ever.

Slimey had meanwhile decided that he was going to be the star of the entire show and so insisted that he fight the largest of the largest of the Heimatwehr in the very last fight of the tournament, which was the one that was supposed to settle the final question of honor regarding the ruckus between Kratzkopf and the Old Kaiser.

Everyone thought that this final fight would be a lousy disappointment after all the fun that they had just had because, although Slimey Stefan was the tallest of the S.A. team, he was in fact as skinny as a bean-pole. At the same time, the guy that Papa had kept to be his opponent was as big as a block-house, so that just one punch from him would feel like being run over by a bull-elephant.

Indeed, everyone really believed that Slimey would just scream mercy the moment that this fellow – who was nicknamed Buster Balls – even so little as just tickled him. To see the way that Slimey was running about the roped-in ring, however, hammering his chest away like a chimpanzee on coke and jumping up in the air like a jack-in-the-box, you would have thought that he really had lost all of his marbles.

"Come on, you big, fat slob!" Slimey practically screamed at the monster lad, even though some people had already begun leaving, having no time left for a joke fight. "What? You've got no spunk left in your buster balls?! Well, let me BUST them open for you!"

Slimey then let out a punch in the air in his warm-up show that probably wouldn't have even dazed a fly. Buster Balls meanwhile just sat on his stool in his corner saying nothing, waiting for the first bell to ring whilst staring at his opponent as if he were stark, raving bonkers and would need to be put out of his misery in a jiffy.

"Don't give ME that dumb-cluck look of yours, you baby elephant!" Slimey fired back at Buster Balls. "It's me who's the one who's INVINCIBLE and it's ME who is going to knock the holy crap out of you!!"

At this some of the crowd roared with laughter, which drowned out the ringing of the first bell.

9: The Unexpected Hero of the Day

Buster Balls then stood up and slouched his way towards Slimey as if he were about to knock the thin lad to Kingdom Come and God bless the fool. Slimey meanwhile kept prancing hither and thither on his two legs as if they were four whilst constantly whirling his fists around in his circles as if he were doing cartwheels with his arms.

Sure enough Buster Balls then let out a powerful jab that would have sent most mortal men flying towards the floor. However, Slimey ducked it at the last milli-second with the speed of a fly. No sooner had he done so then he let out a simple rear hook that completely caught Buster Balls off guard and hit him neatly in the chin. The crowd gave a huge gasp of surprise and everyone who had begun leaving suddenly rushed back to see what they had missed.

Buster Balls then staggered back a little and was about to go for a lead uppercut before suddenly staggering back once again. It was clear that Slimey had punched him a lot harder than we had at first imagined and might even have damaged his jaw. However, there was no time for considering all this stuff because Slimey suddenly let out a lead uppercut himself that forcefully hit Buster Balls right front-center in his unprotected mouth.

"Wow! That was a beauty!" I heard someone cry behind me as blood and teeth suddenly splattered out of Buster Balls´ gigantic face.

"Do it again!" I then heard one of the S.A. team cry out.

Slimey did – and this time he hit Buster Balls so hard in the nose with a rear hook that it must have gone half way into his brain. With that the mountain of a creature simply went cascading to the floor and was immediately out for the count.

"Come on, who wants to challenge Herr Invincible?" Slimey then shouted at Papa´s team of Heimatwehr men, whilst their best man was carried off ignominiously on a stretcher.

Needless to say that Slimey was soon slugging each of Papa´s lads down one after the other, as they kept volunteering one after the other in the ever more vain hope that someone would eventually manage to bring down the indeed apparently invincible Slimey.

"I would never have believed that Slimey even had it in him to keep on winning like this!" Dani shouted down my ear. "You´ve got to admit that he´s bloody-bloody good!"

"That´s because he´s so disciplined, which I must admit is something that I didn´t at all expect from the likes of him," I answered, whilst carefully noting how Slimey was managing to dish out another dose of medicine to another Heimatwehr boy. "I mean: just look at the way that he manages to tuck his chin in whilst always looking for the right moment and then – bang! wollop! – in goes his south paw and it's curtains for the Heimatwehr yet again!"

"Oy vey!" Dani cried in surprise. "I didn't know that you knew so much about boxing!"

"I don't," I answered. "I'm just watching what these guys are doing."

I must admit that I had then suddenly found a morbid fascination in watching these young men and older boys knocking the bejeezus out of each other. The disappointing thing was that as Slimey Stefan kept knocking seven bells out of one Heimatwehr lad after another, the volunteers for another fight kept getting both smaller and smaller and weaker and weaker.

Eventually there was no one left as Papa's younger boxers (and who weren't even out of school) finally called it a day – except, that is, for one small boy of thirteen who hadn't even been registered to fight because he was too young. Yes, you've got it: my dumb, stupid older brother Seppi.

"I'll take you on any day, Herr Supposedly Invincible!" Seppi cried, suddenly standing up and jumping over the ropes and into the ring whilst throwing off his shirt.

To be precise, Seppi certainly looked far more like Slimey Stefan's little brother than my older brother. Although he was smaller than Slimey, being nine years younger than him, Seppi was nonetheless tall for his age although also as skinny as a bean-pole, whereas I was short and stumpy.

Meanwhile, in an almost comical way, Slimey kept trying to tell Seppi that he was not interested in fighting him: but this seemed to only encourage Seppi even further, as he kept running around Slimey with his fists in the air. In fact Seppi now looked for all the world like a neurotic Jack Russell terrier trying to have an argument with an alsation. No doubt Seppi thought that the secret of Slimey´s success had just been a dizzying display of physical agility and that two could play this simple game, without realizing just how much agility of the mind was also required.

During all this time Papa had kept trying to physically stop and hold Seppi tight within his arms but Seppi just kept managing to shake and kick himself free again before running off once more around Slimey. Eventually Seppi managed to annoy Slimey enough by suddenly hitting him right where it hurt, so that Slimey then just as suddenly finally lost his temper with the wincy brat and immediately began playing vicious games with him.

"Come on, do you really want to know how one of my knuckle-sandwiches tastes?" Slimey then asked Seppi as he now began running around my brother instead of Seppi around him.

This wasn´t idle boasting either as Slimey soon began raining little punches down on Seppi – but never too much but rather just enough to hurt the young teenager without killing his desire to carry on trying to fight.

Indeed, watching Slimey slowly knock the bejeezus out of Seppi was like watching a cat teasing a mouse that he had just caught before finally eating it alive. Meanwhile, it was by the grace of goodness gracious me that neither Mama nor Maria were there to see the carnage or else they would have indeed had a fit.

"So you still haven't had enough, have you?" Slimey cried with a merciless grin, after landing another punch that sent Seppi reeling backwards over the ropes and into the crowd. "You're always welcome to come back for another portion of what you love most!"

By this time many in the crowd had decided that they had seen enough.

"Let the poor boy go!" they cried, or "Come on, Stefan: he's already had more than he can take!" and "You've made your point! It's time to cut the poor sod loose!"

What's more, even the S.A. men and boys were now also shouting at Slimey to call it a day.

"Why should I?" Slimey shouted back as Seppi climbed back over the ropes and into the ring again. "Let the little perisher have what he wants!"

It was at this moment that Seppi suddenly made a lunge at Slimey by tucking his head down and running at the tall bully like a cannon ball on spider legs. With another unworldly grin, Slimey simply swung his arm around like a windmill and suddenly hit Seppi full in the face so that the boy was literally catapulted into the air before landing spread-eagled on his back and all but unconscious.

"Okay, that's enough!!!" Papa suddenly roared as he jumped into the ring to check out his son's injuries. "You don't need to commit bloody murder!"

If Slimey Stefan thought that he was going to receive an applause for his massively unfair victory then he was sorely mistaken, for numerous people now rose up in disgust whilst giving him the thumbs down, as if he should be fed on the spot to the lions.

"Well," Slimey said, as my Papa pulled his much mutilated boy out of the ring before someone put him on a stretcher, "it seems as if nobody else wants to fight me."

Seeing the way that Slimey now grinned at everyone as if they were all suckers and schlumps, it was then that I suddenly snapped with outrage.

"You want a goddamn fight!" I cried, quickly throwing off my own shirt as I also leapt over the ropes as Seppi had done not so long before. "Well, then, I'm here to finally knock the living crap out of you, you over-grown bullying turd!"

I really cannot say who was more astonished – me, my Papa and Max, the crowd or Slimey Stefan himself. I may have been no fan of Seppi but seeing a member of my family being knocked about by that bully and coward Slimey whilst he knew full-well that the boy didn't have a ghost's chance against him really got my blood boiling.

In fact, my rage was so intense that it never even occurred to me that I was not only smaller and younger than Seppi but, unlike him, hadn´t even had a boxing lesson in my life. However, as if believing that I were possessed by the devil, everyone seemed to be taking me seriously, including Slimey himself: who, all of a sudden, seemed to have lost his cockiness.

"Well, come on then: what are you waiting for?" I cried out, standing solidly at the ready with my fists clenched just before my face. Unlike Seppi or Slimey, I wasn´t going to stage my fight by jumping about like a cat on hot bricks. I instead stood fast on my ground as I waited for my opening, whilst also making damned sure that I didn´t offer any openings myself.

As such I let Slimey return to his standard play of running around me whilst bopping this way and that way with his skinny fists. Whilst faking this punch and that punch towards me again and again and again he certainly kept me on my guard as I never knew when the real and fatal punch was going to suddenly strike me in the face.

However, I wasn´t going to let Slimey make me nervous so that I began flailing all over the place in idiotic directions, as he had already done with everyone else. No, sir, I kept waiting for that one tiny opportunity when he would let his own guard down so that I could then dish him out a sizable dollop of his own medicine. And come that tiny opportunity did, with my getting in a nice uppercut that just so happened to gash his right eye-brow open, so that blood suddenly splattered all over his nice, white gym shirt.

The crowd immediately rose with a cry of gory astonishment but I wasn´t going to let myself sit back on my newly won laurel. Seeing that Slimey had himself lost some of his concentration as he stroked the blood off his brow with utter disbelief, I immediately punched him another whopper that went straight into his chin. This knocked Slimey so off his balance that I was able to land him another punch, this time in the stomach.

From then on Slimey became my punching bag, even though I had no idea where any of my punches would fall on him. I instead just kept hitting them out every time another opportunity arose, which they did more and more often whilst the crowd kept roaring with delight.

"What´s the matter, with you?" I asked Slimey, taunting the bully as if he were now the mouse whilst I were the cat. "Are you getting tired of an eleven year old knocking the stuffing out of you?"

This really rattled Slimey, so that he started doing stupid things, like letting out wild and frantic punches that I could easily see coming all the time.

Someone suddenly shouted out "Bulldog" because, I later found out, they thought that, with my short and stumpy legs, I both looked and fought like one. Before long other people in the crowd were also shouting out "Bulldog" whilst the boxers of both teams began to shout out things like "Come on Bulldog!" and "You can do it, Bulldog!" Needless to say that hearing his own team now supporting me instead of himself – that is, the underdog and not the bullying star – nettled Slimey more than anything else that I had said to bait him, so that he really started to pull some really stupid stunts.

Soon enough Slimey was just staggering around like a drunk so that I was able to throw a whole barrage of punches at his belly before he suddenly collapsed on the floor. Needless to say that the crowd was roaring like a volcano as Slimey was finally counted out, including the S.A. boys, who seemed to have completely fallen out of love with their supposed star and instead in love with me.

"Where on Earth did you learn to fight like that?" my Papa asked, suddenly rushing into the ring and shaking my hand for all that it was worth, whilst looking at me for the first time in my life as if he were proud as punch that he was my father. "Have you been clandestinely taking lessons behind my back?"

Before I had a chance to respond all numbers of other people also began vigorously shaking my hand, including Max, who cried at me:

"By all the Saints! Where were you when that bullying **Napoleon kept invading Austria** and no one could work out how to defeat him?"

To add to this bizarre twist of events, the Nazi S.A. boys then whipped me up onto their shoulders and began parading me around as their own champion. I even heard one them say to another:

"This kid is solid gold. We´ve got to make sure that he becomes one of us."

I naturally felt that I was everybody´s hero of the day except for, that is, Slimey Stefan´s and his father´s (who had actually put an enormous wager on Slimey winning every match). However, none of this adulation gave me any pleasure. As far as I was concerned, I had only won the fight because Slimey had already been exhausted after so many fights when I came roaring along with all my cylinders firing with pure rage. Okay, I had also managed to contain that rage and keep my cool and use my brain but I guessed that had just been a one-off.

However, it wasn´t a mere one-off for Slimey Stefan. Without realizing it, I had REALLY humiliated him that day – and it wasn´t something that he would ever be prepared to forgive me for.

10: Treason in our Family

After the match I came to be called "Bulldog" by almost everyone, including my Papa, Max and even Seppi, though not Mama, Maria or even Pete. It was a name that stuck with me for the rest of my time in that village. On the other hand, the actual meaning behind the name would diminish during this time, just as I never heard any more from the two S.A. men who had wanted to enlist me amongst their ranks. This was because, like Max, I had no interest in fame or playing the village hero and certainly didn´t want to make a hobby of what I now considered to be a blood sport in its own right.

As such, some people began to believe that my brief moment of glory had been a mere flash in the pan and that I knew better than anyone else I would never be able to pull it off again. Indeed, there were even some people who later completely forgot that I had once been the hero of the village, in spite of the fact that they had actually witnessed the event with their own eyes – and probably thoroughly enjoyed it too.

My Papa, of course, kept begging me to join his club whilst its younger members, especially Seppi, all thought I was raving bonkers for passing up the chance of a career in boxing when I absolutely had the talent for it. No doubt Papa also thought that he could make a pretty penny out of me but why, I kept telling him, should I pass up my Saturday afternoons just to spill blood in stinky, smelly rings in foreign villages when I could instead spend them peacefully enjoying the mountains in my own backyard?

In fact, the only advantage that I saw in having beaten Slimey Stefan was that Seppi – who had spent most of my match lying delirious on his stretcher before hearing all about my victory from everyone else – never dared to annoy me, let alone try to punch me in the ribs, again. On the other hand, in a definitive case of supreme irony (or of sheer stupidity, depending on how you view it) Seppi did not decide to make the guy who had gone out to seek vengeance for his sake (that is, myself) his hero but instead the very guy who had beaten him to a pulp (ie. Slimey Stefan).

In Seppi´s book of fantasy, Slimey was now the perfect example of manhood and God only knows what else and was only too pleased to follow him to the ends of the world. As such, Seppi tried again and again to get on board with Slimey Stefan, pestering him almost non-stop to employ him as Slimey had once employed myself.

"What use would you be to me?" Slimey was rumoured to have cruelly told Seppi on more than one of these occasions. "If that imbecile Pete didn´t already have the position of village idiot, you would be it."

However, sheer tenacity is a virtue that should not be underestimated and so, whilst Seppi was no "Bulldog" like myself, Slimey must have eventually come on the notion that Seppi was like one of those dumb sorts of dogs who you can kick again and again for a laugh and they will still keep loving you for it. As such, Seppi eventually got a part-time job at the Berghof cleaning out the jacks and emptying the pig swill and garbage whilst being paid peanuts for it.

Indeed, Seppi was probably the only person who even liked Slimey at that time for, whilst sympathy for the Nazis hadn´t actually diminished after the boxing tournament, Slimey´s own popularity apparently really plummeted. This wasn´t just in the village but also with the Nazis in the other villages, so that Slimey really had to work hard to get their trust in him restored. Even then, some five years later, people who hadn´t so easily forgotten the past only had to say "Bulldog" in his face in order to rattle him whenever they wanted.

When winter finally came round again, I immediately missed the perks of being able to use the ski-lifts that I had so enjoyed whilst working for Slimey the previous year. On the other hand, with so few tourists from the hotel now around and there being even more snow than ever, I often had entire landscapes of pristine white virgin snow all to myself. In fact, there was nothing like skiing down a slope that no one else had yet used and then turning around at the bottom to admire the only track through the knee-deep powder snow that I had just neatly carved out.

As things turned out, however, I did soon start having to work again during the Christmas holidays

– although not at the Berghof but with Mama beside the miniature lake directly before the hotel. For some reason she had decided to set up a **Gluehwein** Hut of her own on the frozen lakeside after having managed to get the concession for it from the Gemeinderat. Ironically, the Gemeinderat was still made up of the very same members that had kept steadfastedly refusing to give Kratzkopf such a concession a year before: a snub which made Kratzkopf very sore indeed.

"You can always organize a re-match between your boys and our boys," the Old Kaiser told the closet Nazi Buergermeister with a huge grin. "Perhaps this time you would like to hold a ski-race in front of your hotel. I´m sure that Bulldog is more than ready to teach your son a few more tricks again."

To our surprise, everyone was soon rushing to Mama´s Gluehwein hut, where we also sold roast chicken, donuts (both sweet and savoury) and cookies, as well as schnapps, brandy and a thing called **"Hunter´s Tea"**. Kratzkopf was firmly rattled because, having decided to keep his own terrace permanently open to the public as a result of the "Thousand Mark Barrier", he now discovered that we were pulling in his visitors as well. After all, who wants to sit on a terrace with the snobbish Nazi hierarchy (even if you have a bird´s eye view of the lake) when you can be having fun with your own kind sitting directly on its shore?

When Mama managed to get hold of a gramophone record player and began playing all the usual Christmas and Austrian folksong favourites, Kratzkopf very childishly employed his oompah-oompah brass band again, even though he was probably now making a loss doing so. However, far from the band being able to blast Mama´s music to Kingdom Come, the villagers instead all joined in in singing the carols and folksongs themselves, so that they were soon even louder than the already noisy band.

Sooner than later, the Nazi guests on the terrace started telling Kratzkopf to stop the band as they couldn´t hear what the F they were saying to one another. However, they needn´t have bothered as the band also couldn´t properly hear what they were playing, especially with all the singing din that was going on. They therefore suddenly banged down their instruments and tore off in a huff, never to come back again. When an oompah-oompah band did finally appear on the terrace again four years later it was a different one.

All the villagers beside the lake of course had a huge laugh about this, including Mama and myself. I had, however, not been Mama´s first choice to help her. She would have preferred Maria because she was used to helping her with all the kitchen work: but Maria was the only person who could properly take care of Pete since he had been blinded by Slimey.

Then there was Seppi, who Mama thought might well prefer a better job. However, Seppi steadfastly refused, preferring to keep working for Slimey for peanuts whilst still cleaning the jacks – and even though Slimey had dropped him down the staff´s own out-house jack as punishment for doing something extremely petty. Thus I was the one left holding the baby, so to speak.

As things turned out, Mama and I got on like a house on fire, working in perfect tandem with one another and never treading on each other´s feet or getting on one another´s nerves. But then, that was the way with Mama: she got on well with just about everybody. I meanwhile gave up my winter excursions so that I could continue to help my Mama at the weekends whilst also returning for most of the Fasching holidays. In fact, Fasching was even busier than Christmas had been, with it being a little lighter in the late afternoons and people being therefore less inclined to stay at home during the festivities.

We even began drawing in visitors from other villages at the weekends, whilst Kratzkopf tried to get in on the act by offering them overnights at knock-down rates. Fine as all this might have sounded, they weren´t having any of it after what they had heard about the Berghof from our own villagers. The fact that the hotel was still flying the Nazi flag instead of the traditional German one (although, as before mentioned, they were now technically entitled to do) certainly didn´t help.

"Business is really great," Mama said, rubbing her hands together one evening as we all sat down to a supper that Maria had prepared for us. I´m hoping that the Gemeinderat will grant us another concession that I´ve already put in for the summer months. In fact, we might even be able to turn it into a restaurant one day."

"That all depends on who gets to be elected on the new Gemeinderat," said Papa, being as practical and as unromantic as ever. "Besides, you will need to get a five year license to run a restaurant."

"Then Erich could work for Mama as a chef!" Maria chirped in enthusiastically whilst completely ignoring Papa´s realistic but dreary comment.

"How?" I asked Maria, just as unenthusiastically as my Papa. "I don´t even know how to cook a proper meal."

"Well, of course you would have to do an apprenticeship first," Maria answered, sounding for all the world as if she were the older sibling, if not an already experienced adult.

"Well, I´m not going back to THAT place, if that´s what you mean," I said, whilst taking a long, hard stare at Seppi as if he were a traitor for going to work at the Berghof after all that had recently happened.

"Well, there are plenty of catering apprenticeships going in hotels in the other villages," said Maria, still sounding as if she were many years older than her actual self. "What are you afraid of ? Are you too chicken to leave home and find work in another part of the Wipptal?"

"No," I answered: "but what I really want to do when I leave school is to work as a mountain guide and ski instructor like Max."

Papa laughed at this pipe-dream of mine: which hurt all the more because Max wasn't there to defend me.

"Well, then, if you really want to do that, dear," Mama said, "then you will have to look for a job in another village because, as you well know, it's only the Kratzkopfs who employ such guides and instructors in this village."

All of a sudden I felt like a proper Charlie because, lost in my world of perfect dreams, I just hadn't considered these realities.

"What's more," said Papa, whilst getting his long Tyrolean pipe ready for an after-supper smoke, "even Max's job is now hanging by a thread."

It soon turned out that Papa was perfectly right on that score because it was only a couple of days later that Max came roaring into our house just as we were settling down once again for supper.

"Would you believe it?" he roared, whilst throwing his hat so hard into the corner that it ricocheted straight into the open oven and immediately caught fire. "I've been fired – kicked out – given the boot – slung out – pink-slipped – given my marching orders!"

"Sit down Max, my dear: you're just in time for supper," said Mama, being more concerned in her brother-in-law´s stomach than in his employment situation – or even his hat.

"Wow!" Seppi exclaimed, suddenly looking awfully smug with himself. "Don´t tell me that the Berghof now thinks more of my talents than they do of yours!"

"Don´t be cheeky!" Mama snapped at Seppi. "If you talk like that in front of Herr Kratzkopf then you WILL get the sack as well!"

"So what happened???" Maria asked, with her eyes bursting with curiosity, whilst looking for all the world as if she had just changed from being a career advisor to a star journalist on the look-out for a scoop.

"The old Nazi goose simply called me into his office and told me that my services weren´t required anymore," Max answered, whilst stabbing at his giant dumpling as if it were Kratzkopf´s head. "He didn´t even thank me for these so-called services, not even after all these years!"

"But what did he suddenly give you the boot for?" Papa asked. "I mean he must have had a damned good reason for doing so without even giving you a warning."

"Maybe old Kratzkopf couldn´t stand the sight of Max´s face any longer," Seppi said, with one of his huge and merciless grins.

"FACE! FACE! FACE!" Pete suddenly cried over and over again, whilst also starting to throw food all over the place.

"Seppi!" Mama also shouted. "Can't you be quiet? Now you've started Pete off again!"

"Well???" Papa asked Max, ignoring everyone except his brother, whilst looking at him as if he must have a crime to confess to. "What did you do WRONG?"

"I didn't do anything WRONG!" Max cried back.

"WRONG! WRONG! WRONG!" Pete cried, whilst starting to laugh with the encouragement of Seppi.

"Well, you must have done something," said Papa.

"I did do something," Max answered. "But I had to because the guests were starting to annoy the villagers."

"Ooo-h???" said Papa, suddenly sounding very open to reason.

"Oh-hhhhhhhhhhhhhhhhhhhhh!" said Pete, just like a parrot as he tilted his head to one side whilst making his bird-like noise.

"Yes, I had a group of six of these Germans," Max continued, "and every time that one of the locals passed anywhere near them they gave the Hitler salute whilst laughing all the while. Well, I had to say something to them, Josef. They were upsetting the villagers."

"Quite," said Papa, now clearly understanding Max's predicament. "So what did old Kratzkopf have to say about all this? That Hitler salutes are okay when made by Germans? The man should be locked up for this!"

"He literally threw the book at me," Max answered, "whilst roaring at me that what the villagers think isn't at all important but only what the guests think."

"Ooooh," said Seppi with a whistle. "I don't think that the Gemeinderat will like that at all."

"Nor will Kratzkopf either if you don't keep your mouth shut about all this at the hotel!" Papa shouted at his eldest son.

"What's more," said Max, starting to now speak like the prodigal son who had had to finally return cap in hand to his family, "I've no longer got a room to stay in."

"Well, you can't stay here!" Papa snapped instantly back, suddenly showing no sympathy again. "We've got no empty rooms for you! The house is full!"

"He could always sleep in the pig sty with Franz," Seppi suggested with a giggle.

"You be quiet," Mama told him, "or else you will be sleeping in the outhouse."

"But this is as much as my house as it is yours," Max told Papa. "You only got to have full use of it because I haven't needed it these past years."

"Max could always move in with me, Papa," I suggested. "We could make another bed out of the wood in the shed and put it in my room with my bed."

"Not on your nelly!" Papa retorted. "I'm not having a grown-up man sleeping with a young teenage boy under my roof ! It's indecent! Whatever would the neighbours think?"

In the end, however, a solution was found, with Max being allowed to move into Seppi's room whilst Seppi was ordered to join Pete in his room. This, of course, didn't go down with Seppi, even though he got a new bed out of it.

It was I, however, who had suggested all this, telling Papa that because Seppi had refused to help Mama out in the Gluehwein Hut because he had wanted to instead stay on with the old Nazi goose Kratzkopf, he should be punished for his wicked deed. Although Papa didn't quite like the way that I expressed my notion, he did nonetheless agree with its sentiment.

"I only hope," I said, as Max and I manoeuvred Seppi's new bed into Pete's room as soon as we had finished carpentering it together, "that things don't get too fiery with you and Papa now being under the same roof every night."

I also felt like adding, "You know that you two together are like fighting cocks set on each other" but quickly decided that that was a bit too cheeky.

The next bout of fireworks and cock-fighting, however, came a lot sooner than I had expected.

"Hell's Bells!" Max suddenly cried, flying into the main room one Sunday morning with a newspaper in which he had hoped to find some job openings. "Have you seen this? You remember that

´**Civil War**` that occurred in Vienna during the same week as Fasching? Yes, the one between the Social Democrats and your Christian Socialist friends, who now call themselves the **Fatherland Front**? Well, Dollfuss not only banned the Social Democrats that same week but he´s now also going to hang **twenty-four of them**! Just tell me that this autocrat hasn´t gone full-blown Fascist, just like Mussolini."

"Well, he had to," said Papa, trying not to look rattled as he sat in his rocking-chair with his long Tyrolean pipe. "These are, as you can well see, dangerous times that we are now living in. It was only last **October that that Nazi assassin** tried to kill Dollfuss with a revolver. Dollfuss therefore had no choice but to reintroduce capital punishment, as well as martial law."

"Yes, but that was a bloomin´ Nazi!" Max practically screamed. "Social Democrats aren´t radical right but nice people who want a fair and peaceful, democratic world."

"Well, they were hardly peaceful or democratic when they decided to attack the police in February," Papa scoffed back at Max.

"What do you mean they attacked the police?!" Max suddenly roared. "That´s the dumbest and most stupid thing that I´ve ever heard! It was the police who started the fighting because they were trying to break into the offices of the Social Democrats."

"Only to search the premises for secretly stored weapons," Papa tried to calmly reply without shouting back himself. "It wasn´t their fault that you tried to stop them."

"It wasn´t their fault that your lot then brought the bally army in!" Max yelled back. "350 people died in just four days because of your stupidity – and all for nothing!"

In the meantime – and even without her wonderful plans for a restaurant – Mama had clearly bitten off too much with her Gluehwein Hut enterprise, with the extra workload that it brought now beginning to irritate her even more than the frequent eruptions between Max and Papa.

With Maria also returning to school with Seppi and I after the Fasching holidays, Mama was again left having to do the bulk of the housework at home, the cooking and cleaning, feeding the animals and, of course, the endless re-patching of clothes. In a day when only the richest bothered buying new clothes as soon as the old ones started to look worn out, mothers and wives would be sewing and darning new patches on their family´s clothes every night until the blessed garments literally fell apart in their hands.

The simple solution was that Max would take over the Gluehwein Hut. However, since this was Mama´s pride and joy and she was often the reason for people keeping on coming, she refused to give it up completely, so that they would often alternate their shifts working there. However, when Max, unusually for a man in those days, offered to help

Mama with the dishes after supper one evening, Papa nearly had a fit.

"I don't mind a man helping my wife to run a hobby-horse business to bring in a few extra Schillings," he yelled whilst almost swallowing half of his pipe, "but I'm damned if he's also going to start playing the part of a kitchen maid!"

"Heaven's sake, Josef!" Max cried back. "Stop being so old-fashioned and stuck in the mud! You're beginning to sound like a legitimist! We should all be doing our best to help each other in this house!"

"And you're beginning to sound like a damned Socialist!" Papa roared back.

On top of all this was Pete, who was growing more and more a handful for Mama to look after as Seppi literally began antagonizing him every night that he had to sleep in his room. At first Seppi seemed to have begun subtly annoying the silly child late at night whilst he was trying to sleep but then Seppi began playing all sorts of wicked tricks on Pete that often had him screaming and yelling in the middle of the night.

Things got even worse when Seppi began teasing Pete at the dinner table as he had used to tease me – except that whilst suddenly punching a slightly younger brother in the ribs may be one thing, suddenly doing so to a blind and mentally handicapped child is quite another.

Eventually Seppi got so damn cheeky and disrespectful that when Papa shouted at him to stop it one evening supper, Seppi simply coldly replied with an evil grin: "But he´s an imbecile – and as such he will always be a millstone around your necks! I´m just making things a little more light-hearted for you!"

"THAT DOES IT!!!!!" Mama suddenly screamed, rising up out of her chair so quickly that I thought she were about to shoot into space like a rocket. "I don´t know where you get these stupid notions from but I DO KNOW that, although my dear Pete will always be like a helpless child for the rest of his life, he will always love me more than anything else in the world – and if that isn´t a Gift from God then tell me what is!!!!!"

As I have said before, Mama was not the type to snap very often, let alone have an atomic reaction like this. Much preferring to suffer in silence, the most that she had ever done when she had snapped before was to slap her napkin on the table with a few quick words of admonishment. In this way, Mama and Papa were complete opposites, for whilst Mama wore her heart on her sleeve but very rarely got angry, Papa rarely showed any emotions except for that of anger. Max was somewhere in between: being capable of displaying a whole spectrum of moods, from being as happy as a sandman one moment to suddenly spitting the dummy out the next.

In the meantime, with Mama having unexpectedly just put the fear of God into everyone, we all sat in silence for a while and with our heads in our dinners before Maria wisely observed:

"He´s getting these stupid notions from working with Slimey Stefan."

"Well, then, he can jolly well stop working at the Berghof!!!" Mama cried, slamming a metal tray down on the table so loudly that all the ornaments on the shelves above us rattled as if there were an earthquake. "In fact, I ORDER Seppi not to work in that damned place any longer!"

This was a bit of a strange thing to demand since, once again in those days, it was not a woman´s place in the house to make such decisions. That was the role of the head of the house, who was, of course, the father. As such, Papa gave Mama a rather curious look as he reached for another slice of bread, although he didn´t say anything.

Seppi, although visibly shaken, managed to hold his cool instead of having a tantrum.

"Well," he said, calmly putting his napkin down on the table before standing up and leaving his dinner only half-eaten. "If that´s the way that you want it then I won´t obey any orders at all. In short: you´re rid of me."

Seppi then wandered upstairs and soon came down again with his few worldly possessions packed in a bag over his shoulder, whilst we all sat in silence with mixed feelings of bewilderment and sorrow. Mama seemed to be especially confused, with her heart now cut into two: with one half being proud that she had stood up for her handicapped child whilst the other was scared that she had lost her eldest child because of it.

"WAIT," said Papa, gently putting down his fork as Seppi moved towards the door. I thought he was about to ask Seppi for forgiveness on behalf of Mama but he instead told him very coldly: "If you go out of that door now then you will no longer be one of us. You will be a traitor to the family. You will NEVER be again welcome in MY house."

Seppi slowly looked at Papa as if wondering if he really meant what he said.

"I´m not bluffing," said Papa. "I NEVER go back on a promise."

Seppi then nervously laughed under his breath and left the house, whilst I saw a tear trickle down Mama´s cheek.

"But where will he go?" Mama asked. "He won´t even be fourteen until the summer."

"Isn´t it obvious?" Maria answered, having read Papa´s thoughts all this time. "He´s got a room at the Berghof."

If it might seem that our Papa had gone way over the limits in his role as father of the house, it should be remembered that in those days children were expected to grow up fast so that they could become reliable workers in the family. There was no molly-coddling or worrying about feelings because, as my Papa would have put it, such a luxury could only have been afforded by the rich. As you can see, these were still what we today call "old-fashioned times".

Meanwhile, as if this weren´t enough excitement for just one month it was only a couple of days later that Mama suddenly came running into the house first thing in the morning and all in a tizzle, after having just gone out to check on the Gluehwein Hut. Instead of shouting and screaming, however, she was as white as a ghost and shivering with fear.

"What´s the matter?" Papa asked, suddenly showing a rare glimmer of concern for his wife.

11: The Mystery of the Star of David

Mama, however, was too shocked to speak.

"A neat shot of brandy will set her to rights," said Max, suddenly dashing for the drinks cabinet.

"Leave my brandy alone!" Papa roared back. "There´ll be no drinking in my house at this ungodly hour!"

"Shouldn´t we call the doctor?" I suggested, as Max instead began to settle Mama into one of the arm-chairs.

"She´s coming round," Papa said, holding his wife´s hand and staring into her eyes for what must have been the first time in yonks and yonks. "What happened, dear?"

"It´s them," she said, accepting the brandy that Max suddenly managed to procure in spite of his brother´s forbidding it. "I know it´s them. It´s the German guests who must have done it."

"What did they do?" Papa demanded. "Did they give you the Hitler salute?"

"No," Mama replied, not even laughing at the absurdity of the idea that that would upset her.

"Or did they play oompah-oompah Nazi music first thing in the morning on the terrace?"

"No, nothing like that," Mama answered, delicately tasting the brandy. "Somebody has painted the Star of David and the word ´Jew` on the front of the Gluehwein Hut."

"WHAT?" Papa cried, more perplexed than angry. "Why in God's name would anyone want to do that? We're not Jewish, are we?"

"Not unless you've suddenly changed your religion," Max answered, facetiously.

"But it's OUTRAGEOUS!" Papa cried after a pause. "These blackguard cowards can't even get our religion right! Unless it's a joke, of course. But what a stupid joke to make."

"Maybe it's a mistake," suggested Max.

"Oh, don't be daft, you brainless leprachaun!" Papa shouted back at Max. "Who would make a mistake like that in a village where everyone knows everything about everyone?"

"Then it must be one of the German guests," Max answered. "Somebody must have told them that we're Jewish. For a laugh."

"But who would want to do a dumb and vicious thing like that?" Papa asked.

"Slimey Stefan," I answered. "That's exactly the sort of senseless nonsense that he would get up to."

"THAT'S ENOUGH!" Papa cried, suddenly clapping his hands together as if I had just called his last bingo number. "Max and I are going straight off to the police station to get a band of men together to have this stupid swine arrested. Maria: you must stay here to look after Mama. Bulldog: you had better come with us in case things get ugly."

It was no co-incidence that we passed Dani's house on the way to the police station and that Papa knocked his father up, Herr Maggid the tailor.

"Have you noticed any anti-Semitic behavior going on in the village or do you perhaps know of anyone who might think that my family is Jewish?" he asked the much-surprised Jewish tailor.

With the answer being negative we moved on to the police station without my even having a chance to speak to Dani. We soon had our band of mixed patrol men and Heimatwehr troops put together and then marched with a purpose on the Hotel Berghof, whilst the Old Kaiser hurriedly tried to keep up with us.

"We demand to speak to Herr Kratzkopf Junior," Papa practically shouted at the young receptionist.

"Will that be hotel or private business?" the young receptionist asked with a clear-as-a-bell north German accent, clipping his words as if he were also clicking his boots.

"Damn your impertinence!" Papa snapped. "Just tell us where the fellow is!"

"Oh I can do that for you," said Herr Kratzkopf, suddenly appearing out of the back-office whilst speaking with his usual grandiose and resonating Buergermeister voice. "Although I´m afraid that you can´t see him. That´s because, my dear good men, he is now in Germany, visiting some friends of mine."

This certainly took the wind out of Papa´s sails for a moment – but not for long.

"Then I demand to search the premises!" Papa said forcefully, whilst I couldn´t help noticing the guests in the dining-room opposite us beginning to look round to see what all the commotion was about.

"Have you got a warrant?" Herr Kratzkopf asked with a bemused, sneaky look.

"We don´t need a warrant," Papa answered, now beginning to impatiently tap the palm of his gloved hand with the tip of his truncheon.

"I think that you´ll find that you do," said Kratzkopf, turning towards the Old Kaiser. "Hauptmann Kaiser: do your officers need a warrant so that they can search my hotel? Yes or no?"

The Old Kaiser, who had until very recently been famed for marching at the front of his men instead of standing behind them as he was now doing, answered timidly: "Yes, Herr Kratzkopf: the police do need a warrant."

"Well, then, officers: I think that that settles the matter," said Kratzkopf, just as young Seppi suddenly sailed into view whilst dressed as a page. "Now, then, if you will excuse me: I think you are upsetting my – "

"Seppi!" Papa cried.

However, Seppi – looking as pale as candle wax – merely gave his once-upon-a-time Papa a cursory glance before disappearing into the dining-room opposite us.

"I´m damned," said Papa, as we once again settled down to supper that evening, "if Kratzkopf hasn´t somehow got his claws into that old goat the Kaiser. Warrant indeed! No one has needed a warrant anymore since Dollfuss passed his last emergency laws."

"I agree with you for once, big brother Josef," said Max. "By the time that your boys manage to get a warrant those Nazis will have got rid of any paint that they may have used."

"Yes, the Old Kaiser is really getting soft on the Nazis these days," Papa went on. "We couldn´t even get a Putzscharren organized to clean the Gluehwein Hut for you."

This was true enough, with Max and I having to spend all day trying to clean the Star of David and the word "Jew" off the front of the Hut, using a ton of strong acetone and almost burning off the skins of our hands doing so. Surprisingly, however, a lot of sympathetic villagers came round simply to make a special visit to our hut whilst buying a lot of stuff and asking all the while if Mama were okay.

Mama, however, was clearly very despondent during supper that evening, with Maria again having cooked everything for us. Indeed, I began to have that sore feeling that Mama would never want to even see the Gluehwein Hut again, let alone work there. All the same, however, it still came as something of a surprise when, as soon as Max had quickly finished his supper and left the house because he had promised to meet his old friend Kabinett the furniture maker that evening, Mama suddenly said that she had something to tell us.

"Maybe it is because I am Jewish after all," she said.

There was a sudden silence, followed by the loud clattering of everyone dropping their forks on their plates – except for Pete.

"What do you mean?" Papa asked, his mouth suddenly wide open for the first time that I had ever known.

"Well, maybe Kratzkopf knows something about me that he shouldn´t," said Mama. "I mean, you know my story, Josef."

"Story?" Maria asked, who was always curious about any stories, regardless of whether they were good or bad ones.

"You may as well tell them, Josef," said Mama. "They will have to find out sometime and now is as good as any time. I mean, these two angels are old enough to understand when something is serious and that they mustn´t go blabbing it to anyone else."

This seemed to me to be a dig at her unworthy son Seppi.

Papa gently took hold of Mama´s hand on the table whilst Maria and I kept looking at him expectedly.

"Your mother," he presently said, "doesn´t have a family of her own that we know of."

"Wow," said Maria. "That would explain a lot: I mean, why we don´t have any relatives on her side."

"She was born in the hospital of the **Kloster** of **Saint Jerome** in Sachs," Papa continued, ignoring Maria. "Her mother was found destitute in the streets of Innsbruck and died shortly after the birth."

"Goodness, that´s so sad!" Maria exclaimed. "I´m so sorry, Mama!"

Maria then got up and went to our Mama so that she could put her head on her shoulder and her cheek against Mama´s.

"That´s alright, my dear," said Mama, kissing her daughter in return before continuing her story on her own. "It was Kratzkopf himself who went to the Sachs Kloster in 1915, looking for a girl to employ as a cheap chamber-maid for his new hotel, the ´Berghof`."

"New?" I asked.

"Well, relatively new," Mama answered. "As you probably already know, Kratzkopf had married that German woman some five years before in 1910, which was when they also took over his mother´s old guest-house ´The Edelweiss` and re-named it before beginning to re-build it. I was just fifteen years old when I went to work for the Kratzkopfs, just as Stefan was just a little boy of four."

"Did Kratzkopf treat you well?" I asked, clenching my right fist as I thought of what I would like to do to Kratzkopf if he hadn´t.

"Yes," Mama slowly answered, whilst also tilting her head to one side as if she weren´t fully sure of the answer. "More or less. The irony is that I sometimes had to look after Stefan as well and that we got on really well. That was probably because he was glad to get away from his parents, who treated him very strictly – and yet just look at the way that he has now turned out."

"But why does that make you Jewish?" I asked, avoiding being digressed by the tale of Slimey Stefan´s upbringing.

"Well," Mama answered, after biting her lower lip as if she were getting ready to tell a long story. "I had only been working a year at the Berghof when the receptionist gave me a letter that had come from the Kloster. In it was both a copy of my mother´s marriage certificate and my own birth certificate, as well as a kind letter from the Mother Superior. Apparently my father had been a Jew and my parents had been married in a civil ceremony in Innsbruck. Both of their families were dead against the marriage on religious grounds, so that when it occurred they were both cast out without a penny from their families."

It was at this point that Mama seemed like breaking down as several tears came trickling down her cheeks, so that I guessed that all this reminded her of how Papa had just cast Seppi out of the family.

"Well," Mama continued, dabbing her cheeks dry again, "there was worse to come because it was not long after the marriage that my father was killed in an explosions accident on the Brenner railway. The nuns were supposed to tell me all this after my **Confirmation** when I turned fourteen. However, it all seemed to have been forgotten when there was trouble with the Mother Superior and she had to be replaced. It was only after I had left the Kloster that they found what were now legally my certificates and remembered my story. Hence the certificates being sent on to me with the covering letter from the new Mother Superior."

"Wow," said Maria, sympathetically. "That must have been traumatic for you."

"In a way it was," Mama replied, "but in a way it was also a blessing. Even though I didn't have a single photograph of either of my parents, the two certificates and the covering letter that explained the entire story were like a family album to me. As such, I've always kept them locked up in a box in a safe place, whilst the only part of the story that I told your father was that I had been an orphan. Also, as a practicing Christian I just felt uncomfortable telling anyone – even Josef – about my blood being half-Jewish. I hope that you will forgive me for that, Josef."

"That's okay," said Papa. "It's of no account to our marriage."

There was a magical moment when Maria and I watched our parents in silence as they communicated their years-long love for one another simply by Papa's gently squeezing his wife's hard-working hand in his.

"So how did the Kratzkopfs cotton onto all this?" I eventually asked, by which I meant the secretive part about her father having been a Jew. "Oh no: surely Seppi hasn't been snooping around your things? He couldn't have gone off and told Slimey Stefan all about this?"

Papa now looked at Mama with considerable concern.

"Oh, no," Mama answered, "I would have noticed if someone had opened the box – but I´ll tell you what had been opened and that was the registered envelope that the letter and certificates came in. As a registered letter it should have been given to me directly and signed for by me – but it wasn´t. Instead, as I said, the receptionist gave it to me, although she wasn´t the type who seemed likely to hold a grudge against anyone – or even to want to simply pry into anyone else´s business. Instead, I merely thought that it must have just been a mistake on someone´s part, especially when I asked myself why anyone would want to know about a poor chamber maid´s past? So I simply entirely forgot about the incident whilst being glad that I now had at least something to remember my parents by. Indeed, it never ever occurred to me that Kratzkopf or even his young German wife might have had something to do with it. Until now, of course."

"Y-e-e-e-s-s-s-s," said Papa, stroking his chin as if the pieces of an age-long puzzle were starting to fit together, whilst along looking for all the world like Sherlock Holmes with his pipe. "I can now see why Kratzkopf gave you a pig for our tenth wedding anniversary. He was teasing you. He may even have thought that you were a closet Jew."

"Oh my goodness," said Maria, catching on fast, as she always did. "And the fact that Mama has never wanted to kill Franz for dinner would only make Kratzkopf even more suspicious."

I nearly blurted out that we would have to make a show of slaughtering poor Franz and publicly eating him for our next feast but managed to stop myself in time.

"But what difference does any of this make, anyway?" I instead asked. "If your father had been a Jew, so what? You were born and raised and even confirmed as a Catholic."

"But don´t you get it, dummy?" Maria snapped back at me. "Nazis hate the Jews. They want to bait them into non-existence, especially the ones who they see as a threat to themselves. If Mama is half-Jewish, then they´ve got a stick to beat her with."

"You know what?" I said, ignoring Maria and suddenly suprising myself with my own smartness. "Knowing the characters of both Kratzkopf and his late wife I would say that if anyone were doing any snooping around and opening letters that weren´t for them then it was her. And although one is not supposed to speak ill of the dead, I wouldn´t put it past her not only having told Kratzkopf what she had found but also later telling Slimey Stefan when he was older – even perhaps whilst he was still a teenager. And of all three of them he´s the real crackpot."

"What worries me," said Papa, again stroking his chin but now with what looked like real consternation, "is that if Kratzkopf and Stefan have got a grudge against Mama because she is half-

Jewish then they may also someday have a grudge against you kids for being a quarter-Jewish. We are going to have to tread with our feet very carefully in the future if this whole thing isn't going to completely blow up in our faces."

"Well then, what about Dani and his parents?" I asked. "They're full-blown Jewish. I haven't heard anyone hold anything against them yet."

"Well they've been lucky because so far they've lived in a village where anti-Semitism isn't a thing," Papa answered, before suddenly talking down his wife again. "Then again, they've hardly been provoking the Kratzkopfs by running a rival refreshment stall right in front of their noses."

The events that day still hadn't come to an end as I was woken up during the night by an horrendous crashing of furniture downstairs, followed by what was clearly Papa yelling for all that he way worth:

"Sit down there! And don't you dare try to get out of that chair, not unless you want a swastika painted all over your idiot face!"

12: A Test of Courage

At first I dreamily thought that Papa was yelling at Max for coming home too late at night and being drunk – but then I properly woke up and realized that Max never did such things. Needless to say that I was soon creeping out of my bedroom and taking a carefully concealed position at the top of the stairs, so as to get a bird´s eye view of the strange proceedings in the main room below.

To my astonishment, I saw Seppi crouched in the rocking-chair, whilst two Heimatwehr men were standing immediately behind him as if they were about to break his neck. The poor boy (and, yes, I did feel sorry for the poor, bleeding sod just now) was visibly shaking with fear at what his ballistic father might do to him next.

It was then that I noticed that Mama, Maria, Pete and even Max were also standing directly behind myself in the shadows at the top of the stairs, clearly being just as curious as I was of what the commotion was all about – whilst looking particularly terrified about what Papa might do next to Seppi.

"I´ve never seen Josef behave like this, even whilst having one of his worst tantrums," Mama whimpered whilst biting nervously on the collar of her nightie. "Not in all these years that I´ve been married to him."

"Oh, I have," Max quietly answered.

"So you thought that you could pull another fast one on your dear mother!" Papa shouted at Seppi, who was still visibly shaking. "Here, look at me when I´m talking to you! What you didn´t know is that I´ve had two men watching that damned Berghof all day to see if they try to get rid of the offending paint somehow, whilst having these two titans keep watch all night to boot. Ha, you didn´t see that coming, did you? What – no answer? Answer me, boy, when I ask you a damned question!"

"Yes, sir – I mean, no, sir," poor Seppi stuttered, unsure of what his answer should be. "I didn´t see it coming, sir."

"Neither did I! Don´t you see what position this puts me in if any of this comes out? The very idea of my own son writing Nazi graffiti all over my wife´s hut?! It wouldn´t just kiss Goodbye to the promotion to Chief of Police that I´ve been striving for all these years but could very well mean my getting the boot from the force altogether! And just in case you didn´t know: I´m the main breadwinner of the family here!"

"Yes, sir," said Seppi, still visibly shaking and still not sure what to answer.

"Worst of all, you´ve shaken the living daylights out of your very own mother," Papa continued, barely able to contain his volcanic anger. "What on Earth possessed you to paint the Star of David on a Gluehwein Hut with the word ´Jew`? Whatever that might be called in Nazi Germany, here it´s called 'persecution`. It´s a game that we do not want to play and will not play!"

"If you please, sir, I thought it was just a harmless prank!" Seppi suddenly screamed out of fright. "I thought that ´Jew` is just another word for ´jewelry` and that the star was just a symbol for a diamond. It was a way of saying that Mama is a jewel."

"WHAT?" Papa cried, scarcely able to believe that even his stupid kid could be that bally dumb. "Is that what Stefan Kratzkopf told you whilst conveniently making sure that he wasn´t anywhere around when you did it? I am, I believe, correct in assuming that it was the moronic son who put you up to this and not Kratzkopf himself?"

"Yes, he said it was a ´Mutprobe`: a test of courage to see if I were man enough to be part of his gang."

"A ´Mutprobe`, you say? There´s nothing courageous about scaring the hell out of your own Mama."

"Let him go, Josef," Mama said, coming down the stairs in her nightie and gown. "You can see that he meant nothing malicious by his action."

"Well, it´s a damned funny way of showing affection for anyone," Papa said, "but if that treacherous boy ever hangs out with those damned Nazis at the hotel again I´ll have him skinned alive and torn apart limb by limb! I´ll also have that damned Kratzkopf charged for kidnapping and slavery!"

To see the way that Seppi now flew into several convulsions the same way that Pete was always having them, it was clear that Seppi really did believe that Papa would have him skinned alive and torn apart limb by limb if he ever dared to return to the Berghof and the likes of Slimey Stefan again.

"From now on," said Papa, decisively, "Bulldog gets to sleep in Pete's room and Seppi gets Bulldog's room. That should put an end to all this quarreling in this house. In the meantime, dear, I'm sorry that I've made such a mess of disciplining this rather special case of a boy these last few days. I hope that you will forgive me for these mistakes."

"That's okay, Josef," said Mama. However, Mama seemed to be more intent on forgiving Seppi as she went to the back of his chair and tenderly embraced him from behind.

Papa, of course, tried to make sure that the fact that Seppi had been the one who had actually committed the dastardly crime with the Star of David on his mother's Gluehwein Hut stayed under wraps. Of course, there was no knowing if Slimey Stefan might later spread it about that not only had Seppi done it but that he had also done it entirely on his own initiative.

Mama's grandiose plans for one day turning the Gluehwein Hut into a restaurant meanwhile came to naught before the summer had even begun. On May the First Dollfuss introduced his new Constitution for Austria, which gave him and his government even wider powers and Austria stricter laws to follow.

"Well, I hope that you are proud of what you and your Fatherland Front have now gone and done!" Max cried out, storming once again into the house as soon as he heard the news about the coming Constitution. "Bang goes any semblance of democracy and proper free elections in this so-called **Staendestaat**."

"It's better and fairer than traditional democracy with political parties always at one another's necks," Papa answered. "You saw what's happened in Germany."

"It's the same stuff! Fascism and Nazism are both on the same side of the same coin except that Nazism is even more extreme! Keep going on like this and we'll soon all be Nazis!"

"No, we won't. Stop over-reacting to everything. Yes, that man Dollfuss is a bit of a dictator but he means well and certainly isn't another Mussolini. Besides, Austria's now being a corporate state means that the federal, state and local governments are represented by chosen delegates of commerce, trade, industry, tourism, arts, science. It's a system that goes right back to the Middle Ages."

"Yes, well we're now living in the Twentieth Century, in case you haven't yet noticed, with things now being a whole lot different."

"Oh, you're just mad because the **First of May** is no longer a Socialist Day in Austria but is now to be commemorated as Constitution Day. But you needn´t worry, you´ll still be able to dance around the Maypole and hopefully finally find a suitable maiden to marry whilst doing it."

"It also means," said Max, ignoring Papa´s childish jibe at his bachelor status, "that we´re also going to get a whole new Gemeinderat as well as a new Buergermeister without having the slightest say in the matter. I´ve even heard that they want to start calling it the ´tag` instead of the ´rat`."

Max turned out to be perfectly right, with even the new Gemeindetag of staunch Fatherland Front supporters quickly turning down Mama´s Gluehwein Hut concession for the summer. Whilst this came as no surprise to anybody, what did come as a surprise was that Kratzkopf had somehow managed to retain his position as the Buergermeister, in spite of the fact that most of his guests, not to mention stupid Slimey Stefan, were openly Nazi.

It therefore seemed that Kratzkopf, whilst pretending on the outside to now be a member of the Fatherland Front that had been formed out of the Christian Socialists and other right-wing parties, was managing to cunningly wield a tremendous amount of power behind the scenes as a full-blown Nazi collaborator, if not already a secret member of the Nazi Party himself.

With Mama´s refreshments hut now gone, Max was out of a job again. However, as luck turned out and in a stroke of irony, the new Gemeindetag relaxed the laws on hunting so that Max was able to scratch a living as a hunter by supplying fresh game twice a week to both Kratzkopf and Fleischklops the butcher. Naturally Max was in two minds about his new work, for whilst he hated the idea of killing defenseless animals, he loved his re-gained freedom in the mountains.

Max would therefore disappear for days on end before suddenly returning with, very often, a stag on his back and all kinds of animals – such as falcons, buzzards, badgers, stoats and weasels, as well as many rabbits – hanging from his grossly overladen belt like the trophies of a voodoo witch-doctor.

Some of the game meat we would keep for ourselves, so that we soon became the best-fed family in the village. On the other hand, we always used to sell the skins and fur for astronomical prices to a travelling market furrier that Max knew. Besides, although Mama didn´t mind eating the game meat since she hadn´t slaughtered the wretched creatures herself, she was jiggered if she were going to dress up like a diva in the furs of a bear, hare or fox.

Since I also no longer had to help Mama with her culinary endeavour in the hut, I naturally joined Max on his hunting expeditions in the holidays and at weekends. Max not only showed me how to hunt better than Papa ever had but, to my astonishment, he even showed me his secret hide-away. This lay high up on the hanging Messner Valley behind us and had a magnificent view of the Gletschberg village far, far below.

"This is where your grandfather used to bring your father and I whilst teaching us how to hunt when we were still boys," he said, as we walked uphill towards a small wall in the mountain that was partly covered by the forest that covered the Holzbauer Ridge to our right. "It´s called the Andreas Hofer Retreat because it is supposed to have been built by the leader of the Tyrolean freedom fighters himself whilst hiding from the Napoleonic armies in the early 1800s."

However, my first impressions of the hide-away were one of bitter disappointment – indeed, almost of laughter.

"But this is only a small cave!" I exclaimed after we had climbed through some foliage and around a huge rock. It was, I had to admit, a well-hidden cave but it was still just a grotty cave that was hardly the epitome of a cozy hide-out to play runaways in.

"Wait," said Max: "you haven´t seen anything yet."

13: The Summer of the Long Knives

Indeed, had Max not shown me it then I would probably never have noticed the little wooden door that was hiding in the shadows and behind more rock at the back of the cave. However, even more thrilling was that, as Max opened the door with a large, clanky key that he had brought with him, and we slowly stepped inside, I gradually began to feel a growing sense of déjà vu.

"But I´ve been here before!" I eventually exclaimed in utter amazement. "Perhaps in another life! Max: do you think I was one of the freedom fighters? Perhaps I was even the great Andreas Hofer himself?"

"If you were," Max answered, clearly amused, "then you came to a grisly end because you were shot by a firing squad in Mantua in the South Tyrol during the winter of 1810. You had been taken alive after hiding for months in the mountains, having already fled Innsbruck after the debacle of the Battle of the Bergisel the previous summer."

"Stop pulling my leg!" I cried. "I´ve been here ages ago – donkey´s years ago! I KNOW I HAVE!"

"Quite possibly," said Max, now grinning with open amusement. "Your grandfather used to bring you up here in his rucksack whilst you were still a toddler."

The hideaway was a huge cave that was filled with the carpentered interior of a small house, with not only three (albeit cramped floors) but a cellar to boot, as well as little garrets at the top in the rock. From these little window-like openings with tinted glass one could see right across the hanging valley down to Gletschberg and over to the Kricklhorn – but without any danger whatsoever of being noticed one´s self, even when the candles were brightly lit inside the Retreat.

You might be asking if Dani continued to join us on our trips. Well, the answer is "No" and that is because Dani and his family had meanwhile moved down to Innsbruck, with his old man deciding that he could earn far more as a tailor down there in spite of the stiff competition. Dani would, however, often visit us for coffee and cake in Gletschberg on a Saturday afternoon, whilst it never cost him a bean as he soon worked out which of the goods trains that went up and down the Brenner Pass he could clandestinely hitch a ride on.

Dani also managed to build a monolithic-sized radio transmitter for each of us so that we could communicate with one another outside his visits, although we had to be damned careful that the authorities didn´t find out we were using them as we didn´t have a license. Worst still, as my own Papa was one of the authorities I could hardly have installed my transmitter at our house. Knowing, however, that Papa simply never ever visited the Andreas Hofer Retreat any more, Max and I managed to drag the damn heavy contraption all the way up the blooming mountain to said Retreat.

Eventually, however, my transmitter went the same way as the walkie-talkie, except that I didn´t manage to drop it down a ravine this time but simply blew it up by over-loading it, as well as nearly burning the house in the cave down to boot. Well, I can certainly tell you that Max wasn´t at all happy about that and therefore banned all electrical appliances in the Retreat from that day on although, to my mind, candles and fires inside were just as dangerous.

It was whilst my transmitter was still alive and well and busy crackling that Dani told me the electrifying news of the so-called Roehm Purge at the turn of July, otherwise known as the "Night of the Long Knives". Hitler had got worried that Ernst Roehm and his S.A. paramilitary wing had grown so large and violent that it was now a threat to his leadership. His sycophants therefore went on a three day binge of not only murdering **Roehm** but at least eighty-four others – indeed, some say it could have been hundreds.

"Max!" I cried, suddenly skipping down the Retreat´s ladder-like stairs two at a time and into the main room at the bottom. "Have you heard? Adolf Hitler has had the leader of the S.A. murdered, as well as a whole bunch of his cronies – and all in **one night**!"

Of course Papa was also full of the news when Max and I finally arrived back at home in the village with our latest booty.

"There!" Max shouted, having another go at Papa. "That´s exactly the stuff that these fascist swines all get up to when in power! They start killing each other, as well as everyone else!"

"That´s not what´s worrying me," answered Papa. "You remember how that Nazi tried to kill Dollfuss with a knife last October and nearly succeeded? Well, what´s to stop them trying again now that they´ve had a proper taste of blood?"

Papa´s prophecy was amazingly accurate because, before the month was out, a small army of Nazis invaded Dollfuss´ Chancellery (Kanzler Office) in Vienna.

Max and I had once again been hunting in the mountains, with the school summer holidays now being in full swing. Before we got anywhere near the village on our return we could already hear a tremendous commotion coming from it, as if everyone were shouting at each other.

"Great Heavens!" Max cried out as he took a look through his massive hunting binoculars. "It looks as if the Heimatwehr has put the Berghof under siege! They have their trucks posted all around it whilst their men are running about everywhere!"

"What?!" I cried back, trying to get Max to give me his massive binoculars. "Do you mean to say that we´ve now got a Civil War in our own village?"

"I don´t know," answered Max, obliging me with the hunting binoculars. "But it certainly looks as if something mighty big is about to happen!"

Needless to say that Max and I couldn´t run down the meadows fast enough with our heavy loads of catches so as to get to the scene of what looked like the beginnings of a full-scale battle. By this time, however, the Heimatwehr troops had calmed down, although the guests at the Berghof apparently hadn´t. They were busy hurling torrents of abuse at the troops – and especially at the police, who were at the forefront of everything – as they stood on the wooden terrace, shaking their fists and giving Hitler salutes.

"What the devil´s going on?" Max asked Papa as soon as we found him at the very front of the forces, along with the Old Kaiser.

"Good Lord!" Papa replied with a shocked face. "Haven´t you heard? Dollfuss has just been shot dead by one of those damned Nazi cowards in the Kanzler Office! He tried to flee from the Nazis before he collapsed from his two gunshot wounds. Even when it was clear to the Nazis that they couldn´t get away they simply let Dollfuss bleed to death instead of giving any kind of first aid assistance or even calling for a doctor. It was only by the grace of God that the other ministers in the Kanzler Office all managed to get away."

"So what´s all the ruckus for?" Max then asked. "Has there been a coup or not?"

"Oh, the Nazis had planned a coup alright but the army stopped it before it got beyond the Kanzler Office. There were supposed to be a hundred and fifty Nazis involved, all dressed up as Austrian soldiers and police. They had counted on the Austrian army falling in line with them but our boys soon told them where they could stick it. Unfortunately, the Nazis managed to take over the main radio station in Vienna and broadcasted a fake message that was a signal for Nazi uprisings all across the country."

"So are we now in a state of civil war?" I asked the village chief of police.

"Not really," the Old Kaiser answered. "At least not here in Tyrol. The police and Heimatwehr and other militia have thankfully had little to fight off, unlike other parts of the country, such as Schladming and Leoben in Styria, which both ended in bloodbaths."

"Then why all the bally fuss here?" Max rather rudely then asked. "Surely Kratzkopf and his hotel guests aren´t planning to run over the village in their Sunday best? No wonder they´re all so mad at you."

"Good God, Max!" Papa suddenly burst out in his superior´s defense. "Have you already forgotten? All those guests are high-ranking Nazi officials, even if they may look like harmless castrated penguins in their tuxedos! Besides, there´s also that villain Stefan to worry about. We´ve no idea where the hell he now is or even if he had anything to do with the murder of Franz Hickl just now."

"Franz Hickl?" Max echoed.

"Yes, the Chief of the Innsbruck Police who visited us not so long ago. He was gunned down by another one of these damned Nazis on the very doorstep to his office, I ask you! Thankfully there were passers-by who were able to stop and hold down both him and his accomplice as they tried to escape through the Old Town."

"The most unsettling thing of all," added the Old Kaiser, "is that Hickl´s murder was utterly pointless. By the time that he was killed the coup in Vienna had already been quashed so that, without that lead, all the regional coups eventually crumbled as well."

The Old Kaiser eventually called the siege off, leaving the guests – and especially Kratzkopf – in a stinking, foul mood. In fact, even the goodies that Max and I now brought into his hotel kitchen didn´t cheer Kratzkopf up. Meanwhile, we didn´t hear any more about Slimey Stefan for nearly another four years, since he had apparently now suddenly done a moonlight flit from Innsbruck and over the border into Nazi Germany.

However, worse was to come. Hardly two days had passed since the failed July Coup then both the Old Kaiser and his wife were found shot to pieces in their car on a remote farmer´s track road nearby in the mountains. They had been brutally machine-gunned down whilst driving to the shores of a delightful glacier lake so they could spend the Kaiser's one free day of the week picnicking there.

No one was ever able to find out who the assassins were in this Mafia-like attack – or at least that was what Papa's official line was as the new Chief of the Gletschberg Police. In private he told us:

"I don't know how Kratzkopf managed to get his claws into the Old Kaiser – I thought it might be bribery but we found no money hidden anywhere – but Kratzkopf certainly felt betrayed when the old man besieged his hotel after Dollfuss and Hickl had both been murdered."

It was not, of course, the way in which Papa would have liked to have been promoted to his dream position. Indeed, both Mama and Maria were terrified that Papa would be picked off next and that we would soon be fatherless. However, Papa kept talking about having to do his "duty", although I could see that he was clearly enjoying his new-found powers.

"Just make sure that we are not the next ones that are carried off in boxes like those two," said Mama as we attended the Old Kaiser and his wife's funeral as members of the new Chief of Police's family.

"That's why I don't have a car, sweetie," Papa jestfully replied with one of the few quips that he ever made.

Unsurprisingly, the only Nazi to be seen at the funeral was Kratzberg, being the Buergermeister, whilst still parading himself as a Fatherland Front man. Considering how much he liked to keep a low profile in anything controversial, I wondered if he had really ordered Old Kaiser´s assassination, as Papa clearly believed. Of course, if he had done so then he may have given the actual unsavoury task of execution to Slimey Stefan, which might also explain Slimey´s suddenly doing his bunk over the Bavarian border immediately afterwards.

It was only now that I noticed that Kratzkopf wore the same officer´s insignia on his military uniform as Papa did on his ceremonial police uniform.

"Max," I asked my uncle, who just happened to be standing beside me at the funeral, "I didn´t know that Kratzkopf had been a major in the War like Papa."

"Oh, he was," Max answered with a rare moment of recognition for his brother´s past glories, "but whereas your Papa earned his rank by being a war hero, the Queen of Sheba used her considerable influence to see that Kratzkopf joined the War as a ready-made major, before helping him to skive off his army service after just one year because he had hurt his thumb."

Just three years later I would also be a member of the village police force. By then it was 1937 and I had already turned fifteen in March. With this being a normal age in those days for children to leave school if they had a job on offer, I became a police cadet. Of course the fact that Papa was the village Police Chief was a big help in getting the job offer, as well as the other fact that no other sod wanted to join the police after all the recent events and incidents.

14: A Little Piece of History

Besides, with there being no chance of my ever being employed by the Kratzkopfs as one of their mountain guides or ski instructors, my old dreams of one day being such had simply melted away like the tips of a glacier. Of course I knew that I could have tried my luck as a guide or instructor in some other nearby village but, at my age, there was little chance of anyone taking me seriously if they didn´t already know me.

I could perhaps have scraped in a few Schillings by hunting full-time with my Uncle Max but this "blood sport" had eventually sickened me so to the core that I had stopped joining him on his expeditions. With perhaps the exception of the fish in the streams, rivers and lakes, I found the slaughtering of defenseless animals and birds and then returning home with their blood dripping all over myself was just becoming more and more stomach-turning as each new season approached. Besides, there was no telling what the Fatherland Front Gemendetag might do next, such as suddenly repealing all the hunting licenses and leaving me unqualified for the future.

Indeed, I guess that I was now developing much more into a serious and practical person like my Papa and less and less into a dreamer like Max, as I had previously been. I was also becoming quite a book-worm, with Papa being a prolific reader and having several bookcases that were full of books on history, as well as a few classic novels.

The only thing that Max ever read were the newspapers because, like Papa, he was nuts about politics, on both a local and a national level (which included the threat of Germany). As such, they had been arguing eternally about politics. Growing up as I now was, it therefore seemed to be only natural that I would not only take an interest in politics but even occasionally join in with Papa´s and Max´s fiery arguments, usually on Papa´s side. Sometimes, however, it didn´t even have to be politics for me to want to join in their verbal bun-fights.

"You know what your problem is, big brother Josef?" Max shouted at Papa one day when Mama was out. "You´re too soft with Kratzkopf. You´re letting him play you like a fiddle. Stand up to him, man, and DEMAND that he and that dumb Gemeindetag allow Lilly to have that concession for a hut on the lake again! Because if you otherwise carry on behaving like a sop like this you´ll soon be a Nazi collaborator!"

Of course Max didn´t know anything about Mama´s little secret about being half-Jewish and that Kratzkopf might well have been using it as leverage to control Papa.

"Don´t talk to me about collaborating with the Nazis!" my Papa suddenly yelled back at Max like a tiger leaping on an overgrown kitten. "What do you think you have been doing all your damned silly life? First you were actually working for them and now they are your best customer!"

I had to agree with my Papa so I decided to also give my own dollop of "mustard", as the Germans and Austrians like to put it:

"If you ask me, Max, Papa is doing a pretty good job of keeping this village ship of fools on a keel as well as Kratzkopf and his Nazi ambitions under wraps."

Max then looked at me as if wondering where on Earth I had learnt to talk like a creepy swot, before giving me his own dollop of mustard:

"You can say what you like, Bulldog, but if this isn´t the quiet before the storm then I don´t know what is."

"Nonsense," said Papa. "Kratzkopf doesn´t want to do anything sinister in Gletschberg unless he is provoked into it. All that he wants is a nice, quiet place for his nasty friends to have a holiday whilst minding their own business for a change. Of all people you should know that. The real trouble-maker was his son Stefan all along."

My Mama meanwhile said that I had become much more like Papa because I had finally left school and was smart enough to now realize the responsibility of leading a grown-up life. I even joined the police boxing club to please Papa, although I wasn´t quite as phenomenal as everyone had expected and still didn´t fancy taking part in any Saturday afternoon tournaments in other villages.

My Papa was also well-pleased with my quick progress as a police cadet.

"You'll make a fine policeman," Papa told me one morning as he put his hand on my shoulder as an extra sign of encouragement – a thing that he rarely did at the best of times. "Who knows: you may even one day also rise to the rank of Chief of Police."

As I now pictured the Old Kaiser and his wife lying punctured by bullets in their machine-gunned car, as well as Franz Hickl being shot down on the very front doorstep of the Innsbruck police headquarters, whilst also imagining other guys having the times of their lives as guides and ski instructors in the mountains, I suddenly wondered if I had made the right career choice after all.

One kid who did seem to be utterly content with his career choice was Dani, who had just begun to work on the railways in Innsbruck. Seppi had already begun working on the railways two years before: but in Gletschberg – or, more specifically, the "West" part of Gletschberg in the Wipptal Valley. Seppi had even managed to get a surprisingly large room of his very own on the top floor of the railway station for next to nothing. However, he kept saying on the few occasions that he did unfortunately visit us for Sunday dinner, that what he really wanted to do was to join the German army and fight for the Third Reich.

At the time of this story the Brenner Pass was still just a narrow country road, with the motorway that now runs along the Wipptal Valley not being built until the 1960s. As such the railway, which had been built between 1864 and 1867, was the main transport route for especially goods and had already begun to bring much needed income to Gletschberg. This was because this part of the Wipptal Valley was particularly wide, so that there was plenty of room for a large shunting station for the many goods trains as well as the "new" village of Gletschberg West, whilst still leaving the lion´s share of that part of the valley as farming land.

As well as this, the advent of wealthy weekend visitors and rich holiday makers from as far away as Germany was also starting to shape up – although it was still only just a beginning. Max had also told me that, like the Brenner Pass road, our main village had looked pretty rugged and medieval until the tourists started bringing money in with the development of the Hotel Berghof.

Unfortunately, unless you happened to be rich and either came by car or were picked up by the Berghof´s own taxi, or were lucky enough to catch one of the very few omnibuses in the area, anyone perambulating between Gletschberg proper and Gletschberg West had to do so by foot.

That meant either wandering up and down the pretty but nevertheless rough and somewhat lengthy Gletschberg Pass or taking the so-called Gletschberg Climb. This was a very steep and narrow footpath that led straight up the hill between the two parts of the village. Some kind soul had bothered to build a few wooden steps into it but it was still a bum to climb, especially if one had to drag one´s bags up as well if one were staying in one of the pensions that later began sprouting up in the village.

Of course, since tourism in the Wipptal was still in its infancy, most of the trains that passed through Gletschberg were the ungodly goods trains: with their huge, ugly, stinking steam locomotives plus dozens of wagons coupled behind them. Indeed, they seemed to me to look like long boa constrictors made of iron as they tiredly crawled uphill with smoke bellowing everywhere.

Being a nature freak, I couldn´t stand the stink of this thick smoke, the roar of the engines or their screeching whistles whilst imagining that this must be what all of Innsbruck must look like. I was therefore mightily glad that we didn´t live anywhere near the railway line in the west but instead on the edge of the meadows in the south-east.

Of course the Brenner Pass is by far and away the most important pass between the (North) Tyrol of Austria and the South Tyrol that now belongs to Italy. It is not only a veritable jugular artery of commercial traffic between the two countries but is also a major route to and from Germany, just over forty miles to the north.

I say North and South Tyrol because they belonged for centuries immemorial together: a single "Grafschaft" or dukedom whose natives were always German speaking. There is even a much smaller East Tyrol that still also belongs to the Austria, even though it has no border with North Tyrol but only South Tyrol and yet belongs as part of the North (now called Austrian) Tyrol. You may therefore be wondering how the South Tyrol came to be an amputated part of Italy, even though almost everyone there spoke a Tyrolean dialect of German as their mother language?

Well, the legend goes that, whilst the Treaty of Saint Germain was being drawn up in 1919 to decide what was going to be done with Austria-Hungary now that they had just lost the Great War, a delegation of pompous no-nothings decided to take a quick whirlwind trip through the South Tyrol before they finally decided on its future fate. Needless to say that, because they all already had their luxury hotels booked into as permanent holiday homes in other parts of Europe, their only interest in the South Tyrol was what class of railway carriage they could have in order to quickly travel through it and how luxurious their snacks, dig-ins and booze might be.

Enter the Italian government of the time, who quickly had all the railway stations' place names changed from German to Italian. Result: "Oh, I say, dear chap: just look at all these stations' names: they're all in Italian – what – what! We must simply give the South Whatsit to the Italians! Now hand me some of those Garibaldi biscuits and Prosecco, old bean!"

The Truth, however, is even simpler than that: namely, the Spoils of War. The Allies wanted to reward Italy for changing sides in the middle of the War and nuts to what the Tyroleans felt about the matter – north, south or east of the Brenner Pass. It would be like having half of England given to the French. It was also something that no less than the Grand Man of Great Britain Winston Churchill would repeat after the Second World War. Mind you, he was also all for chopping Germany up into bits and pieces and continuing the already long Second World War, this time against Russia . . .

Needless to say that tempers would keep rising in the South Tyrol with the call for Unity during the next few decades – and even included some acts of terrorism. However, Father Time is supposed to be a great healer and so the two Tyrols have both since come to **reconcile themselves with the split**, especially when the South Tyrol became much more autonomous from the rest of Italy in the 1960s.

But I am getting way ahead of myself. In the meantime, back in the world of the mid-1930s, Hitler's Germany was being a right pain in the backside of Austrian politics. Dollfuss's successor was a South Tyrolean called Kurt Schuschnigg. Like Dollfuss he wanted Austria to remain an independent corporate state like Italy and a nicer, kinder and, most of all, supposedly Christian version of what Germanic fascists could get up to, as opposed to that Hitler Hell-Hole that was Nazi Germany. This did not stop him, however, from keeping 16,000 people locked up for political grievances, although "only" fifteen Nazis were executed for terrorist attacks, with all but two of these being for the July Coup and three of the remainder being also for murder.

Like Dollfuss, Schuschnigg also naturally looked towards Italy for support against Austria´s bullying Nazi brothers. However, the apple cart got completely knocked over when Mussolini decided to invade Abyssinia in October, 1935 just so that he could pretend that he were another Napoleon or Caesar or whoever. To do this he needed Hitler´s backing and that meant that he could no longer protect Austria from the conniving little weasel with the toothbrush moustache and who excelled in toddler tirades.

By 1938 Hitler was putting so much pressure on Schuschnigg and his half-fascist government that Austria was already starting to crumble apart. On the Twelfth of February Hitler ordered Schuschnigg to get his backside to his own "Berghof" in Bavaria in order to sign the so-called "Berchtesgaden Agreement" that would finally allow the Nazis to infiltrate Schuschnigg´s government.

A very bookish-looking Austrian Nazi called Arthur Seyss-Inquart was ordered to be Schuschnigg´s Minister of the Interior and Security – in other words, Austria´s Number One Bully Boy. On top of that Seyss-Inquart made Schuschnigg agree to the Nazis publishing whatever propaganda that they now wanted to in Austria and basically be able to do whatever the hell that they wanted. So much for being a banned and illegal party in the **red-white-red republic** of Austria.

Reading between the lines, Schuschnigg gave a defiant public speech to the Austrians on the Twenty-fourth of February, shouting out "Until the Death! Red-white-red Austria!" whilst still defending the independence of Austria from Nazi Germany. Hoping that the majority of Austrians would now give Hitler the stink finger, Schuschnigg announced in Innsbruck on Wednesday the Ninth of March that he planned to hold a referendum the following Sunday the Thirteenth for the Austrians to decide for themselves on whether or not they wanted to become a part of the German Reich.

Fearing that the Austrians might indeed give him and his Third Reich the stink finger, Hitler suddenly decided that the Germany Army should get their marching boots on pretty sharpish and make a one-way weekend trip to the Edelweiss Republic first thing that very next Saturday morning. As things turned out, the only thing that he and his boys were given on that sadly unforgettable day in Austrian history were flowers and cheers galore . . .

15: The Death of Austria

Austria would later officially claim that it had been "invaded" by the Nazis and therefore been the victim of the Third Reich and not its accomplice. The Truth was a lot more sinister. Austria was indeed a victim of the Third Reich but not simply because of the invading German army that marched straight across Austria´s many borders on the morning of Saturday the Twelfth of March without the Austrians so much as firing a pop-gun or even throwing a rotten egg at their pudding-bowl helmets.

These guys were simply the back-up force to all the coups that had taken place in every city, town and major village the day before. Ever since the failed July Coup of 1934 the Nazis had been carefully planting the seeds for a meticulously organized take-over the length and breadth of the country. If nothing else, the Nazis were masters of terrorist organization and propaganda. On top of all this, tens of thousands of Nazi "exiles" who had been forced to flee to the "German Reich" because of the Fatherland Front suddenly returned to their homeland just a couple of days before the planned "Anschluss" or "Annexation".

One of these returning Nazi exiles was none other than Slimey Stefan, who took part in one of the so-called "Jolly Rides" of motorcades that went cruising up and down the country immediately before the Anschluss. On the morning of Friday the

Eleventh of March he came riding up at the front of such a motorcade of civilian cars that was steadily climbing the Brenner Pass before driving up our own Gletschberg Pass. I remember this day very well because it was not only the very day before the actual "Einmarsch" of the German Army and Adolf Hitler but was also my sixteenth birthday.

In the meantime, Slimey Stefan´s motorcade tooted and hooted and honked their horns whilst flying Nazi flags galore, singing the Horst Wesel Song and giving no end of Hitler salutes. The entire population of Old Gletschberg seemed to have come out to watch the spectacle from the top of the rough Gletschberg Pass as the noisy convoy made the last curve up into our village square before the church.

Even I was there – just before I rushed back to the police station to change into my uniform and join my Papa on the front steps of the Rathaus. Many were shouting, some were even waving small Nazi flags that they had gotten from I do not know where but – I am still quite sure – the actual majority just watched them in silence whilst no doubt wondering what on Earth was about to happen to their futures.

As if directing a circus parade that had decided to play our village, Slimey Stefan was now standing upright like an erect penis in the front car, whilst giving Nazi salutes as if he were a rejuvenated Adolf Hitler. Even more bizarre than this was the fact that he was now dressed in a full-blown, shiny black **S.S.** ceremonial uniform – a bitter and grotesque coevality considering that his nick-name was also "S.S."

The convoy was soon joined by a brass band, which then marched through the village and propped itself up on the wooden terrace of the Berghof, whilst playing the same happy and victorious oompah-oompah music that we had all heard from the other band five years before when Hitler had first come to power in Germany.

Kratzkopf then offered half-price drinks to the villagers, so that the entire terrace was soon choc-a-bloc full with Nazi dignitaries and Nazi sympathizers as they swirled amongst each other as if taking part in a gigantic and orgiastic Bacchanalian festival. It was clear that, for most of the villagers, little work was going to get done that day, as if an official public holiday had been declared, with an evil bigger one planned for the morrow.

However, if the Berghof were now the site of jolly fun and games, there was a much more sinister scene soon playing out in the middle of the village, where Slimey Stefan and his boot boys in brown had taken up arms before the Rathaus. Papa had been well aware that this would happen as the Nazis prepared to raid the government building and take over the business of running the village and its borough. Once again the various local Heimatwehr forces were called in but this time their resources were stretched all over the Wipptal Valley as they had no idea which village Rathauses would be stormed and which would not.

Papa had meanwhile barricaded the entire perimeter of the government building with barbed wire and **Czech hedgehogs**, as well as having several **Fokker-Leimberger machine-gun**s from the Great War menacingly poking out of several of the windows. Rather than looking like a scene out of a modern day war movie, however, it looked more like a revolution, with the Nazi boot boys constantly jeering at the armed Heimatwehr men posted around the building as if a New Order were about to break out at any moment.

I and my Papa were standing at the back of this loyal legion of Heimatwehr and policemen, perched up on the front-steps of the Rathaus whilst wearing our great capes like a pair of defiant birds that were refusing to be made extinct. It must have indeed been a grotesque sight to behold: with my Papa standing tall and alert and with all the dignity of a royal about to be kicked off the throne, whilst I was short and stumpy and played the part of the quintessential defiant little schoolboy cadet as I faithfully stood by my old man´s side.

Was I frightened? Of course I was. I genuinely believed that although the only things that were being hold at us were insults and curses that these might well soon escalate into bricks and firecrackers, possibly even hand-grenades and knives, to say nothing of hidden pistols.

"Where is the Gemeindetag?" one of the Nazi locals shouted, shaking his fist at us. "Have they all scarpered off like the jelly-fish that they are?!"

"Where is the Buergermeister?" someone from the Heimatwehr in front us shouted back. "Is he also on the piss like the rest of those damned Nazi boffins whilst trying to fool all of you with empty promises?"

Of course the members of the Gemeindetag were nowhere to be seen but not because they had cowardly scarpered off by clandestinely bolting out through the back windows but because they simply hadn´t been scheduled to hold a meeting on that day. As to all the regular civic workers: Papa had told them all long before to make themselves scarce as things might well turn out messy that day.

What´s more, if things did indeed get spicy then this wouldn´t be another innocent tournament of fisticuffs in which I could be churned out to the chants of "Bulldog! Bulldog! Go get him, Bulldog!" This was about actual killing, with people getting shot at close-range and knifed in the back. Neither would it be another Battle of Hitler´s Birthday. That had been a spontaneous free-for-all, smash-up-the-joint kind of bun-fight that had gone horribly wrong. This would be a determined onslaught and calculated bid for power.

However, whilst the Nazis kept jeering us whilst we and the Heimatwehr remained standing stoically before them like stuffed mannequins whilst saying very little in reply, the crowd of locals around the Nazis kept growing larger and louder.

It was at that moment that I realized what the power of a large minority really meant and that I had just been wrong about everyone having gone to the road exit of the village to watch the entrance of the Nazi motorcade. This was not "The People" or even a majority of the People just because they were managing to fill the streets with their sheer numbers. It might have looked as if the entire village were out on the streets but that was only an illusion, a question of optics. The majority of people were still going about their daily chores and minding their own "business". Little did they seem to realize that their "business" would soon also be the business of the new Nazi government.

Yet it was this large minority that was now calling the shots whilst its numbers seemed to be swelling like bees being given the promise of honey – or like children being told that it was Christmas Eve but that they mustn´t yet open their presents until the next day.

"But in Germany and Austria we get to open our presents on Christmas Eve!" I could almost hear them shouting in my imagination, with the next day being Christmas Day as Adolf Hitler and the German Army marched over the borders into Austria.

Encouraged by the swelling crowd and the band music coming from the Berghof in the far background towards the meadows, the Nazi boot boys kept lurching towards the Heimatwehr troops standing guard before us as if about to take them down in a rugby tackle. The Heimatwehr kept pointing their own guns and rifles at them but had strict orders not to fire a single shot – not even into the air – until the command was given by my father. Indeed, this cat and mouse game of taunting and bluffing between the Nazis and the Heimatwehr went on for quite a while until someone suddenly shouted:

"At last, the Voice of Reason!"

"Let´s finally get rid of this Sunday school Fatherland autocracy," cried another in the crowd, "and put a real People´s Government in its place!"

"Let the National Socialists take over!" someone else cried. "They´ll soon get the economy on the up and up again!"

"Let´s make Austria great again by joining the German Reich again!" came a distant voice from the back of the crowd. By this I assumed that this person was having sweet memories of the long-defunct Holy Roman Empire as Austria had never been a part of the modern German Reich of 1871.

Finally, a cheer suddenly went up in the crowd as I saw the giant Tyrolean hat of the Buergermeister bobbing brightly towards us through the mass of villagers. Soon enough, the large presence of Kratzkopf appeared before us, grinning like a Cheshire cat that had just found the prime cream whilst his golden mayoral chain glinted almost as brightly as his teeth now did.

"Come, my dear Major Schilling," Kratzkopf addressed my Papa, whilst looking more like a festive phoenix bird in his get-up of traditional costume and ceremonial decorations. "Let us be reasonable about all this. We don´t want any bloodshed on this beautiful spring day, do we? What´s going to happen is going to happen, even if just a few of us might not like it."

This was, of course, a huge understatement for I was sure – and still am to this day – that many of us were not at all happy about the new impending arrangements. However, it was then that Kratzkopf quietly said something to my father that shook me to the core:

"After all, we don´t want to forget our own little understanding between us, do we, Josef ?"

It was then that I realized just how much leverage that Kratzkopf did have over my family with his likely clandestine knowledge that my mother was in fact half-Jewish. In fact, I was so taken up by this alarming thought that I must have gone into a completely dreamy state as my Papa simply gave the order to let the Nazi boot boys into the Rathaus, along with their own set of thug-like boffins to form a new Gemeindetag that would this time fall completely in line with Kratzkopf´s Nazi ambitions. As such, my Papa was allowed to keep his position as Chief of Police. Buergermeister Kratzkopf now completely had him by the short and curlies.

By the time that it was early evening the Austrian flag had been taken down and the Nazi swastika banner hissed up in its place before the Rathaus building. Likewise, the Austrian flag before the Berghof hotel had also been removed and replaced by a second Nazi flag, just as there were also swastika flags draped over each of the balconies.

"Well, it´s official," Papa solemnly said at supper that same evening. "We now have a Nazi Gemeindetag and our Buergermeister is finally flying his true colors."

As if the village could not get enough of these damned flags of spiders bathing in a pool of blood, dozens of private houses also had them flying out of their windows, doors and gate-ways like a devil´s version of a Chinese red lantern festival.

None of this would have been possible had similar coups not also taken place in Vienna that day, as well as Innsbruck, the capital of Tyrol. No one, least of all the police and the Heimatwehr and Heimwehr, had the stomach of starting a bloodbath with the Nazis whilst so many of their adoring fans were already swarming around, so that any pretense of a defense soon fizzled out. Indeed, not wishing to lose their jobs, many of the Austrian police rolled up for work the next (Saturday) morning also wearing swastika arm-bands.

Indeed (as Dani would later explain to me) the enthusiasm for German Nazism and a bright future with the now prospering German Reich seemed to be engulfing the entire population of Innsbruck like a tsunami wave as more and more thousands of sympathizers meanwhile took to the streets of the Old Town to join in the Nazi celebrations that weekend. However, it is, as I said just before, only too easy for a large and noisy minority to look like the vast majority, just as a glass-full of spilt milk can look as if it is a bucket-full.

That same Friday evening we listened to a radio broadcast from Kurt **Schuschnigg**. He asked the Austrian people not to let any German blood be spilt the next day, having always considered Austrians to be part of the German family even though he also considered that they should live in their own house. To clinch the Nazi coup he then announced that he would be resigning his chancellorship at midnight that night and finished with the futile words, "God save Austria!" as if he were the captain of a sinking ship taking his last gasp of air before going down under the waves.

Schuschnigg´s immediate successor was none other than that other Nazi Schweinhund, Arthur Seyss-Inquart. Seyss-Inquart would later become Hitler´s right-hand bully in the Netherlands and responsible for the forced labor and deportation of over a hundred thousand Jews into extermination camps. As such, Seyss-Inquart became one of the twelve top Nazis who were sentenced to death at the Nuremberg Trials.

Of course there was little chance of any blood being spilt the next morning as literally thousands of Nazi sympathizers were up bright and early to line the roads into Austria to cheer the incoming marching troops on. Waving their little bloody spider flags whilst believing all that crap of shiny new things to come, they little realized that, like the Germans, they were being duped into embarking on a long voyage with international pirates and slave-makers that could only end with everyone being sent to the ocean bottom.

These scenes were no different when the first of the German troops marched into the heart of Innsbruck in time for morning coffee, except that the cheering crowds had themselves already had time to have a decent breakfast before the great event. Austria was now de facto Nazi and, just to put the cherry on top of the brown cake and make everything look supposedly above board, Hitler announced that he would hold Schuschnigg´s referendum a full month later on the Tenth of April.

However, this was no typical democratic referendum where you could quietly disappear into an enclosed box, discreetly mark your cross on a form that had two simple choices, slide it into an envelope and then drop that through the slit of a ballot box with no one any the wiser. No, sir: you had to put your cross down in the open and throw your ballot paper into the box unfolded whilst gorilla-sized S.S. men watched you do it. Try to quietly do so in a corner or even fold the paper then you were remembered.

In short, a typical Nazi ballot with, as per usual, almost a hundred per cent going to Adolf Hitler. Indeed, it was only in the backwater region of East Tyrol that a lot of people decided to say nuts to the gorillas and pen in their crosses where the hell they wanted – and, I´m glad to say, that was also the case in our own backwater village on the Brenner Pass.

To my surprise our Mama was allowed to vote, even though Jews and part-Jews were officially excluded from the referendum. This seemed to show that Kratzkopf was at least keeping his side of his bargain with puppet Papa and that Slimey Stefan wasn´t managing to meddle in our affairs.

In the meantime, many would say afterwards that Austria´s prosperity and social well-being took off immediately after the Anschluss, with the Nazis putting a particular emphasis on starting sports clubs for the youth. There were also bold new plans for major infrastructure projects, including a sparkling new **Autobahn along the Brenner Pass** with sky-scraper-sized bridges galore. As things soon turned out, however, most of these projects never even took off from the ground since World War Two broke out just eighteen months after the Anschluss. Austria sure drew the short straw with its bet on the Nazis.

On the other hand, there was absolutely no doubt that Austrian tourism suddenly boomed after the Anschluss, with Germans holidaymakers pouring in as if there were no tomorrow (and how true that would soon turn out to be). Indeed, even our tiny backwater village, high up on the Pass and just below the Italian border, also immediately felt the seismic effects of the German tidal wave of tourists. Suddenly we had guesthouses and pensions mushrooming all over the village, in people´s backgardens and on their terraces, with concessions for jerry-built alms being given all over the meadows, although none were ever given to my Mama.

Most of this was encouraged and promoted by Kratzkopf himself, with even a brand-new and larger cable-car being built to replace the old one that went up the side of the Kricklhorn. In fact, Kratzkopf did so well in managing to do all this in just the one summer season that the Gemeindetag decided to make him an "Esteemed Citizen of the Gemeinde", along with Adolf Hitler (who had to first be made an "Honorary Citizen of the Gemeinde").

In the meantime yet another oompah-oompah band came to the terrace of the Berghof and went on to remain as its big feature. Not only that but Kratzkopf won the concession for building a large snack-bar called "The Pavillon", with its own lakeside terrace on the shore of the miniature lake just before the hotel. In fact, it stood on almost the exact same spot that Mama´s Gluehwein Hut had stood four years before, whilst being much bigger. Ironically, Maria began working part-time at the Pavillon snack-bar bussing tables, before "moving up" to the main terrace of the Berghof on account of her infectious friendliness.

Indeed, far from all the horrible things that we had expected of the Nazis to come to our quiet backwater village, the spring of 1938 seemed to indeed be heralding an age of peaceful prosperity for us as our tourist industry began blooming as quickly as the flowers on the meadows. Little did many of us realize that even before the mock referendum in April the Nazis had already begun rounding up any potential trouble-makers that they knew of and sending them to their concentration camps. Worse still, in order to make life even more like Hell for those that he didn´t like, Hitler then appointed one his favorite sadistic maniacs as the new **Gauleiter** of Tyrol and Vorarlberg, just as summer was beginning at the end of May. It was an appointment that would have a devastating effect on the lives of my family.

16: The Terror of Franz Hofer

In every society there are some people who, when they feel massively wronged and ill-treated, just end up losing control of their minds whilst seeking vicious revenge on all sorts of imaginary enemies. When, however, they actually see the harm and injuries that they alone have caused, they immediately break down into a deep sense of bitter remorse and wonder how they will go on living with their terrible guilt.

Then again, as we all know, there are those few sadistic maniacs who don´t need to be wildly angry and out of their minds in order to inflict wicked harm on others but positively ENJOY seeing the excruciating pain that is the result. Indeed, some would say that these "monsters" are not maniacs at all but that they cold-bloodedly know exactly what they are doing and are simply EVIL at heart.

Franz Hofer was one of them. Slimey Stefan was another.

At the same time, the worst of all this is that they also often have an unquenchable thirst for controlling people and whipping up anger amongst them in order that they may inflict the maximum amount of vicious harm on those that they decide they don´t like.

And if all that wasn´t bad enough the Nazis – the masters of organization, with evil geniuses like

Goering, Himmler and Goebbels at the very top – produced a system whereby the only way to achieve anything in civic life was by towing the party line. Anyone who wanted to keep their job as a teacher or as an administrator, let alone get promotion in the future, had to join the Nazi Party. Worst still, many plum jobs were only available if you were first allowed to join the elite S.S., whilst at the very least pretending that you were a fanatically loyal Nazi.

Most of all, anyone who was not seen openly cheering the party and merrily attending its frequent festivities was soon ostracized as a trouble-maker. And trouble-makers had a nasty habit of winding up in the concentration camps that the Nazis had immediately begun building when they had risen to power in 1933.

And even if you were cheering the Nazis on from the roof-tops, that still didn´t mean that they wouldn´t make you their enemy if they decided that they simply didn´t like you, such as if you were gay, were severely handicapped in any way or even if you just so happened, as in our case, to have some Jewish blood in your veins. The Nazis, as we all know, pathologically hated the Jews, with the botanist Heinrich Himmler going full-blown racial when he introduced the Nuremberg Race Laws in Germany in 1935.

Himmler had in fact studied agricultural gene research and had developed a mad professor obsession with the racial "purity" of human beings that was based on the cultivation of plants and crops. As such these laws not only annulled the citizenship of all German Jews but also demanded that everyone else carried passes detailing exactly what proportion of their ancestry was German. These same laws were introduced with a vengeance in Austria in May, 1938, just two months after the Anschluss and the very same month that Franz Hofer was made the Gauleiter of Tyrol and Vorarlberg.

Franz Hofer was without doubt one of Adolf Hitler's favorite nutters, having crawled his clever way into the inner circle of the Fuehrer before begging for the prestigious and magnificently powerful job of Gauleiter. Indeed, Hitler had even lent Hofer his own private plane to fly him out of trouble after he had escaped imprisonment in Innsbruck in 1933.

Like Hitler, Hofer was also an Austrian, having been born in Salzburgland, which is Tyrol's neighbor to the east. And, like both Kratzkopf and Goering, he was also large and jolly, although that largeness was more in the waist than in the height. In fact, he would have made a great ice hockey player because he would have filled the goal.

It was not long after Franz Hofer's appointment to being the Gauleiter of Tyrol and Vorarlberg in Innsbruck that he began showing up at the Berghof at weekends. Even so: for all that we knew he might have been there before because all sorts of high-ranking Nazi bigwigs would show up there without making an exhibition of who they actually were.

However, now that he was Gauleiter and had all the trappings that went with it, Hofer clearly wanted to depict his self as being some kind of German Reich prince as he began turning up in his brand-new, open-roofed **W150 version of the 770 Mercedes-Benz**. Decked out with swastika flags and a massive obnoxious horn, Hofer was at first accompanied by a suitably large escort of cars and motor-bikes.

Even so, Hofer either soon got tired of having a motorcade of body-guards following him all over the place, or just couldn´t find lodgings in Gletschberg to put them all up for the weekends or simply began popping up spontaneously without any time to organize such a parade because he started showing up in Gletschberg with just one extra car of bodyguards behind himself.

Franz Hofer´s frequent spontaneous visits meant that Kratzkopf had to permanently make sure that his oompah-oompah band was always there on the terrace for weekends, as well as that the champagne glasses were constantly kept full. Max was also kept busy supplying these dudes with fresh game, even though Hofer occasionally liked having the odd blast himself in the meadows. However, due to his large size and lack of sports, he never got very far up the mountains.

"Just make sure that you don´t bring him back here," I heard Papa once say to Max after Max had guided the flailing Gauleiter on one of these futile expeditions.

However, as if Papa had tempted Wicked Fate by saying the very thing that he didn´t want to happen, Franz Hofer and his elite boys, all dressed up in their smart uniforms, came marching towards our chalet one Saturday afternoon in early September. Slimey Stefan also came trailing at the back in his own glittering S.S. uniform, whilst grinning all over like the cat who had been allowed to join the cream train.

Whether it was Slimey who had deliberately or Max who had accidentally let out where exactly we lived I don´t know – but the timing couldn´t have been worse, with Papa still at the police station and Max away in the mountains. In fact Mama would have been completely alone with Pete had I not gone off sick with the ´flu and Maria been given the entire weekend off at the last moment in lieu of holiday money that she was owed from the Berghof. Thus, we were both able to join Mama in meeting the pompous Gauleiter as he marched straight through our front door and into our hallway without so much as a by-your-leave.

Fortunately, he didn´t bring in his entire entourage of bully boys inside with him but left most of them standing outside to guard the fortress, as it were. However, Slimey also came in, still at the back and still grinning wildly away as if he had just scored the sweep of the century.

"You have a very nice chalet here, Frau ???" Hofer said, as he admired our hall´s interior, including its pictures and ornaments, whilst bobbing his head up and down with a gentle, sneaky smile.

"Schilling," Mama immediately answered, straightening her dress whilst taking her apron off, as well as trying not to let her terrified fear of the man show through her pretense of politeness. "Frau Schilling."

"And I suppose that this must be your dear son," said Hofer, now eying me up like a prize bulldog whilst still keeping his gentle grin. For a moment I thought he was about to start touching me up all over the face as Adolf Hitler was prone to do with children and youths, especially boys. Instead, he simply added with a leer of amusement: "I hear that you were once a boxing champion."

"Just the one time, Herr Gauleiter," I answered. "And even then it was only an unofficial match at the end of a village tournament."

"Ha-ha!" Hofer shouted whilst patting me on the shoulder. "Your modesty forbids you from enjoying your own success! I bet that you gave your unfortunate opponent the lesson of his life!"

At this point Hofer laughed out so loud that all his cronies and henchmen felt that they also had to laugh out as loudly as they could, including a very unsettled Slimey at the back. Slimey looked even more miserable when Hofer then actually turned round and stared at him whilst still laughing, so that he was very pained to keep up the pretense of appreciating the ugly joke made at him.

"And this must be your little sister, ???" Hofer then asked, turning around to look into Maria´s sparkling eyes. However, before Maria could answer with her name, Hofer suddenly asked her another question: "Haven´t I seen you somewhere before?"

"Very likely, Herr Gauleiter," Maria answered with a smile and whilst her eyes still kept sparkling. "I sometimes bus the tables on the Berghof terrace."

In spite of Maria´s glowing personality, Hofer did not seem to be impressed by her low position as a mere bus-girl. He instead turned back towards me and told me with a show of bluster:

"You should also come and visit us at the Berghof some time, Bulldog! We´re always on the look-out for young men like you!"

Of all the strange things, it was then that I noticed that Maria´s eyes weren´t so much sparkling because the Gauleiter was looking at her but because she kept looking at Slimey, who was now grinning like a Cheshire cat all over again. Surely to God, I thought, as Slimey more than once tried to return her looks without making it too obvious, there wasn´t something going on between the two of them?

As such, it took me all my will-power to calm down, especially as Maria was still only fifteen whilst Slimey was already twenty-seven. However, I also tried to tell myself that this was reason enough for my probably imagining things and that I was probably just being a jealous, over-protective older brother. However, my thoughts were soon interrupted when we all suddenly heard a loud, wailing sound coming from behind the closed door of the main room.

"Hallo? What´s that?" Hofer just as suddenly asked before adding very ominously: "Is there an ANIMAL in your kitchen?"

I could see the look of horror suddenly show on Mama´s face as she almost leapt to the door whilst saying, "Oh, there´s nothing in there! It´s only the kitchen!"

"But there seems to be an animal in distress in there," said Hofer, slowly moving towards the door as if he would be more than glad to have Mama physically removed out of the way if he had to. "Surely you don´t want to have any animals in distress being left alone in your kitchen?"

"Oh, please go away!" Mama suddenly blurted out at the Gauleiter. "I´ve got so much to do and my husband will be arriving home pretty soon!"

"Oh, that´s not good," said Hofer, as if giving Mama a ticking off.

However, Hofer did not say this because of what Mama had just said but because he had noticed the large crucifix that was hanging above the main room door. It was a well-known fact that, as well as being especially anti-Semitic, even for a Nazi, Hofer was also especially anti-clerical, even though Tyrol was about as Catholic as one could possibly get. Naturally, a person who entertained such vitriol hate for both Jews and Catholics (and even though he came from a family of Catholics himself) wouldn´t have any empathy for a mentally handicapped person like Pete.

We had, as you have no doubt guessed, left Pete on his stool in the main room. Of course we had tried to bring him upstairs and out of harm´s way as soon as we had seen (and heard) Hofer and his posse marching towards our house through its windows. However, Pete was in an especially stubborn and whiney mood that day and had proved to be impossible to budge. Very stupidly, all three of us had then instinctively sprung into the hallway as soon as we had heard Hofer marching towards the front door, as if we were forming a protective wall to stop anyone getting into the main room and kitchen. By then it had been too late for any of us to go back and help keep Pete quiet.

It was then that my police training tried to spring into action with a tactic of digressions.

"It´s just our baby boy," I said. "He´s just having his sleep at the moment and so it would be bad to disturb him just now."

"Oh, I JUST LOVE BABIES!" Hofer suddenly roared as he just as suddenly pushed his way between us and threw the door open himself before marching into the main room. At the same time that Mama then screamed with fright, poor Pete also began screaming and wailing and having one of the worst fits that he had ever yet had. Miraculously, however, he still managed to stay perched on his stool, even though he was now frantically waving his arms all over the place as if he were being attacked by a swarming army of hornet wasps.

"My, what a foofaraw he´s making!" Hofer jestfully commented, quickly returning to the hallway whilst closing the door again in order to keep out the terrible din that Pete was creating. "That one makes more noise than a suckling pig! We´ll have to do something about THAT!"

I fully expected Hofer to send a couple of gunmen to go into the main room and shoot Pete in the head there and then. However, Hofer did not do this but just left the house with all his men whilst they all looked frustrated at their visit suddenly having to be curtailed because of all the dreadful noise.

"We´ll have to get Pete out of here," Mama said when we were all back at supper that evening.

"Can´t we keep him at the Retreat?" I foolishly suggested.

"Don´t be silly," Max answered. "A boy like that can´t be left on his own in a place like that. He could easily do himself a mischief."

"I´ll think of something," Papa said – although, from the way that he said it, it seemed that he was only saying this so as to try calming our nerves.

With the next day being Sunday, it therefore took us all completely by surprise when the front door was suddenly hammered on (as opposed to being politely rung) as we were all preparing to go to Church together. In fact, we had all been so busy that none of us had noticed or even heard both a van and a car pulling up before our house in an age when there were still hardly any motor vehicles in the village. Perhaps we just thought it were the butcher and the baker making special Sunday deliveries.

Our worst fears were confirmed when, looking out of the windows, we saw an ambulance and a **Citroen Traction Avant** saloon car standing in the road outside. When we let our uninvited visitors in I was surprised that they didn´t seem to include any of the men from the afternoon before – with the one exception of Slimey Stefan. It was, of course, abundantly clear who these other men were and that this was no longer a friendly visit but a grave one of the grimmest magnitude.

This time all but one of the men were dressed in "plain clothes": that is, the typical "uniform" of Fedora hats and long coats – leather, trench and Mackintoshes – that belonged to the Gestapo. The odd one was instead wearing an alpine deer-hunting hat and a traditional woolen "Loden" coat. He also had a soppy moustache and a particularly weasel-looking pair of eyes. Without even showing the curtesy of tipping his alpine hat to us he sullenly introduced himself to us, whilst the others stared at us in stony silence with eyes like knives and as thick as thieves.

"My name is Herr Zeller: Kommissar of the Geheime Staatspolizei," he told us, more as a harsh statement of fact than as a sign of politeness. "I´ve come to arrest Herr Major Schilling in connection to the murder of Herr Hauptmann Kaiser of the Gletschberg Gendarme."

I fully expected my Papa to suddenly roar out "WHAT?!" at the Gestapo Kommissar, as was his wont, but even he understood what a damned dangerous pickle he was now in – and, by extension, all of us. It was, of course, also blindingly obvious that there was more than just a smidgeon of politics here and that Herr Zeller was eating out of Slimey´s hand rather than Kratzkopf´s. There was also no doubt that they would soon be concocting a story where the motivation for murder was that Papa had wanted the Old Kaiser´s job as the Chief of Police.

Whilst Mama and the rest of us simply looked on in horror, Papa calmly took hold of Mama´s hand and said:

"Don´t worry, dear. I´ll be home again soon enough. Don´t forget to keep the dinner warm for me."

It was on this light, jestful note that Papa now left the house whilst surrounded on all sides by the Gestapo henchmen as if he were being kidnapped by Chicago gangsters. Many, many more dinner-times would of course pass by without Papa returning home for them.

But if that wasn´t bad enough then there was even more to come: namely, that the Gestapo men had no sooner bundled Papa into the Citroen Traction Avant then Herr Zeller returned inside the house, accompanied this time by two men in white coats who looked more like overgrown thugs than hospital carers.

"There's someone else who we also need to take care of," Herr Zeller then told Mama, as if we couldn't guess who he was talking about.

Mama immediately barred the doorway into the main room but the two overgrown zombies simply butted her aside.

"He's got to be properly looked after," Herr Zeller almost shouted at Mama whilst the zombie thugs grabbed hold of Pete and dragged him screaming and shouting away through the outdoor kitchen door and out into the yard.

"But where are you taking him?" my Mama cried in a fit of hysterics and tears before collapsing onto her knees in front of Herr Zeller.

"To the Cure and Care Clinic in Hall," Herr Zeller replied, whilst Mama began begging for mercy by pummeling his legs with her baby-like fists. "You'll get a letter of acknowledgement from the clinic the moment that he is delivered there."

"But will we be able to visit him?" I suddenly cried in my shrill, teenage voice as Herr Zeller began leaving through the front door again.

"That'll all be in the letter," Herr Zeller answered, speaking to me for the first time and without any of the recognition or admiration that Franz Hofer had at first shown towards me.

Of course we all knew that that meant that even family visits would as likely as not be tolerated by the so-called clinic. Mama also had that magical sixth sense of a mother in that she could tell that far, far worse than mere incarceration would come to our darling boy Pete.

It was at the end of all this painful melodrama that Slimey suddenly sprang up from absolutely nowhere like a pantomime demon, before turning towards Maria and telling her with a devilishly sneaky playboy grin:

"Your Papa may be in prison for a long spell, Maria, so your Mama will be needing some extra cash for the family household. If you like, you can start working with us full-time. I guess that we can EXPECT to see you at eight o´clock sharp tomorrow morning."

"But Maria is still only fifteen!" Mama suddenly cried out. "School begins again tomorrow and she wants to do the final year so that she can take her exams next summer!"

"NUTS to her final exams!" Slimey almost roared back in her face. "Bulldog left school last year when he was still only fifteen to become a police cadet, so Maria can become a waitress with us at the Berghof tomorrow!"

There was no doubt that what Slimey Stefan really meant by this was that if we wanted our Papa to be treated well that Maria had better show up for permanent work the next day, new school year or no new school year. Mama naturally wanted to prevent all this by crying something else out but I gave her a sign that it would be best if we all just remained quiet.

As well as now suddenly being anxious for Maria´s own safety, the fact that I was now well enough again to be also returning to the police station the next day, just as Max also needed to shoot more game in the mountains, meant that Mama would now be entirely on her own during most of the day, with no one to take care of her in these traumatic times. However, there was nothing that any of else could do just now without making things worse – and things were already bad enough.

"It´s okay, Frau Schilling," said Slimey, now turning towards Mama whilst grinning like a fox that had caught its rabbit. "Your daughter will be perfectly okay with my father and myself."

A look of horror suddenly appeared on Mama´s face, especially as her daughter´s eyes still kept sparkling with delight as she kept staring at the tall, dark and (for her at least) good-looking young man in the black S.S. uniform.

17: The Secret Sign of "Oh-Five"

"It's no longer the Law of Kratzkopf in Nazi Gletschberg with me as his puppet," my Papa sighed when I went to take him his breakfast of bread and cheese on Monday morning. "It's the Law of Hofer with Kratzkopf as his puppet."

"And with Slimey as his favorite Bully Boy," I added. "I don't know how much power Slimey has in the S.S. but at least we are now able to humor him in order to protect ourselves."

Indeed – and to my delighted surprise – Papa had not been driven off in the back of the Citroen car to the Gestapo's own headquarters and prison cells in the notorious Herrengasse of Innsbruck: which had been the very place that Franz Hickl had previously had his police headquarters. Instead, we the local police had been allowed to hold Papa in our own prison cell in our cellar: the very same infamous jail-cage where we had kept holding Nazis during the Fatherland Front era. How quickly the tables had therefore now turned on all of us!

To my ever greater surprise, I was even given the job that Monday morning of being prison warder to my own father in the jail-cage. Of course, I could have easily "forgotten" to lock the cage door when I went for a pee and so let my father escape into the mountains but that would have had dire consequences for my family. The Nazi way of doing things had nothing to do with the rule of law but was just a pirates´ pecking order of bullying, with the non-Party civilians at the bottom taking the most stick of all if they ever dared to – or even appeared to – step out of line.

No more was this so obvious than in our own police force. Whereas even the new Fatherland Front constitution of 1934 had meant that, even in a semi-fascist, authoritarian corporate state, the police still mostly had to follow protocols and set rules, the police today could run the country like a Wild West show. Indeed, they wouldn´t get any stick for it just so long as they didn´t tread on anyone´s steel-capped boots in the S.S., Gestapo or any of the other many secret police organizations of the Third Reich.

Moreover, it might be argued, that had the Fatherland Front been as ruthless with the Nazis as the Nazis now were with them, the Nazis might never have been able to stage the multiple coups on the Eleventh of March: coups that had thereby allowed the German Army to simply swan across the borders the next day without being given so much as a Stinkfinger.

As such, Papa had already had major problems with discipline within his force so that he had ruled more by consensus than by his position. His diplomacy with his men had, however, meant that he had won their overall sympathy, although just how long that would last with the fake accusation that he had been responsible for the murder of the Old Kaiser and his wife remained to be seen.

Papa and I spent most of the morning trying to play chess together at a small table in the jail-cage but our minds were so busy with thoughts of Pete´s incarceration, the Gestapo´s all too obviously concocted suspicions that Papa was a murderer, Slimey´s treatment of Maria at the Berghof and Mama´s now being all alone at home with the farm- and house-work that concentration was simply out of the question. It was just about noon when I had just served Papa with a bowl of warmed-up pea soup that another prisoner was brought down into the cellar.

"Father Murrsea!" my Papa shouted with mixed surprise, joy and worry, whilst jumping up so suddenly that he almost spilt the pea soup all over me. "What have they now gone and charged you with? Also murder?"

Father Murrsea merely shook his head in sorrow, as if there were things worse than even murder in the eyes of the Gestapo.

"I should be so lucky," he replied, finding a stool on the outside of the cage to sit on before simply stepping through its unlocked gate with it and joining us on the inside of the cage. "The whole village is talking about your being charged for the murder of the Old Kaiser and his wife and no one believes it, so I think the Gestapo will have a hard time trying to pretend that it was you who did the terrible deed and not one of Slimey´s lot. On the other hand, they´ve only got to say that I´m a priest and that´s enough reason for them to shoot or even

guillotine me. Just encouraging the worship of God amongst the community is like devil-worshiping to these Nazis, although it is they who are the devil-worshipers, what with their countless rituals of kissing the swastika flag, their torchlight processions, bonfires of books and fiery swastikas on the mountain sides."

"Oh, come on, Father Murrsea," my Papa said, "you know how popular the Catholic Church is in Tyrol. In many villages the Church is their very life, soul and back-bone."

"Really?" said Father Murrsea. "Do you know just how many people have left the Catholic Church in recent years? Well: most of them are young people. That's because Hitler is like a wicked uncle who keeps giving his children candy and toys so that they love him whilst all the time he is in fact stealing the candy and toys from the children of other families. Furthermore, there have even been Catholic societies who have also been supporting the Nazis because they believed that the Nazis would treat them even better than the Fatherland Front fascists had done, even though the Nazi Party was not formed out of Christian Socialists like the Fatherland Front. Indeed, there is as much chance of any of that ever happening as there is of the Habsburgs even being given back the Austrian throne or the Hohenzollerns the German throne by the Nazis."

Wow! I thought to myself. If Father Murrsea's sermons had been as fiery and straight from the heart as this epistle, I would have been looking forward to them every week. On the other hand, it would have probably got him locked up a lot quicker as well.

Father Murrsea´s troubles had all begun with the school. First the Nazis had ordered that all the crucifixes be removed from the school walls, along with the bibles and all religious books. Then Father Murrsea had been forbidden to teach anything even remotely religious and, finally, was told that, as a priest, he was not allowed to teach at all in the school and must instantly resign his teaching post there and then.

I later learned that this had in fact been standard practice all over Austria and Germany – but Austria and southern German states like Bavaria, Baden and Wuerttemberg had strong Catholic traditions and many villages weren´t keen to change completely from Catholicism to Nazism. Indeed, rather like the way that the first Church boffins had had to mix Pagan traditions into the Christian rituals in order to make their "new" religion more palatable, so too did the Nazis realize that they couldn´t go the full hog with the Catholic church goers. At least most of them realized this. Top psychopathic Nazis like Franz Hofer, as I mentioned before, and in spite of the fact that he himself had had a Catholic upbringing, were not only fanatically anti-Semitic but also anti-clerical.

It was during the afternoon when both Father Murrsea and Papa had taken to sleeping on the hard wooden beds placed around the sides of the cage, whilst I also began dozing off somewhat whilst sitting on my perch at the door out of the cellar, that Father Murrsea got a visitor.

"Begging your pardon for disturbing your siestas," one of our policemen cheerfully said as he came through the cellar door, "but a certain Father Gabriel wants to talk to Father Murrsea for a few moments."

Up till then I had always thought all priests were grey-haired, humorless men but this one was middle-aged and bouncy with scruffy brown hair. Indeed, in spite of his priest's cassock and **cappello romano** hat, he looked and moved about as if he were some kind of eager, young farm laborer who was just busting to get through all the work that he could do in just one day. As such, there was an air of defiant optimism about him, as if he were a man on a mission that he was determined to accomplish and in spite of the fact that he was now bringing bad news to Father Murrsea.

"I ask you for your blessing, Father Murrsea," he began, blending clerical formality with not only a deep sincerity but also a boundless energy as if there were some magical Hope in all that he said. "I am Father Gabriel from the Kloster of Saint Jerome in Sachs. I have been sent here to look after your parish for the duration of your absence here, however long that might be. In the meantime, I have the unpleasant duty of having to now inform you that Herr Zeller will be coming here shortly to take you to Innsbruck."

Of course we all knew that that meant either the Gestapo Headquarters in the Herrengasse or the Concentration Camp in Rossau.

"Thank you Father Murrsea for your graciousness," said Father Murrsea, without even a spark of nervousness. "You are being very kind indeed and so I also ask you for your blessing."

"Perhaps I may therefore suggest," Father Gabriel added, "that we now say a prayer of thanks and one of forgiveness."

"Yes, that would be a very good idea," Father Murrsea replied, whilst smiling for the first time as if he found the circumstances somehow amusing. "As you can see, I have nothing to pack, so we have plenty of time for prayer."

It also astonished me that neither of these priests suggested a prayer asking for a "Get out of Jail for Free Card", as if egocentricity and self-preservation were something that they had long since learnt to live without. Even more astonishing was how the priests immediately got down on their knees inside the cage and began praying together as if everything around them had ceased to exist.

Stuck at a loose end with what to do instead of just watching these two wise and selfless priests chanting their prayers out loud together, Papa and I decided without speaking to each other to join the two priests with their praying on their knees. It would have therefore been pretty humorous if Herr

Zeller and his henchmen had then entered the cellar and found all four of us on our knees in the open jail-cage and praying together. On the other hand, I would have probably lost my job and career as a policeman on the spot whilst Papa would have also as likely as not lost all chance of ever returning to the station as a simple policeman, let alone to his old position of Police Chief.

In the meantime, I must say that Father Gabriel absolutely fascinated me and I could not help thinking that he was exactly the sort of enthusiastic and inspirational teacher that I would have loved to have had at school for my lessons. Naturally, like Father Murrsea, he was not allowed to teach at the school as in accordance with the new Nazi rules, whilst the sermons that he then began giving in our church were considerably toned down from religion.

Instead of harping on about what the Bible said and did not say every Sunday, Father Gabriel became more like a motivational speaker whilst encouraging natural human qualities like optimism, hope, determination, discipline, loyalty and looking out for others. He did, however, omit the Christian qualities of compassion, forgiveness and universal love whilst putting a clever emphasis on team spirit and getting on with others.

As such, he managed to endear himself to Nazis like Kratzkopf, although I never managed to work out if Kratzkopf had ever actually believed in God, let alone a compassionate and forgiving Christ, or just felt that he at least had to pretend that he was a

Christian in our ultra-traditional village. As to Slimey Stefan, he might as well have been Simple Simon when it came to understanding anyone´s sermons. I, on the other hand, was so captivated by everything that Father Gabriel had to say that I often volunteered for church duties that I had never done before.

Fortunately for us all that afternoon, Herr Zeller took some time in arriving, although Father Gabriel soon had to leave us on our own again. It was then that Father Murrsea moved his stool closer to where Papa had returned to our own stools in front of the small table in the jail-cage where we had been playing chess that morning. He looked very closely into each of our eyes as if searching our souls before saying in a low and absolutely calm voice:

"There is something very important that I must tell you – and because we haven´t much time I must also ask you to please listen very carefully. You must remember for the future the **code name for Austria, which is Oh-Five**: that is the letter O and the number 5. If you see it written anywhere then it means that they are friends of ours and not of the Nazis. Likewise, if you decide to use it yourself, it will mean that friends will know they can contact you. Most importantly, if you want to buy anything then I suggest that you try the butcher, the baker and the furniture maker. Oh, yes, if you think that you need to confess anything, then I know that you´ll find Father Gabriel an excellent priest for that."

As if Father Murrsea had already known exactly how much time Providence had set him aside to tell us his secret, Herr Zeller and his men came marching down into the cellar the moment that he were finished. As the day before, Herr Zeller and his men were all dressed in Fedora hats and long coats whilst Smiley still stood at the back, still wearing his glittering S.S. uniform and still grinning like a cat on crack.

What I would have given to have squeezed the last living breath out of Smiley there and then for snitching on us I cannot say but I managed to control myself, whilst I´m sure I was shaking with fury and certainly not with fright. As to Father Murrsea: I was again astonished by just how calm he still was, even though he might soon be being tortured out of his mind.

"Gentlemen," he said, as cool as a cucumber and as polite as a prince´s courtier as he rose up and picked up his own cappello romano hat, I am at your service."

No one said anything as they led him out as if merely making a formal visit to the headmaster – except for Slimey, who unnecessarily stuck his foot out so that the noble Father nearly went flying over it before being able to stop himself crashing into the floor.

"Lieutenant Kratzkopf!" Zeller shouted at Slimey sharply. "You know how I detest shows of exhibitionism."

"Jawohl, Herr Kommissar Zeller!" Slimey snapped back, suddenly clicking his boots together with a sharp crack that must have frightened every mouse in the building.

Slimey then waited for everyone in the entourage to begin walking up the stairs so that he could again follow at the back. However, just before he also tagged on, he turned round to Papa and myself and said mirthfully:

"Oh, by the way, little Maria seems to have had a good day today! You wouldn´t believe how all the fellas love her now that she is also serving them on the Berghof terrace instead of just bussing their tables!"

18: Wild Passions of the Heart

I could not believe that such a remarkably clever person as Maria could be so naïve and stupid when it came to the tall, dark and ugly Slimey Stefan. All that he had to do was to make moony eyes at her, grin like a cat on opium, make silly jokes and she was all his. Talk about it all being mere optics on the one side and the zero use of brains on the other.

Maria was no eye-catcher when it came to good looks but she did have a sweet and innocent knack for grabbing fellas´ attentions simply by the way that she carried herself and looked at them. Her sparkling eyes, coquettish side-way glances, twinkling smiles and the simple yet irresistible way that she would quietly move towards people before casually appearing close to their sides like a cat wanting to be stroked, meant that all the men – from schoolboys to grandpas – were not only taking notice of her but were also reading all sorts of fantasies into her unintended gestures.

Put simply, Maria was sending out all the wrong signals to the male sex and she had no idea that she was doing it.

Meanwhile, I returned home that evening after giving Papa his supper of bread and cheese again, whilst being determined that I would bring him something more substantial from our own family kitchen the next day. In the meantime, two Nazis who Papa had once locked up himself during the Fatherland era were now found to guard him at night, whilst being armed with pistols. I only hoped that they wouldn't try to inflict some kind of revenge on him by organizing an "accident" of sorts.

On arriving back home at seven, I was surprised that Maria hadn't yet arrived home herself from her first full day of work at the Berghof. I therefore found Mama sitting all on her own at the kitchen table whilst looking thoroughly miserable as she kept looking at poor Pete's empty stool on the opposite side.

"I've made a stew with dumplings for you and Maria," she said, trying to brighten up as I entered the main room.

"Thank you Mama," I answered, giving her a kiss on the forehead before sitting down close beside her. None of this was out of habit but because I now genuinely feared for my parents' well-being and the safety of all of my family. "It's good to see that you are keeping yourself busy, Mama. You need to keep yourself busy if your thoughts aren't to spiral out of control."

"There's plenty to do around here," Mama said nervously, whilst her well of tears had long since dried up. "How's Papa?"

So I told my very relieved Mama that I had been able to look after Papa all day long and that they were keeping him here in Gletschberg. Also, that we had had a game of chess together. In other words, I told her only the good things whilst deliberately missing out that Father Murrsea had also shortly been with us before being dragged off to certain Hell in Innsbruck. I also left out telling her until a better time (if there were such a thing as a better time these days) that I was the only one in the family allowed to visit Papa.

"Of course it would be easier if Maria were still here," said Mama, as if her mind were still wandering back and forth.

Talk of the devil, Maria now arrived home. I was surprised how business-like she began giving out the bowls and spoons for our stew before sitting down herself on her own stool as if this were a day like any other day. For a while I wondered if she had completely forgotten that we were now only half the family that we had been just two days before, when she suddenly asked how Papa was? So I told her what I had just told Mama.

"How was work?" I then asked Maria.

"Good – good," Maria answered, non-committedly.

"So you enjoyed it?" I then also asked.

"Yes, yes," Maria again answered, whilst putting too much bread dumpling to fit in her mouth easily. "I think I like working full-time. It certainly gets me out of the house and learning new things."

I then looked at Mama to see if Maria had inadvertently hurt her feelings but Mama seemed to be oblivious to our conversation. So I looked at

Maria again and gave her a nod towards Mama as if to tell her to mind Mama's feelings.

"Mama," Maria then said, "why isn't Max here?"

"You know that Max has to keep disappearing on his hunting expeditions," Mama answered – but only after Maria had had to ask her the question for a second time.

"I think," Maria replied, "that Max should be here more often to look after you so long as Papa can't be here every evening. You know that Max doesn't have to earn quite as much now that I'm also bringing money into the family."

"That's very kind of you, my dear," Mama said with a quaint smile as she touched Maria's hand with her own.

Of course it was obvious (at least to me) that Mama found it sweet that her daughter thought that she might be earning anything like as much as what Max made, whilst not mentioning that Papa would probably no longer be earning his much larger Chief of Police salary.

"It's a pleasure, Mama," Maria answered, as if she had suddenly discovered that she was someone important in the world.

I found it very difficult to sleep that night – but not so much because I was worrying about Papa being guarded by the two Nazi villains that night, although that certainly didn't help. No, it was because I kept thinking that something else had changed about Maria, all in just one day. Yes, she had suddenly become more confident, if not also a little bossy as well, but there was still that something else that had changed. Indeed, it was not until after I had finally dropped off to bed in the small hours of the morning that I suddenly woke up with a start: yes, the sparkle had gone out of her eyes.

As things turned out, Max did start spending more time at home, so that we should have at least begun to resemble a small family, with a grown man and a grown woman in the house (even though one was the brother-in-law and uncle) and two almost grown-up children. Likewise Maria began bringing in a lot more money and better tips than I had ever earned at the Berghof – or had even dreamt was possible.

Papa, in the meantime, was still allowed to stay in our jail for what might well be weeks on end, although I was immediately taken off being his warder the moment it was found out that I was bringing him extra food. However, the more that Max seemed to stay in the house the less Maria seemed to also be there. Or was that, I wondered, just my imagination running amok again?

Things then came to a head when, towards the end of September, a rather cocky Maria arrived late at supper, gave Mama a whole pile of coins that she had earned that day, gobbled her food down and, whilst still shoveling the last spoonful into her mouth, quickly rose up from her stool and declared:

"I've got to go now! I've promised to get back to the Berghof straightaway. I've decided to move into a room there!"

"Not over my dead body!" Mama suddenly screamed, having one of her rare fits. "You've no business staying there overnight – not for one night, two nights, a whole week or even a whole season! This is where you live!"

"But Mama," Maria replied, "you've still got Max and Erich – and I'm sure that Papa will be back soon. I promise that."

Unfortunately Max wasn't there that evening: otherwise he might have knocked some sense into my stubborn and insensitive sister. However, I was there: so I was waiting in the hallway as Maria ran down the front stairs, having just gone up to her room to collect some of her things.

"Don't you get it?" I asked, grabbing her by the arm so that she couldn't get past me. "Your mother NEEDS you! You can't go gallivanting off like Seppi at this crucial time of our lives, least of all to go and live under the same roof as that Nazi lot!"

I expected Maria to suddenly go on the defensive and to tell me to leave her arm alone and to mind my own rotten business. It therefore came as a big surprise when she instead gave me one of her affectionate smiles of old and said compassionately:

"Erich: I know that you mean well and want to be both the protective big brother of myself as well as a loyal son to Mama but I NEED to do this! You see, if I play my cards right, I'm sure that I can get Papa out of prison!"

I was so stunned at hearing this that I could hardly think for the moment. In fact, as Maria was about to open the door to leave, I suddenly blurted out:

"Maria! Maria: you're not – I mean, you're not in love with him, are you? Not Slimey?"

Maria suddenly laughed out loud as if I had just said the most stupid thing that I could have thought of.

"Of course not!" she answered with a big smile and whilst, I was sure, her eyes began to sparkle again. "Of course not, Big Brother 'Bulldog`!"

Maria then left the house in a flurry of laughter, whilst leaving me wondering if girls really did grow up faster than boys or if they just learnt to flirt sooner than them.

Of course I could not help remembering over and over again how Maria had said, "I NEED to do this" and "If I play my cards right" and wondering exactly what she had meant by these two strange comments. Indeed, it worried me so much that I went to Father Gabriel and asked him about it.

"Ah, Puberty and all the Wild Passions of the Heart that come with it!" he said, as if embarking on one of his lively sermons again.

Apart from this Father Gabriel didn't seem to have much to offer: either because he didn't have much experience of women or (as I felt much more likely, considering how all the ladies were so easily charmed by him) because he was simply blissfully unaware that he was supremely attractive to the fairer sex. On the other hand, one good thing that did follow when Mama began talking to Father Gabriel about Maria after one of his services was that Mama then began spending a fair amount of time helping Father Gabriel in the church.

This was naturally a great way of getting Mama finally out of the house and keeping her mind occupied with things other than Papa´s internment in the cellar of the police station and Pete´s incarceration in the Hall clinic – especially as Max had soon found out that he really couldn´t afford to neglect his hunting business for too long. As to Max´s view when I approached him on the subject: he didn´t seem to even know the meaning of the word "puberty", so that I seriously wondered if he had ever even had a crush on a girl or woman in his entire life.

It was therefore to my surprise that it was Seppi who provided us with some answers as to why Maria was behaving the way that she now was, although they were certainly not the sort that we had wanted to hear. It was during one of those rare occasions that he had decided to come and visit us for Sunday dinner, with Maria no longer being able to come to them because Sundays were always the Berghof´s busiest day for waitressing.

Seppi turned up in tremendous spirits whilst we (Mama, Max and myself) were, as always these days, pretty down in the mouth. Worse still, Seppi didn't even bother asking about Papa, even when Mama said a prayer for him at the beginning of the meal.

"Of course," Seppi said, knocking down Mama's cooking as fast as he could as if he hadn't had a decent meal at the railway station in yonks and yonks and yonks, "Bulldog has probably told you that they've closed the police boxing club now."

"No," said Mama, looking towards me as if it were another piece of information that she had noticed I had been withholding from her recently.

"I mean," said Seppi, barely stopping gobbling his food down as he went on speaking, "they had to: what with Papa being its one and only organizer and coach whilst, at the same time, having to be kept under lock and key in the very same cellar that was always held."

Mama looked at me again whilst it was obvious that Seppi was deliberately rubbing the painful fact that Papa was still imprisoned even deeper into our minds.

"So long as the weather is still sunny," Max suggested, "they could still hold the club outdoors, if they wanted to."

"That's just it," Seppi answered. "Hardly anyone wants to be in any clubs these days unless they are being organized by the National Socialists. There must be at least a dozen of them now, including boxing and fencing, athletics and running, cycling and hiking, climbing and pioneering: and they're all super popular."

Seppi then looked at each of us in turn whilst waving a liver dumpling in the air with his fork as if he were making a decisive point.

"I´m telling you all," he told us. "National Socialism is the new All Good Things to all Good People. You guys should really be trying a lot harder to get on with this merry lot. They hold all the cards, you see."

"What about Maria?" I asked, suddenly remembering Maria´s own comment about cards. "Have you seen her lately, as you say that you occasionally go to the Pavillon?"

As I said earlier, Kratzkopf had managed to get a concession for the miniature lake and built a small snack-bar for the public on its shore, whilst now keeping the terrace only open for his hotel guests and Nazi dignitaries. However, with Franz Hofer visiting the Berghof so often, the Pavillon snack-bar soon became a bee-hive for Nazis without rank, whilst most of the village now avoided the lake altogether.

"Oh, absolutely," Seppi replied, "but only from afar as she only works on the hotel terrace these days, serving all the bigwigs. However, it´s not difficult to see that she flirts like the devil´s OWN business with them all."

"SEPPI!" Mama suddenly cried. "If you don´t mind! Not in front of your own mother, if you please, and at the dinner table as well!"

"But it´s true!" said Seppi, as insolent as ever. "She´s forever sitting down on their laps and drinking out of the same glasses as them. I´ve ever seen her sing and do a little naughty dance on more than one occasion. She must make a fortune in tips."

"She does," I said, for once agreeing with Seppi. "She brings home more money than even I do now!"

"Yes, but you´re only a cadet," said Max. "She´s working as a full-time waitress and there´s no knowing how much money those wealthy Nazis are willing to throw around."

"And there´s no knowing what else she is willing – !"

"SEPPI!" Mama again shouted. "If you PLEASE!"

"Oh that´s ridiculous," I said. "She´s not like that at all."

"Oh, really, Baby Brother?" said Seppi, now turning round and looking me full in the face with a mischievous and sick grin. "Do you think that you really know her? I´m telling you all: she positively glows with happiness whenever she´s with the big Nazis – but most of all when she´s with Lieutenant Kratzkopf."

"You mean, Slimey Stefan?" I asked.

"Well, if you want to call him by that childish nickname from our Kindergarten time," Seppi answered, "then yes. Fact is, though, that if those two aren´t together than I´m a Chinaman´s uncle."

"WHAT?" Mama, Max and I all seemed to roar together before adding, "You´ve got to be joking!"

"Don't be absurd!" and "Now you're making it all up!"

"No!" Seppi cried back. "Gospel truth – cross my heart and hope to die if it's not!"

Hard as the fact was to swallow, it was equally hard for us to deny it for, as much as Seppi enjoyed taunting us, he only ever did so with truths that would stick and never with lies. As such, I could just see Maria's eyes sparkling like diamonds every time that Slimey Stefan so much as winked in her direction and it made me rock-bottom sick. Likewise, from their own looks of shock and horror, I could see that it certainly made Mama and Max feel grossly ill just to imagine everything that Seppi now told them, just as it would have undoubtedly turned Papa's stomach around several times if he had heard any of this.

"If you don't believe me, then go there and see for yourselves," said Seppi, as if hammering the final nail in a coffin.

"I don't think so," I said. "I don't think I would be very popular in that circle now."

The fact was that, since Papa had been accused of murder, the less and less popular and respected in the village he was becoming with each passing day, even though not a single shred of evidence had yet been presented against him. This was also true in the police force, which he had previously been more or less able to unite under his leadership. Now, however, the force had been taken over by a couple of Nazis from another village and they would have gladly sent Papa to the Innsbruck Gestapo headquarters if they had been given the orders to do so.

As to myself, I was only still being tolerated in the force because that was apparently Slimey´s wish for whatever perverted reason (or so I guessed). Indeed, had it not been for the fact that I was able to keep an eye on Papa at the police station, I would have gladly resigned my cadetship, even though I had no idea what I could have done instead.

"Then come with me," Seppi suggested. "You´ll be alright with me."

I politely declined Seppi´s offer without a reason and we spent the rest of the dinner eating in silence. However, as soon as Seppi had gone, Mama, Max and I anxiously picked up the conversation from where we had left it.

"I can´t believe any of this," Mama said, burying her face in her hands as if she were about to suffer a complete breakdown. "My own daughter can´t be like this!"

"I have noticed that she has been dolling herself up lately," said Max. "Like a movie star with too much make-up on."

"Thanks, Max, but you´re not being very helpful," Mama sharply replied.

"Yes, that may be so," Max nevertheless went on. "I didn´t want to mention it whilst Seppi was still here but I do actually occasionally get to see Maria at the Berghof. Don´t forget that I make my deliveries at the back and sometimes see Maria passing through the kitchen."

"Yes, but I hardly think that there will be any guests in the kitchen for her to flirt with," Mama again replied sharply.

I don´t think that any of us slept well that night, knowing what we had just heard, nor the night after that – and so on and so forth. For myself, I was beginning to have nightmares about Maria dolling herself up so much that her face was beginning to look like an evil clown´s face, whilst sneering and glaring at us as if she were deliberately playing us for fools.

Worse still, what did she do with Stinking Slimey Stefan behind closed doors? Did she kiss him? Of course, she must have! And if so, how often and how passionately? And if that wasn´t bad enough, if they were living under the same roof, then did he ever invite her into his own bedroom? Did she set any limits in order to curry favor with him?

However, it was only when I had asked myself this last question that I began to understand what she had meant by "if I play my cards right". Far from being in love or a coquettish whore, she was playing a power game with the Nazis and especially Slimey.

By pretending that she might be willing to return any affections that he might have for her, she was hoping, in her over-confident and inexperienced way, that she might be able to turn the tables on

Slimey: that instead of her being the daft young girl who was blindly eating out of his hand the whole time, that she would turn him into the fool that he really was and have him doing everything to help our family that she subtly whispered into his dopey ear.

That would explain why her eyes only sparkled whenever she was actually looking at him. It was all an act that she could put on at a drop of a hat, whilst people who are genuinely head over heels in love with someone cannot help lighting up and glowing all over the place, whether they want to or not.

However, I now began to wonder if Slimey was really as stupid as Maria and I had always taken him to be. And even if he was, the rest of the Nazi dignitaries with whom he surrounded himself as guests of his father´s hotel were legend in being as sharp as tacks and as smart as whips.

At some point one of them would get wise to her trying to play them for fools and it would be curtains for her. In short, Maria was playing a deadly game of "Dare to Bluff" with vipers. As such, I kept wondering if I should tell Mama and Max about this – and especially Papa – but also kept deciding that that would only make them even more anxious.

Another week then passed, as the promise of a bright and colorful October was suddenly blown away by a bout of wild, rainy, windy weather. Maria hadn´t visited us as such during that time but we had begun to occasionally find that the petty cash box had suddenly gotten full overnight, presumably with her tips and most of her daily wages. We meanwhile asked Max to try and keep an eye on her but she hardly ever seemed to be around on the few occasions that he came by with his new catches.

In the end I had begun wondering if I shouldn't cook up a reason for visiting the hotel when Maria suddenly came racing through the yard door and into the main room from out of the pouring rain very late one Saturday night, looking for all the world as if she had just stepped out of an eternity in Hell. It was clear that she had been beaten black and blue, whilst her dress had been ripped open so that we could see her torn knickers, whilst blood was dripping down her legs.

"MAMA!" she cried, plunging across the kitchen into my mother's arms. "Mama!"

"Oh, my God!" Max said, making a bee-line for the hall door. "I'll run to find the doctor!"

19: A Day of Tragedy

"No, don´t do that," I said. "Doctor Zirrhose has turned Nazi lately. Try to get Father Gabriel."

Max looked at me as if I were talking nonsense because Maria would clearly need more than prayers and a warm fireside chat.

"He´s also a trained doctor," I said, although I knew full well that that wasn´t perfectly true.

I could have wept as Maria now knelt before our mother as Mama cradled her dear daughter´s head in her arms and let her sob over her knee.

"Mama, you don´t think that I will – ?"

"That´s alright, my child," Mama answered, whilst looking for all the world like the **Pietà** and as she kissed Maria softly on her neck. "God will have mercy on you for what you have done."

"It wasn´t my fault," Maria almost whispered between her sobs. "HE made me do it."

Whilst I prepared a pick-me-up for Maria and got some towels and blankets for Mama to dry her and wrap her up when Maria was ready for it, Max thankfully managed to find Father Gabriel. They returned just as we had finished drying and wrapping up Maria, so that she was sitting in the rocking-chair as comfortably as one could expect for a young teenage girl who had just had her body soiled and her soul torn apart.

Getting straight to the point, Father Gabriel quietly pulled a stool up before Maria and gently put each of his hands on her own as they lay on her knees.

"Maria," he said with a calm and soft voice whilst looking intently at her, even though she was too distraught to be able to return the look. "This is Father Gabriel. This is not a time for Judgement or reflecting upon the Past but merely a time for comforting you in your hour of need. Your family is here beside you and will take care of all your needs. Please try to get some sleep and think of only peaceful things like your mother and her love for you."

Father Gabriel's soothing voice seemed to have a hypnotic effect on Maria as she was not only soon asleep but was indeed also sleeping peacefully – a small miracle, in my opinion, on Father Gabriel's part. Father Gabriel was not there to be a doctor or to play the part of the priest or even that of a psychiatrist but simply to put Maria's mind at rest, at least for the night.

Throughout that night, Mama kept vigil over Maria in the main room, as well as looking after her throughout the whole of the next day. In fact, she looked after Maria through every hour of the next couple of weeks. Maria even moved into Mama's bedroom, sleeping on the side of the double bed where Papa had always slept. On one night I heard Maria through the door suddenly crying out:

"Oh, Mama: he kept calling me a Jewish slut over and over again whilst he tore at my hair and twisted my arms! Why do people think that being

Jewish is such a bad thing? Are they not humans like the rest of us?!"

The sting of all this was not just that Slimey also believed in the idiot Nazi creed that Jews were somehow inferior to everyone else: but that it did indeed confirm our suspicions that Slimey had known all about Mama´s half-Jewishness when he had gotten Seppi to paint the Star of David on her Gluehwein Hut.

Mama meanwhile agreed with me when I suggested that it would be best to now let Max on her little "secret" that her father had been Jewish – that is, before Slimey began shouting it all over the village in order to save his own face whilst telling his own side of the story.

As I was the only one in the family who was allowed to visit Papa it was therefore also up to me to tell him about everything that had happened with Maria, although I had no idea how I would do so or how he would take it. As it was, he hardly said a thing other than that I was to tell Maria that he wished her all the best and to continue to be brave.

"Shall I also tell her that you love her?" I asked.

Papa looked at me as if he were surprised by the question and answered after some reflection: "No, I don´t want this sounding like a **schmaltzy Berlin movie**."

"But you do love her, don´t you?" I asked, with similar surprise at Papa´s answer.

"Well, of course I bally do!" Papa suddenly blurted out with even more surprise. "Just make sure that none of this gets out or the village really will be making hay out of it."

We of course had no choice but to get Doctor Zirrhose to examine Maria´s body, especially as Father Gabriel was not an actual qualified medical doctor. Of course there was nothing that Doctor Zirrhose could yet do for Maria except check that nothing had been damaged and to take a urine sample for a lab pregnancy test.

After being as being as quick as he possibly could with Maria in my our parent´s bedroom, the cold-hearted doctor hurriedly left the room, rushed down the stairs and bolted out of the front door as though he were disgusted by the entire matter.

Indeed, if Doctor Zirrhose had ever taken an Hippocratic Oath regarding his patients, then he certainly didn´t seem to regard it as applying to unmarried pregnant girls or partly Jewish patients. As I had predicted, Slimey had speedily broadcasted to the entire village that Mama was half-Jewish but, worst still, the no-good doctor was also soon announcing to everyone the fact that Maria was now with child and that Slimey was the father. As such – and with one fell swoop – the village split itself clean into two camps of judgement.

On the one side were the Nazis, which included all the Gemeindetag delegates and other bigwigs of the village, as well as all of their loyal Nazi followers. They also included the regular weekend guests of the hotel, even though they were not officially part of the village populace. They were of the opinion that Maria was indeed nothing but a slut with Jewish origins and that she had gotten everything that she had asked for.

The fact that it would have normally been any honorable officer's duty to accept the responsibility of his actions and, at the very least, offer to financially support the future baby throughout its entire childhood and youth, if not actually ask the girl to marry him and start a family with her and his child, was for them neither here nor there.

On the other side was the rest of the village, who only made a pretense of being Nazi sympathizers in order not to be ear-marked for their own ostracization. In reality they were almost entirely made up of the Catholic conservatives who had once supported the Christian Socialists and Fatherland Front and were still faithfully attending church services.

At first I thought that many of them would also condemn Maria for having actually encouraged Slimey's depraved urgings, so it was to my complete and utter astonishment when I gradually found out that they were supporting Maria's innocence, right down to every man, woman, youth and even small kid.

However, whether this was also because they still hadn't forgotten what a bully Slimey had always been in the village or because they had extreme respect for anyone who was the daughter of the recent Chief of Police in their village, I could not tell. What I could tell was that even the police force was now also split into two camps of judgement and that the two new Nazi chiefs were now having a devil of a time keeping all their men in line.

In the meantime Maria presently started helping Mama around the house and the farm again in the same way that they had always used to, whilst bonding more than ever before, perhaps because Mama had finally had to accept and respect her child as now being a woman.

However, it was difficult for them to even begin feeling cheerful because October was still being atrocious with its weather, with it raining almost every day. In fact, the deluge was so bad that even the River Sill on the other side of the railway line in the Wipptal Valley began swelling to such dramatic proportions that the farmers´ neighboring fields were almost flooded.

It was also feared that **Kirchtag** would also be wash-out. This religious and traditional folk festival always came at the end of October and was often the last Sunday of autumn joy before the gloomy month of November began. This year, however, it seemed as if November had also eaten the whole of October up.

On top of all this, Mama now also missed her dear Pete more than ever because Kirchtag had always been Pete´s favorite day of the year. For one thing, it was not only one of the liveliest and most merry festivals of the year but it also had none of the masquerading that came with Fasching or the harassment of the **Krampus and the Perchten** during Advent.

Such Advent traditions used to scare the beejeezus out of Pete and had nothing to do with the Church´s own traditions. In fact, in my opinion, they were just an excuse for wild youths in the village to let their brainless frustrations out on others, especially younger children. As such, they were village traditions that the Nazi youths particularly loved.

Indeed, the Nazis loved folk festivals, from small village market affairs like ours to the enormous Oktoberfest of Munich, as they were a chance to bring all classes of society together and make them feel like a homogeneous united group, rather the same way that some firms have jolly outings for all the staff and managers to have a good time together.

However – and as I have already mentioned – the Nazis took a very dim of the Church and its own festivals, even though many of the folk festivals are just a civic extension of a religious festival, which means first having to go to church. A big exception is the May the First celebration, with villagers dancing around a Maypole (called a "May tree" although it is just a tree-trunk) in a pagan way that no doubt goes all the way back to Time Immemorial.

A pagan "tree" similar to the Maypole is also put up for Kirchtag, even though it is also a religious holiday and not just a folk festival. This tree is simply called the "Kirchtag Tree" and has a doll or puppet called the "Kirchtag Michl" (that is, "Kirchtag Micky") stuck on its top. As you can see, the pagans loved trees and the worship of nature, with even the Church eventually accepting decorated Christmas trees not only on their grounds but even in their churches and cathedrals.

But what had made Kirchtag especially exciting for Pete had been the endless Tyrolean Kirchtag doughnuts that were on offer. Yes, there were also doughnuts galore during Fasching but these were different because you didn´t have to get through the masquerading buffoons to get to them. Also, whilst Fasching doughnuts were round, filled with apricot jam and called "Berliner", Tiroler Kirchtag doughnuts were rectangular and filled with either poppy seeds or plums.

Naturally it was the baker, Herr Datschikoenig, who produced all the doughnuts. As such, he was always looking for help at Kirchtag (as during Fasching) to help produce them, as they literally sold like hot cakes. This year it was I who had offered to help, beginning early in the morning and before taking a break to go to church together with the rest of the still-faithful in the village.

For a while, it was seriously suggested that the village stalls be set up in the cramped quarters of the Rathaus but, although the rain kept going on and on and on like an Indonesian monsoon, the weather forecast kept predicting that the weather would suddenly and magically clear up on the very night before Kirchtag. In fact, I remember that Kirchtag

Sunday morning very well because that was exactly what had happened, with a bright blue sky now promising a month of Indian Summer, whilst the dying leaves of the trees suddenly shone in a glorious colorful blaze of good cheer.

However, it was just as I had walked out of our home´s front gate that, full of excitement of what joys awaited us that day, I suddenly noticed that someone had painted a Star of David all over the side road-facing wall of our chalet, along with the words "Jewish whore".

For a while, I just stared and stared and stared, totally incapable of accepting that any of this was really happening to us and especially to poor, beloved Maria. The question of how the hideous perpetrator of this wretched crime had managed to paint all of this during the night without waking up any of us did not cross my mind. Instead, the only question that entered it was how anyone could be so utterly and despicably cruel and cowardly.

My next thought was how to tell Mama and Max without Maria ever finding out, especially as one of us would now have to spend the morning cleaning it without Maria noticing. I thought that Mama and Max could perhaps take Maria to church with them – but Maria was still not in a fit state to want to be seen in public, even amongst sympathetic church goers.

Extraordinarily, Maria´s intellect and ability to tune into everything that was going on around her was still as sharp as ever, in spite of feeling that she was standing on the Abyss of Hell. As such, whilst I was quietly telling Mama and Max what had happened whilst we were in the main room, Maria was already tip-toeing down the front staircase into the hallway and out of the doorway to find out for herself what it was that I was so keen to talk about.

It therefore came as a big surprise when I then walked into the hallway and found Maria sitting on the wooden floor and huddled up in the corner, whilst looking as if she wanted to knife herself. As such, it was as clear as daylight that any progress that Mama had made in managing to keep Maria out of her depression had been completely swept back by this manic act of unnecessary callousness.

I therefore rushed back into the main room to tell Mama, who immediately ran to her daughter and sat in the corner with her for I´ve no idea how long. It was somehow decided that Max would run to the baker and take my place whilst I immediately began desperately trying to wipe off the graffiti as quickly as I could. Max had wanted to wipe off the graffiti because he was much stronger than I was but I wanted to be near my sister and Mama in their hour of need. However, I did manage to persuade Mama to go to the church service without Maria because she was so religious that she had never yet missed a church service in her life. I had also told her the day before that Father Gabriel wanted to thank her before the entire congregation for the tremendous help that she had been in arranging the flowers for that day.

As such, we had tucked Maria back into Mama´s bed again and given her a sedative from Doctor Zirrhose in the hope that she might get some rest. I then continued my efforts to wipe off the graffiti, somewhat glad that our Catholic festival day services often went on a long time as there was an awful lot more paint to clean off than when Seppi had defaced Mama´s Gluehwein Hut.

Some time must have passed by for I was already beginning to sweat from the hard work when I suddenly heard a squealing come from the animals´ stall house beside the yard behind the chalet. Thinking that Franz the pig must have somehow escaped from his sty, I threw my brush down into the bucket of acetone and began running around our house, whilst cursing our luck that this would have to happen on this day of all days and at this time (even though any other day and any other time would have also been inconvenient).

It was therefore to my horror that I found that Franz had somehow slit the side of his neck open and was now rolling about the hay in utter agony whilst screaming to the High Heavens. How in the name of goodness gracious me this had happened was totally beyond me because Mama was always extremely careful that nothing sharp was ever anywhere near any of her animals.

Knowing that all our neighbors would now be at church, whilst hoping that Maria might have fallen fast asleep as this would have otherwise surely sent her round the bend once and for all, I rushed out of the farmyard and through the chalet's backdoor into the kitchen part of the main room. As quick as lightning I then piled up all the sheets and broad bandages that I could find, before grabbing an empty bucket and running out of the kitchen again.

Unlike many other houses in the village, we were lucky to have our own pump in the yard behind the chalet and it was at this that I filled the bucket with much-needed water. I then rushed back to poor Franz and began trying to save his dear life.

Unfortunately, in spite of all that I did I was unable to save the poor hog's life. I was naturally just as upset that the unfortunate creature had had to die so suddenly and in such agony as that it would be yet another tragedy for Mama to have to bear in our now dark, dark life. Feeling as if the whole world were falling apart for us all, I then cleared up my things before leaving Franz's now lifeless corpse finally at peace and alone in his sty.

I was also convinced that Mama would demand that he be buried behind the stalls just before the meadow with a cross to mark his grave, instead of being sold off to Fleischklops the butcher for him to cut up and sell in pieces.

With these thoughts in mind I returned to the pump and tried to wash out the bloodied cloths as well as I could before hanging them on the line. I then returned to the kitchen and walked slowly and mournfully up the steps to see how Maria was – only to find that she was no longer in Mama's bed. It was at this moment that Mama entered the house through the front hall door and called out my name before asking how Maria was.

"She´s not here," I replied, climbing back down the front stairway into the hall.

"But she must be somewhere," Mama replied. "She can´t have gone far. After all, it´s only a small house."

The first place that we looked was, of course, the hallway where I had found her earlier that morning.

"Perhaps she´s in the outhouse," Mama suggested – but Maria wasn´t in there either.

"Maybe she´s decided that she is well again and wanted to feed the animals," Mama then brightly also suggested.

"No-no," I immediately answered, not wanting Mama to find out yet about poor Franz´s death. It was then that I had an even brighter idea as I finally thought of the obvious: "Perhaps she´s gone into her own bedroom to look for something."

Maria´s small bedroom was in the opposite corner to my parents´ room, being at the top of the hallway stairs with a window on the front garden, whilst my and Seppi´s old room were on the other (west) side of the house and were directly reached by the back stairs out of the main room. For some reason, Mama was delayed in the kitchen instead of immediately following me into the hallway and up its stairs straight to Maria´s room.

"Maria," I softly said, arriving on the landing and then softly knocking on Maria´s door. "Are you there?"

Although there was no answer I decided to look inside, just in case – only to find the poor girl's body hanging by a rope from the ceiling of her bedroom. The poor young angel had finally had more than she could cope with and hung herself.

20: In the Jaws of Hell

It was by the Grace of God that our neighbors were at home when this happened, instead of going straight to the village festival after church as they usually did. Max was the first to show up and cut Maria down before laying her down on her bed like a Snow White who everyone wanted to come back to life. Doctor Zirrhose then arrived, grumbling that he was never allowed any peace before officially pronouncing Maria dead as if she were of no more value than a rag doll.

Thankfully, Father Gabriel showed up soon afterwards, even though he were perhaps more busy than anyone else in the village save the baker. He very sympathetically offered a death prayer for the poor girl with us and, although it might have been my imagination, I could not help feeling that Maria´s face slowly began to glow as he was doing so, as if she were finally coming to peace, in spite of her life having been so devastatingly short.

It was decided that the funeral would be held on the following Tuesday in a week, which was also **All Saints´ Day**. Although it was supposed to be against liturgical law to hold a funeral on this day, the diocesan Bishop had the right to give a dispensation of the rules if he deemed it to be spiritually uplifting for the faithful. As our village faithful seemed to agree that this should be done as a message to the Nazis that this was all their handiwork (as was the rest of the suffering and harassment that they kept inflicting on whoever they chose) the dispense was granted.

For some reason, Seppi didn´t show up at all during this time, not even at the funeral, and even though we tried to contact him goodness only knows how many times. As to the rest of my family, I cannot begin to describe how frightened we now were, as if the Jaws of Hell had suddenly opened all around us. We were literally shivering and couldn´t hold anything down that we ate or drank as we simply wept and wept and wept. It was as if a huge knife had just disemboweled each of us all the way from our stomach and kidneys to our brains.

On the other hand, I now seemed to be thinking more clearly than ever before and suddenly seeing everything for how it really was. As I had only recently suspected, Slimey was not nearly as stupid as I had all the time been thinking. He might have kept grinning like a lunatic because he thought that was what made him more accessible to others but deep down inside his mind was a conniving evil that absolutely thrived on seeing terror in the face of others whilst they pleaded for mercy. And Maria, I could easily imagine, must have pleaded and pleaded with him until her heart was broken.

Likewise, there was now no doubt that Slimey had been deliberately riling Franz Hofer up to seek revenge on my family simply because I had once beaten him blue and black whilst humiliating him before the entire village, as well as other nearby villages. Kratzkopf, on the other hand, had simply wanted to maintain a steady ship so that he could make his fortune out of his rich Nazi clients.

Any Nazi plans that I had thought that Kratzkopf might have had were therefore probably just the fiction of my own imagination: indeed, he may not have even had any Nazi convictions at all but was just playing the part solely for enriching himself. However, whether he knew it or not, Kratzkopf was nonetheless playing with fire and, as such, liable to end up burning the whole village down to boot, to put it figuratively .

To my astonishment, Papa was not only allowed to visit his daughter´s funeral but was actually told, just as he were leaving his jail-cage attend it, that he was no longer under arrest because of lack of evidence. It therefore seemed to us that Kratzkopf did have a conscience after all and that he too was sickened by the tragedy that his son´s wayward actions had led to.

Papa, however, had never been one for making a scene unless he were angry – let alone outshining someone else´s moment in the spotlight, even if they were dead – and so left his glowing news for the family and especially Mama until after the very end of the funeral. I cannot, however, say that any of us suddenly shouted out "Yipee!" or began dancing a jig out of joy but the tears did begin flowing thicker and faster when he finally gave us this news, whilst Mama, Max and I began hugging him endlessly.

Of course Papa just remained standing like a wooden doll as we hugged him because, as I just said, he was unable to show any emotion other than that of anger. This was in stark contrast to Mama, who would be chirpy and bubbly at the best of times and nervous and downright depressed at the worst. Indeed, Papa had been totally stoic when I told him about Maria´s suicide in his cage, although I knew that all the emotions of heartbreak, despair, remorse and sorrow were all burning away like a veritable furnace in his mind and heart. Now he was just the same.

Of course Papa couldn´t go back to his job as Chief of Police after his release. He would have had to have been a bona fide Nazi to have got that job back. As such, I gladly threw in my resignation to boot, whilst almost grinning at the new Nazi Chief of Police as I did so and wishing that I could also say to him: "So stick that up your Nazi jumper, you degenerate hoodlum!"

Fortunately, both I and Papa had new jobs to go to: I as an apprentice to Datschikoenig the baker and Papa as an assistant to Fleischklops the butcher. Max, as usual, continued his freelance work as a hunter, providing game to both Fleischklops and the Berghof, as well as helping to feed the family. He had also sometimes helped his old friend Kabinett the furniture maker during the mid-winters. Indeed, Max and Kabinett had been jointly apprenticed as carpenters with Kabinett´s father during most of the Great War so that the two had become good friends.

There was a reason for both Papa and I landing these jobs other than Max putting in a good word for us and our already knowing each other well enough. That was because we had finally tried out the magic code "Oh-Five" with them and they had been more than willing to take us into their confidence. By taking us on as their workers it would be easy enough for us all to meet for a **"Feierabend"** beer in their work-places without raising suspicions, especially as there were Nazis milling about all over the place and trying to watch every move that each of the villagers made.

Furthermore, the butcher, the baker and the furniture maker had all publically renounced themselves from the church, even though the church didn´t officially recognize such apostasy. How they coped with their own religious needs I do not know but they felt that it was a necessary evil to at least distance themselves from the church in order for there to be no connection seen between them and Father Gabriel.

They had disavowed themselves even before Father Murrsea had been arrested, who was not only the leader of their small cell of the new Austrian Resistance but had been the one who had got it going in the first place. They also knew that Father Gabriel would become the cell´s de facto leader if Father Murrsea were arrested, whilst hoping that the elderly patriarch would not crack up under torture and reveal the names of his cell´s members. Indeed, knowing the aged father´s indomitable character, none of us expected him to, although we often prayed together that he wouldn´t suffer too much.

As I have already mentioned, Father Gabriel was completely different from Father Murrsea in his approach to his sermons, putting an emphasis on social needs of the day and almost none on religion. As such he was able to make his work much more palatable to the Nazis, whilst only showing his true religious self in private. In the meantime, Papa, Max and I became a kind of go-between between Father Gabriel and the butcher, the baker and the furniture maker, although we did try to keep the number of times that we kept visiting him for confession to as few as possible.

Resistances had existed before in History but it was during the Second World War that they would become particularly iconic, especially with the much more famous French Resistance. By the time that the War came to an end about a 110,000 Austrians had been in the Resistance, with about a third of these paying with their lives, either through accidents or through torture after capture, as well as 2,700 being executed by the Nazis.

Although the Resistance cells tried to be interactive with each other in order to get rid of the Nazis for once and for all, they varied greatly according to their own political views and their future plans for Austria. Some had been founded by "legitimists" who wanted to also restore the monarchy with the Habsburgs back on the throne, some were communists or social democrats and many were Christian conservatives who had previously also been members of the Fatherland Front. What unified them was a hate of the Nazis, with many cells not yet worrying about what might happen to Austria once they were gone.

With the Nazis having an iron grip on Austria, resistance at the beginning was pretty futile, although it often included hiding persecuted Jews – a crime that was punishable by death. Once Germany began losing the war, however, things began to move a lot quicker as spy networks were established and information passed on to the so-called O.S.S. or "Office of Strategic Services", which was the intelligence agency of the American armed forces.

Perhaps most exciting of all (at least from the point of view of movie-makers that came after the War) were those who decided to blow up things or even assassinate certain dignitaries with no outside help. Although we had no idea what the butcher, the baker and the furniture maker had previously been up to in their cell, it clearly wasn´t blowing things up, as I found out when I now suggested that we blow up Franz Hofer´s car whilst he was still in it. Just eight days after Maria´s funeral, it was our first meeting with all six of us and I was already determined that the cell didn´t become a mere "talking shop" with plenty of brains but no balls.

"Get rid of that sod," I said emphatically, "and a lot of innocent lives will be spared."

It was, of course, blindingly obvious that I wanted revenge for my sister´s suicide, believing that had Franz Hofer not been there to encourage Slimey Stefan to go as far as he dared and fancied, that Kratzkopf would have managed to put a brake on his psychopathic son´s lunacies. Indeed, it was to my astonishment that all five of my fellow so-called Resistance fighters now looked at me with abject horror.

"Good Lord!" Papa immediately cried out so loudly that he even surprised myself. "What about all those innocent people who will also get killed?"

"What innocent people?" I answered back. "They´re all committed Nazis. They know exactly what their Party is all about."

"Heavens above!" Max also said. "But what about your own children in the future? How will they react when they find out that their own daddy-O used to be a murdering terrorist?"

"They will praise me for having been a freedom fighter!" I quickly answered. "And a Hero of the Resistance!"

"But doesn´t the Good Lord say ´Thou shall not kill`?" Fleischklops the butcher asked, ironically for a man who spent his entire life slaughtering animals and then taking them apart.

"Oh, come on," I answered, "if we were to take everything literally that the ´Good Book` says then we would still be living in the Middle Ages."

"Sometimes I wonder if that wouldn´t be so bad at all," said Kabinett the furniture maker, who clearly resented the progress of mass-produced furniture.

"Besides," I went on, being still not finished with Fleischklops, "I sometimes wonder why killing animals shouldn´t be any less a crime than killing humans just because they cannot talk and tell us what they are thinking and feeling."

"You know," Max said in a soft voice as he now leaned close towards me, "I know this is all very, very difficult for you – just as it is also very difficult for us – but you need to calm down. Revenge is a terrible thing to contemplate. It turns us into evil people."

"This isn´t about Revenge," I snapped back. "It´s about saving more people´s lives. Besides, I seem to remember a time when you hated killing wild animals – now you do it all of the time."

Max did not bother to defend himself here. In fact, none of the others took the matter any further, knowing just how upset I still was about Maria´s suicide. They also probably knew that there had been a sense of guilt gnawing at me all this while for not having been the whole time with Maria before her death, even though I had been distracted because poor Franz had himself been in agony.

As such, there now came a long silence: during which time I started wondering if the others were themselves beginning to wonder if I were in fact too immature and emotional for the business of effective Resistance.

It was Datschikoenig who was the first to speak again, whilst I was relieved that he didn´t suggest that I still had some growing-up to catch up on before again joining the cell at least a couple of years later.

"It´s all very well having ideas," he instead calmly told me, "but do we also have the practical means of actually carrying them out? After all, who amongst us even knows how to blow a car up, let alone do so without getting ourselves blown up as well?"

"Oh, I can easily solve that," I answered. "We can easily ask Dani to help us out on that score."

"Dani???" the butcher, the baker and the furniture maker all asked in unison.

"Yes, the son of Maggid the tailor, who used to have a shop here until a few years back."

"Maggid?" Kabinett asked, almost laughing. "But he´s as mad as a hatter. I remember how – "

"Yes, but I´m not talking about Dani´s father," I rudely snapped back. "I´m talking about Dani. He´s a crack-shot at shooting and a master of just about everything that he puts his hand to. He´s also learnt everything that there is to be learnt about demolition jobs from his father. Isn´t that true, Papa and Max?"

"Oh, I´m not at all sure about this," said Fleischklops before Papa and Max even had a chance to consider their answers. "We´re fine with having a smart kid like you on board because we know you and your father and uncle – but another kid (even if he is as smart as you are) and especially one who is the son of a nut-job like Maggid: no way!"

Needless to say that no one was interested in my bright idea and that, seeing how irate I had now become, they all decided to call it a day and break the meeting up. It was a good thing that we did so when we did on that late afternoon because a hell of a freak snowstorm had been brewing all day over the glaciers to our far south-east and now it was about to descend on our village with a vengeance that felt almost biblical.

Everyone in the village must have got their doors and windows closed and their shutters bolted down, whilst making sure that everything that was remotely loose around their houses was shut up in safety. Max and I also had a heck of a job trying to get the animals settled in their stall house, especially the chickens, who seemed to be convinced that the sky was about to fall down on their sweet heads.

Eventually we were all snuggled up in our own house for supper and just as the storm struck all around us. The mad wind was soon trying to batter us from all sides and then kept going on and on and on. In fact, it was so strong that we seriously wondered if the roof of the house would be blown off, to say nothing of all the snow being piled up against the house the next morning so that we would have to dig our way out.

The biting cold wind meanwhile kept sneaking through the cracks and crannies of the wooden outside walls of our chalet As such, when we went to our beds that night we had to make sure that the brutal wind didn´t blow the flames of our candles so far into the air that they actually set the wooden house on fire.

I, for my part, couldn´t sleep for ages as the wind outside kept howling like a giant demon trying to break into the sanctum and safety of our house. Worse still, when I did finally nod off to sleep, I kept dreaming that the ghost of my sister was trying to revenge me for leaving her alone and to lose her mind and commit suicide. Eventually, I could stand it no longer and so grabbed my two blankets around me before staggering down the stairs into the main room. The flame of my candle meanwhile kept dancing about as the icy wind kept managing to blow its icy breath through the crevices of our timbered walls.

I had hardly been sitting at the kitchen table for long, with a cold tea and brandy set before me, when there came a sudden thunder of bangs against the kitchen door, as though the very Devil himself were knocking at it. Scared out of my wits, I wrapped my blankets tighter around myself as I was now shivering out of fear as well as because of the cold. The yard door then suddenly flew open and a spectral shape slowly appeared inside the kitchen before me.

For a moment I thought it really were my sister´s ghost as it looked exactly as she had on that terrible late Saturday night after she had been raped, looking for all the world as if she had just stepped out of an eternity in Hell.

To my astonishment, however, it was not Maria´s ghost but instead Dani´s, as he now stood as white as a sheet and as frozen as the Abominable Snowman. For a while I stared at his expressionless pale face whilst it also stared back at me and as motionless as an icicle – until it finally spoke to me with stammering teeth:

"BULLDOG! Mama and Papa are DEAD!!!"

21: Enemies of the People

For a moment I thought that Dani´s ghost was a premonition of what was about to happen to my parents, even though they were asleep upstairs. However, as the time passed by without the ghost saying anything more whilst the ticking of the clock above me grew more and more intense, I suddenly began to realize that this was no ghost at all but Dani in his real flesh and blood, although still as frozen as an icicle.

Suddenly gathering my wits about me, I sat Dani down at the table and wrapped my own blankets around him whilst also giving him neat brandy. I then stoked up a fire in the kitchen oven and put on a cauldron of water that we always kept ready inside for emergencies. Once the fire was going enough, I sat Dani down on the **in-built ceramic bench** on the side of the oven so that he would really start to feel warm again.

It was a long time before Dani sufficiently came out of his shock so that he was able to begin to tell his story in bits and pieces, with the crux of it being that it had been his own parents who he had announced as being dead. In fact, they had both suddenly and brutally died right before his eyes, with his father being knifed in the heart. His mother had jumped out of the bedroom window of their apartment on the fourth floor and to her certain death in order to escape the horrors and indignity of being raped before her son. In fact the last image that Dani had of her before her suicide was of her quivering and screaming whilst she clutched onto her bed-sheets as if they were the last resort for dignity in a world gone mad.

It was on this Ninth of November, 1938, that the Nazis had decided to stage what became known as the "Crystal Night" throughout the entire German Reich. Entire Jewish communities were to be targeted with brutal violence and even murder, whilst their homes and shops were smashed and pillaged and their synagogues destroyed. The adjective "crystal" was a sickening euphemism for the huge amounts of broken glass that were left lying around after the Nazis had literally smashed everything that the Jews had to smithereens.

Although Innsbruck´s 300-strong community of practicing Jews was miniscule to that of other cities, Franz Hofer had riled up his boot boys to attack the Jews in an even more vicious and brutal way than other Gauleiters had.

With knives, rifle-butts and severe beatings his thugs gladly answered his rallying call that "the boiling soul of the Tyrolean People must rise up against the Jews!" – with the object being that Tyrol would finally become Jew-free, including from the further 400 part-Jews who also lived in Innsbruck. In fact, Hofer did such a good job of stirring up hatred towards other human beings that many non-uniformed Nazis also spontaneously joined in on the savage carnage.

Dani´s parents were only two of several other Jews to be killed that night in Innsbruck. Many more were hospitalized with severe injuries, with at least one of them dying from them and another traumatized for life. Worse still, even the children were not spared, with one family being thrown into the River Sill, whilst only just managing to escape drowning. At least thirteen such victims decided soon afterwards to end it all by committing suicide.

Somehow Dani´s instinct for survival kept him alive, in spite of all that he had witnessed. Leaping out onto the fire escape at the back of the apartment whilst still in his slippers and without time to even grab a coat, he somehow managed to rush down the stairs fast enough to escape the boot boys. Running through the streets whilst other Jews were being dragged out of their houses to be beaten within an inch of their lives or simply stabbed to death, he also somehow managed to make it to the shunting station.

Knowing the schedule of the trains by heart, it was there that he waited in the shadows until he was able to jump onto a goods train that was about to make the long and arduous journey up the Brenner Pass and (unknown to him) our now snowed-up village.

When morning finally arrived, Mama, Papa and Max were surprised to find Dani downstairs in the kitchen with me. We were all less surprised to find that the snowstorm had gone and that the whole of the Gletschberg had changed into a sparkling winter wonderland of fresh snow, with the white mountain peaks now gleaming in the wide-open, clear blue skies.

Like everybody else, we had to dig ourselves out of our house with fully-laden shovels, not to mention shovel the stuff off the roof before it collapsed. I was also mildly amused when I later learned that the only snow-machine in the entire village hadn´t yet been prepared for the coming winter, with no one having expected the freak November snowstorm. As such, even smart-arse Slimey Stefan now had to do some toiling and grafting for a change whilst his father looked on in disgust at his poor performance of snow-shoveling.

I could not help remembering that, whilst we were small kids, the first dump of snow in the year was always an excuse to close the school for the day and to let the kids have the time of their lives in their magic wonderland. Waking up as soon as the sun shone through the window, we would be up and dressed and out like a shot through that same window, not even bothering to first clear the snow from before the kitchen or front hall door. There would immediately be a snowball fight, then a snow-fort with a snow-man-king would be made. We would then be invited back into the chalet by Mama for the warmest and jolliest breakfast you could possibly imagine and wish for – before going off again and sledding down the meadows.

Now, as I brought down my spare clothes and jacket to clothe Dani in, it was a different story altogether. It also nearly broke my heart to have to tell Dani to put Maria's old snow-boots and mittens on, a thing which he was very reluctant to do, in spite of having no choice in the matter because we had to go outside. That was because, Max said, we simply couldn't take the chance that the Nazis in Innsbruck wouldn't soon inform the Nazis in Gletschberg that they had noticed that Dani was missing and that he might have tried to find refuge with old friends. As such, the sooner that I took Dani to hide out at our secret Retreat then the better.

"But isn't it a bit far-fetched to think that the Innsbruck Nazis will want to follow the son of an unimportant tailor all the way up the Brenner Pass?" Mama asked us whilst Dani was taking a turn in the outhouse.

"Knowing just how damned efficient and brutal these Nazi thugs are," Max said, "Dani could run all the way to Timbuctoo and they would still manage to follow him."

"It's not that," said Papa, with his usual air of authority. "Not even the Innsbruck Gestapo or the **S.D.** have the time or the resources to yet notice who has fled the city, let alone follow them all over Tyrol. No: the snag comes if any of the village Nazis recognizes Dani and tells the police."

"Worse still," Max added: "now that it has snowed, Franz Hofer is bound to come here for the weekend and he's always eager to listen to news of trouble."

"Then there's no choice for it," I said, as Dani returned to the kitchen whilst looking remarkably like Maria with her winter togs on. "We've got to get to the Retreat straightaway. We can easily walk all the way up to it with skis without anyone thinking too much about it. They'll just think we're another couple of villagers or hotel guests having a good time."

"No, it's too dangerous to go during the daytime," Max replied. "Someone could easily see you two going out of the house and wonder who the other fella is dressed as Maria. Or one of the villagers might also be skiing on the meadows and want to join you. You'll have to go up at night."

"But what about your tracks?" Mama asked. "You'll be walking knee-deep in snow so people are bound to see them in the morning."

"But who's going to follow them?" Max replied. "Believe you me, there is absolutely NOBODY who ever goes trudging all the way up the mountain in winter apart from myself. And even if one of the Nazi boys did decide to follow the tracks, they would soon give up. They may be great at boxing and athletics and all that jazz but they're absolute wimps when it comes to the stamina needed for climbing up mountains."

"Besides," I added, "we can always spread the snow around with broken branches, as Max has taught me, so no one can see the entrance of the Retreat – not that anyone would be likely to find it anyway, tracks or no tracks."

Thus it was decided that Dani and I would both disappear up the mountain when all the village had gone to sleep that night. Mama saw to it that we had plenty to eat for the next few days, as well as plenty to wear to keep us warm when we were up in the Retreat, for she said that it would be mighty cold without our being able to light a fire during the day for attracting attention. In fact, although I didn´t realize it at the time but much later, Mama seemed to have an awfully intimate knowledge of the inside of the Retreat for someone who had supposedly never visited it.

In the meantime, we certainly didn´t have any trouble with the cold as we began trudging up the meadow behind our chalet, struggling through the knee-deep but thankfully dry and powdery snow with our heavy packs on our backs, along with our skis.

To my surprise I soon got into my stride of marching through the snow up the mountain, even though I had done precious little walking during that terrible summer. Dani was even quicker than I was – although, for all that I knew, he had been regularly sprinting up and down the **Northkette** in his recreational time in Innsbruck.

In total contrast to the previous night it was a clear night with millions of diamond-like stars twinkling in the empty black heavens above us. There was also a lot of light still left from the full moon just three nights before, which meant that anyone who happened to be looking out of the window at the meadow after midnight might have indeed been able to see us two monkeys slowly gliding up the meadow. However, no one called out to us from below, whilst I knew that we were pretty safe when we began passing the forest where Max and I still cut down our family Christmas tree each year.

There is a strange joy to be gotten from scaling up mountains if one is fit. Yes, it is a bit of struggle but as they like to say in Germany and Austria, "the journey is the destination". Indeed, under this especially starry night, I could not help feeling that if this was the way one climbed up to Heaven then I was all for it. Certainly, I felt more at home in the mountains then I did in our actual home, even before it had become a place of tragedy. I was certainly a lot safer up here than in the village, where everybody had a much higher chance of dying if they had been labeled an "Enemy of the People". Of course, this ominous name-tag was given to anyone who either didn´t agree with the Nazi Party or who they simply didn´t like.

For some reason time seems to pass much more quickly at night, whether one is hiking or otherwise busy working in the bakery or the like. Perhaps it has something to do with the fact that the hours of the night are all meaningless, whereas each of the day-time hours has its own special connotations according to what one´s daily routine is.

When we arrived at the Retreat, I nearly passed it, for the scenery of forest and rock walls around it looked completely different under snow and I had never visited it during winter. Indeed, it was Dani who told me I must have passed it, even though he had never even been there before – summer or winter – and in spite of the fact that he was heavily traumatized by his parents´ double murder.

"How the heck did you know that the Retreat is here?" I asked him in astonishment.

"I didn´t," Dani answered with a rare laugh for that week of his life. "I just noticed that your nostrils were flaring up and down like a hound´s and guessed that your sub-conscience knew we had arrived!"

Switching on my battery-powered flashlight torch, I then found my way through the overgrowth and into the small cave, before also finding the door to our Retreat. The trusty iron key worked just as handsomely as it always did and soon we were in the bosom-safety of our cozy refuge.

Yes: it was – as Mama had expected – freezing cold but it was nonetheless our cherished place of safety. Besides, with it still being night, we would soon be able to start a roaring fire with the wood that we always kept there on hand. We would just have to make sure that we weren´t fast asleep when the time came to put it out just before dawn broke. It was, after all, astonishing what curious eyes could manage to find with a good pair of binoculars in the village when looking upwards towards the mountains.

We also had the luxury of running water from an underground stream that conveniently ran through the rock walls of the refuge. As such, our hide-out was almost the perfect place to want to live as if we were some kind of magical kobolds.

Having gone to bed so late after our night hike, we naturally slept through most of the next morning whilst making sure that the fire was out when the new day began breaking. When we finally came back to life in the afternoon we carefully looked out of the look-out windows in the rock wall on the top floor of our Retreat. From there we could easily see the village far, far below, as well as the tell-telling tracks that we had made the night before whilst making sure, as I had said, that we brushed them away with broken shrubs and branches once we approached the Retreat.

With Max´s massive hunting binoculars, which Max had lent me, we could even faintly make out the goings on in the village, although there wasn´t anything out of the ordinary going on apart from snow still clearly being cleared. Certainly, if anyone had decided to try and follow us, they would have had to have been as quiet as mice for us not to have heard them, as it was also as quiet as a ghost so high up in the mountains. Indeed, we could even hear the snow falling from the trees outside although, strangely, from outside it was almost impossible to hear what was going on inside the Retreat.

Realizing that the coast was clear, I went outside for a while to stretch my legs whilst Dani stayed indoors and tried to come to terms with his traumatic shock. Although both eagle-eyed and even friendly enough as he now was, he kept lapsing into bouts of looking as if all the life and will to keep on going on kept suddenly draining out of him. As such, I had talked to him a little but not asked him too many questions. Indeed, I let him do most of the talking whenever he wanted to.

We passed the time with a couple of games of chess, both of which Dani won effortlessly, as well as with some reading, with each of us having borrowed several of Papa's many books. After a little supper we began falling asleep again before the fire for, although we had done precious little that day, we were still tired from the previous night's expedition and all the emotional excitement before then.

Funnily enough, the next day, Saturday, was pretty much the same, with us both still being emotionally exhausted and feeling as if we were now living in limbo. As such, we once again fell asleep early in the evening around the kitchen table whilst we had both tried to do a bit of reading.

It was just after midnight that I suddenly woke up with a start, because I was sure that I had heard something moving just outside the Retreat. Very gingerly I climbed up the wooden stairs to the top floor but I could see nothing moving about in the half-moonlit snow from our secret windows. Climbing back down to the ground floor, I found Dani also awake, clutching his blanket in much the same way that his mother must have done before she had jumped out of her bedroom window to her death.

"I couldn´t see anyone or any tracks," I said.

"It must be Max," said Dani, although clearly looking as if he feared it were the S.S. "Listen: I´m sure that I can hear him moving about outside that door in the cave."

"If it is him," I quietly said, "then he must have forgotten to give us that call of the **golden eagle** that he had promised to first make for us."

"Maybe he did give it but we were just too far gone asleep to hear it," suggested Dani.

It was at that moment that there came the sound of someone trying to put a giant key into the lock of our door. It immediately startled me because I never knew that there was a second key for the door, believing that I had taken the only key with us.

"Christ!" I said, blaspheming in a way that I as good as never did. "I forgot to take one of Max´s hunting rifles with us. Wait, I know what to do."

I immediately lurched to the kitchen part of the room and grabbed a giant skinning knife that we often used for cutting the cheese with. Turning round, I immediately noticed Dani squirm with terror as he remembered how the Nazis had just knifed his father to death before his very eyes.

"Sorry, Dani, but this may be the only chance we´ve got," I said, standing directly before the door as if I were about to begin a boxing match, except that this time it was with a knife.

The key clunked in the lock and slowly opened, to reveal – relief of reliefs – Max indeed standing before us, covered with snow. Only this time it wasn´t the mountaineering Max that I had known all my life and loved so dearly but a Max who had also just crawled out of the Pit of Hell. Just like both Maria and Dani before him, he wore the same haggard look of despair and devastation, whilst also shaking and quivering in spite of his long walk up the mountain.

"Oh, no," I said, thinking of the worst thing that I could now imagine had just happened: namely, that the Innsbruck Crystal Night had now also become the Gletschberg Crystal Night. "Please to God don´t tell me that they´ve now gone and killed my Mami!!!!!!"

22: The Darkest Nights

Max just looked at me as if he were on the brink of losing his mind whilst remaining in the doorway with the giant spare iron key in his hand.

"No," he finally said, "your Mama isn´t dead."

As if unable to say anything else, Max slowly closed the door again and locked it with the key, before slowly walking to the kitchen table and dropping on a stool before it. He kept looking at me as if he were about to say something very, very important whilst trying to stop his tears first clogging up his eyes or himself beginning to choke.

"What is it? What has happened?" I asked, offering to take off his winter mountaineering jacket for him.

I thought that Max was about to finally tell me again when he suddenly asked: "Please? Do you have a brandy?"

So Dani served Max one – a large one – and it seemed to soothe the mountaineer´s shaken nerves a little. I meanwhile sat down on another stool beside him and did what I had seen Father Gabriel often do in these extraordinarily tragic times: I laid my hand on his and said:

"Take all the time that you need, Max, but please tell me what has happened."

Unfortunately, it was a lot worse than even I now expected, beginning with Herr Zeller and his boot boys knocking on the front door just as Max, Mama and Papa were about to sit down to their Saturday supper. They naturally expected that Herr Zeller had found out about Dani´s fleeing Innsbruck and would want to know if they had seen him. Of course, they had already worked out their cover story, answering that they hadn´t seen Dani and that I had taken advantage of the freak snow by going skiing in the Italian South Tyrol. Although Hitler no doubt wanted to unite the South Tyrol with our own Austrian (North) Tyrol, he was very careful not to upset Mussolini by ever making such a claim.

As it turned out Herr Zeller didn´t mention Dani at all, instead having come, there and then, to take Mama away – to be resettled somewhere in the East all because her father had been a Jew. The fact that she had been born in a Catholic Kloster after he had already died, had been raised there as a practicing Catholic and had then actively worshiped as a Catholic all her life didn´t make the slightest difference.

"I wondered how the Hell Franz Hofer and his gang had found all this out," Max told us, "not believing that even Kratzkopf would have told him. "But then I saw Slimey Stefan once again lingering in the background with his stupid grin and in his S.S. uniform."

But that wasn´t all. After Mama was taken away, losing everything that she had ever loved and not knowing if she would ever see her family again, Herr Zeller then told my Papa that he couldn´t remain married to a part-Jew and that he would have to divorce her. Of course, with marriage being a **sacrament**, divorce was an impossibility in the eyes of the Catholic Church. As well as this, my Papa loved my mother dearly and would never ever have considered divorce unless it would mean saving someone else´s life. As such, when he refused, Herr Zeller told him that he would have to instead shoot his own brains out.

"´Of course,` Herr Zeller told your Papa," Max went on, "´if you also refuse to do that one simple thing then we will just have to shoot you dead ourselves, rather as your son should have done with that stupid pig of yours`. It was incredible how much Herr Zeller knew about us, as if Slimey had told him every scrap of information that he had on us. Zeller also knew exactly how to play on your Papa´s emotions, playing the Card of Honor like a master-class."

By this time Max was starting to break up so much as he told the story of his brother´s sudden death that he had to call for another shot of brandy, which Dani dutifully poured out for him. When Dani then offered me one, I declined, instead waiting patiently for Max to down his second brandy before continuing the devastating story:

"So your Papa was led up to Maria´s old room to do the ´honorable thing` with a gun that they now gave him, which means that Zeller even knew that Maria had also ended her life up there and wanted to remind him of it. Zeller also told your Papa that if he tried any funny business like shooting the guard or escaping through the window that they would not only shoot him to bits with a machine-gun but Mama as well. It was not long after that that we heard the fatal shot."

I could easily imagine the scene in Maria's old room. We had turned it into a shrine after her body was removed before the funeral, with pictures of the Holy Maria and several saints on the walls, as well as a small crucifix and a rosary. We even built a little altar in her memory, with candles and holders from the church. As such, Papa had at least been very much in his Catholic element when he had to end his life on this Earth.

We hardly said anything for a long while, but just finished up huddled together in the corner like the Three Bears. This wasn't so much to keep ourselves warm as to share in our sorrows. Indeed, after a while, I couldn't help remembering how that, some ten years before when the world was still good, all three of us would sometimes sit together on the corner-bench of our chalet after an afternoon's mountain wander, with Dani and I still being little kids and wanting to cuddle our favorite uncle as he told us stories.

"But what about you, Max?" I finally asked after some time. "What did they then do with you?"

"Oh, they left me well alone," said Max, as if his life had no more meaning without his brother. "I was therefore able to lay your Papa's body down on Maria's bed as we had already done with Maria, before cleaning up the mess in the room. I then went straight to Father Gabriel and he immediately returned with me to offer a death prayer. We still have to agree on a date for a funeral – that is, if Zeller allows there to be one. After that, I came straight up here."

I began to feel more and more drowsy, being overwhelmed by the pure double shock that I had just lost my Papi, whilst wondering in which man-made Hell Mama now was. I was therefore more than surprised when I woke up the next morning with Max already having made breakfast for us all, in spite of his long walk in the night, as well as having put the fire out.

"You two lads need to keep yourselves busy in your hour of sorrow if you aren´t to go entirely mad," Max told us as he ladled out some hot porridge that he had somehow managed to knock up on the still-warm stove.

"I have been keeping myself busy – at least in my mind," I said, looking at the porridge without an appetite. "We´re going to blow up Franz Hofer´s car – as I keep saying all along!"

"Are you MAD?" Max asked, trying to nod his head towards Dani without Dani noticing it. "You can´t talk about things like that here!"

It was clear that Max didn´t want Dani to know that our "Oh-Five" cell even existed, let alone about my plans for it.

"WHY NOT?" I demanded. "Slimey Stefan has all but turned my older brother into a full-blown Nazi like himself, as well as raping my only sister so that she finished up hanging herself. He has also encouraged Franz Hofer to not only take away both my baby brother and Mama to God-only-knows what Hell-holes, not to mention also as good as ordering my Papa to shoot himself!!! On top of all that Franz Hofer has gotten his Nazi mob to beat up every living soul amongst the Innsbruck Jews, including murdering my best-friend´s parents!!! Sorry, Dani: I didn´t mean to be as blunt as all that."

Dani, however, seemed to be more interested in what I had said just before I began my raging party-piece.

"What´s all this about blowing up that monster swine´s car?" he asked me.

"Bulldog!" Max pleaded with me. "We can´t tell him! It´s none of our business to tell anything without the consent of the other boys."

"NUTS to those other clowns!" I practically roared back. "We´ve got our own demolition expert right here! We can form our own cell with just the three of us. After all, you can´t get more loyal than us Three Bears. If we´re aren´t an actual family with Dani then we´re the next best thing to it, as well as all being actual victims of all this shit!"

I paused in order to tackle some of Max´s porridge. Strangely, my appetite had returned with my fantasies, rather like a fictional author who couldn´t stop writing once he had begun first thing in the morning.

"Listen," I eventually went on: "it´s now Sunday morning. I absolutely guarantee you that Hofer came up in his car on Friday afternoon to enjoy the weekend snow at the Berghof and will be returning to Innsbruck sometime late this afternoon, as he usually does whenever he is here. In the meantime, Seppi is always going on about there being an entire shed of explosives near the railway station, which they keep on hand for avalanche control in times like these. All that we have to do is to get down to the railway today, find this shed and then lay out a whole load of explosives all over the Devil´s Bridge in time for Hofer´s crossing it later today!"

The Devil´s Bridge was a road bridge in the Wipptal Valley that crossed the River Sill as it curled around the Dinkelswald hills to the immediate north of Gletschberg.

"But there isn´t enough time!" Max protested.

"What do you mean?" I cried back. "It´s not even eight o´clock now! We´ve got at least eight hours to prepare everything!"

"All the same there are too many variables!" Max as good as shouted back. "What if someone sees us and starts to ask us questions, or even recognizes us three monkeys prancing all over the railway lines? It might even take us ages to find that shed of explosives, providing if it even exists."

"Dani works on the railways," I interrupted. "He´ll soon be able to find out if there is a shed of demolition explosions or not, won´t you, Dani?"

"Oh, yes, undoubtedly," Dani answered, with as much enthusiasm as myself. "I can sniff out explosives and dynamite just as well as if I were a bloodhound trained for the job."

Max now looked at Dani as if he had also grown as "mad" as his father, the late "Mad" Maggid.

"But what if we don´t have time to set the explosives properly out," Max went on whining, "and they don´t go off as intended, especially with all this snow now lying about everywhere?"

"Oh, they´ll go off alright!" Dani almost shouted himself, before slowly throwing his arms in the air whilst making the sound of an exploding bomb: "KA-BOOM!!!"

"It´s not that I´m a coward, just as I do indeed applaud you for wanting to get knuckled down to the job of resistance, but you two guys are just too hurried. Eight hours may seem like a hell of a lot of time to you two but we still have to do all this stuff whilst making sure that no one at all sees us doing any of it. And even if we do manage all of it, we´ll still look like a right trio of Charlies if Hofer has been sent off on urgent business with Bloody Adolf and are left sitting in the snow with a whole bunch of explosives tied to the Devil´s Bridge, ready to go off at the slightest rumble of an avalanche nearby. No: let me first get back to the boys in the village and then we can see if we three can pull off your job next Friday. Those boys are even supposed to have a contact who knows all about Hofer´s plans at the Berghof."

"Oh, not those three wet fish again!" I cried. "They´ll be bound to tear down my idea again! They´re not interested in action and actually getting things done: they´re just interested in sitting on their backsides whilst drinking beer and blah-blah-blah."

This time Max didn´t bother answering my rude and rather childish comments so that it was Dani who next spoke about something else:

"Max: where is your rifle? I thought that you hunters always carried your rifles with you in the mountains but I didn´t see you with one last night. As to Bulldog, he forgot to bring his."

"Oh, no," I suddenly said to Max: "don´t tell me that they took all of our rifles away in the chalet?"

Max replied in the affirmative, as well as adding that the Nazis had also removed all the big kitchen knives as well.

"Then that means that we´ve got nothing to fight the Nazis with if we need to," said Dani, disappointedly.

"Are you kidding?" Max exclaimed, suddenly pulling up the floorboards below the kitchen table whilst spilling porridge and coffee everywhere. "Take a look at this little lot, my boys!"

"WOW!" Dani exclaimed, as overwhelmed as I now was as we both stared down into a deep cubby-hole that was stuffed with a hidden cache of rifles and ammo. "It looks as if you´re already prepared for the next War with all that stuff! I don´t suppose that you have any bombs down there as well?"

"Don´t be so darned silly!" Max snapped back. "I´m a hunter, not a bloomin´ demolition expert. I shoot the poor bloody animals: I don´t blow them to Kingdom Come!"

Having persuaded us that trying to attack Hofer's car so soon was taking a ridiculously and unnecessarily big chance, Dani and I now agreed that Max should return to the village that same day and continue his job with Kabinett the furniture maker, in order to make it at least look as if he weren't getting up to any trouble. Max warned me, however, not to dare show my face again in the village any more than Dani as Franz Hofer's Nazis were clearly not distinguishing between full-Jews and part-Jews.

As such, and even though I was theoretically only a quarter-part-Jew, my Mama's Fate might also be mine if I was found returning. However, if the Nazis noticed (as they were bound to) that I wasn't even around for my Papa's funeral (which Max hoped to hold that week) Max would have no choice but to say that he hadn't been able to contact me in the South Tyrol. I just prayed that the obvious conclusion that I must have therefore absconded to never-ever-be-seen-again wouldn't mean that Max would ultimately have to pay the price for it.

In the meantime it was decided that Max would try to get as much information about Franz Hofer's planned movements for the following weekend from the furniture maker and his friends, whilst also finding out if Father Gabriel also had any information to offer.

Dani and I were therefore left to twiddle our thumbs and toes for a week in our mountain Retreat. The long winter nights might have been especially cozy at any other time of our lives but now they were the darkest that we would ever know, with both of us dreading falling asleep as we kept having constant nightmares about our parents. To begin with, I repeatedly re-imagined Papa blowing his brains out, with his blood then spraying all over the religious portraits that had been hung up in Maria's memory. I then also kept dreaming that Mama was machine-gunned to pieces whilst trying to escape over the barb-wired fence of a concentration camp.

"You know what," Dani said to me late one morning, as we tried to rise bleary-eyed from our blankets, whilst wondering if breakfast really was necessary. "You talk in your sleep, Bulldog."

"Rubbish," I replied. "You've definitely been dreaming all that."

"No, you really do," Dani went on. "If Max does decide to let us go through with this bombing, then you had better make sure that you don't get caught. At the rate that you're going they will only have to listen to you whilst you are sleeping to get all the information that they want out of you."

"Well, then, I won't bally well get caught, will I?!" I answered, angrily rolling back into my blankets again.

You might think that the Winter Wonderland outside our Retreat might have lifted our spirits a little during the sunny day-time. Indeed, I would have loved to have gone skiing all over the fresh snow or even just gone for a walk around. However, I knew just how suspicious all the tracks that I then left in the snow would be if anyone decided to follow the tracks that the three of us had already made up the mountain (and, in the case of Max, also down it again). As such, our mountain Retreat was now beginning to feel more like a prison than a holiday home.

Indeed, the last thing that we needed were Nazis snooping after us, even if – as Max supposed – they were all supposed to have zero stamina for the mountains. As such, I instead kept a sharp vigilance from the top of the Retreat across the valley below us with Max´s massive binoculars, whilst also keeping an eagle´s eye on all the going-ons in the village.

Max had hoped to be able to get the funeral arranged for the Wednesday afternoon, as well as having everything regarding our demolition venture sorted out by then as well, so that he could be marching back up to the Retreat during that same Wednesday night. That would give us the whole of Thursday to begin our own preparations, before hiding in one of the many farmers´ barns for the night and resting before the final attack on the Friday.

However, as I scanned the village – and particularly the church – that next Wednesday afternoon I could see no sign of a funeral, not even a quiet one. As powerful as Max´s massive hunting binoculars were, I still couldn´t make out exactly who the dark figures wandering around inside its lens were, not even if they were patrolling Nazis in uniform or just ordinary villagers going about their usual daily business.

When night fell in the early evening I began to wonder if we could still expect Max to arrive sometime after midnight, as he had that Saturday morning, or if something were preventing him. As such, I could neither relax nor sleep but just kept on looking out of one of the top windows, even though the waning moon had hardly any light left in it. Indeed, the outside vista now looked like an endless sea of bottomless darkness, with just a few pin-points of light coming from the few buildings in the village that already had electricity. As such, the first that I would see of him was when he shone his flashlight torch just outside the Retreat.

It was about nine o´clock that same evening that I noticed that there was what looked like a huge bonfire burning on the outskirts of the village, with its light flickering across the now snowless meadow beyond it. I wondered if the Nazis had decided to hold a Burning the Books ceremony as they frequently did wherever a library was to be found, no doubt with numerous choruses of the Horst Wesel Lied and endless Hitler salutes. They might even be marching a whole parade of Nazi flags and banners backwards and forwards and even going through the ridiculous motions of kissing one of their swastika flags as if it were some kind of holy relic.

I called Dani to me to see if he could see anything more than just a bonfire far, far below through the binoculars, when he suddenly said:

"But that's not a bonfire! That's a house!"

We both knew what that might mean. As I have said before, with so many of the houses in the village being wooden chalets, it only needed one of them to go up for the entire remainder of the village to also catch light and burn down.

As such, there was always a force of fire volunteers on hand – with no doubt everybody else in the village joining in if ever such an emergency occurred. The snag was, however, if there were enough pumps and buckets on hand. An abundance of snow would certainly help: however, I had noticed during the day that most of the snow in the village had already disappeared.

Thankfully, the fire did not spread – but it did take a long time in being putting out.

"I wonder whose house it was," I casually said when all was over – and before suddenly realizing the significance of what I had just said. "Oh, no, Dani: you don't suppose . . . ?"

23: Ten Little Nazis

As things were, I could not just remain in the Retreat, wondering what the Hell had happened.

"I need to get down there right away," I told Dani. "If I ski down there I will still have plenty of time to walk back up to the Retreat whilst it's still dark."

"Don't be daft," said Dani. "You can hardly see a blooming thing outside. You'll break your leg if you try to ski in that darkness."

"Then I'll walk down and try to make my way up through the forests during the day," I said. "That'll fox the dumb Nazis."

"Then I'll come down with you," Dani said. "There's no point in my being up here if something happens to you. At least if we are together we can look out for each other's back."

"Then we had better take a couple of Max's rifles with us as well as a lot of ammo," I answered, agreeing with Dani.

With our rifles on our backs, we certainly looked like a pair of resistance fighters as we climbed down the mountain that night. Indeed, it would have been awkward if we had met anyone on the way down and been asked us what we were up to. Of course I could have claimed that we had been out hunting and then had to make a long detour, but I still couldn't see that washing very well.

Fortunately, the only person that we were likely to meet on the way down at that time of night was

Max himself, taking that he had somehow been delayed. However, the more that I kept hoping that that was the case the more that my disappointment kept growing as we still did not meet him. Indeed, it was with utter despair when we finally made it onto the meadow before my house and saw – as clear as daylight – that it had indeed been burnt down to the ground.

All children are prepared for the Ultimate Fate that is Death, especially in the Catholic Church: where it is an all too common subject, at least in those days. Some have the unfortunate misery of getting to witness it first-hand at a young age – and some, like Dani, in an especially brutal way. Yet whilst the Church may have prepared me for all this, what I was not prepared for was the flood of once-happy memories that were now lying strewn about the still smoldering timbers of our old home. My sister's old porcelain doll, a framed family photograph and the ball with which Pete had learnt to play "catch" with were just a few of the many objects from our childhoods that now lay broken, battered and burnt amongst the debris.

"Bulldog," I presently heard Dani calling me from the blackened stone walls of what had still been the animals' stall house only a short few hours before. "I think that you had better have a look at this. But you had better hold your stomach in first."

I knew what Dani meant by that before I had even got to the burnt and charcoaled remains of the farm, for there was a rich stench of burnt roast meat coming from it.

"Look," said Dani, realizing that I had to see it in order to believe what had happened. "They must have huddled all the animals into this sty and locked them up before setting everything alight and burning them alive."

"But who in God's name would want to do that?" I gasped in horror. "I can see their sick reasoning behind wanting to murder every man, woman and child just because they believe that they have evil blood in them. It's absolutely diabolical and monstrous but even the utterly insane have a perverted logic in what they do. But this is utterly senseless. Animals don't have ideologies, religions or political views. If nothing else they can be slaughtered humanely for food and yet those damned Nazis just set them all alight for the fun of it!"

"But who could be so wicked as to even think of doing this?" Dani asked me, even though the answer was obvious.

"Slimey Stefan," replied a third person beside us.

Turning around, I was amazed to find myself looking at that treacherous weasel, Seppi. He was smoking a cigarette so calmly that it seemed to suggest that all this smoldering wood and debris from our old home didn't affect him in the least.

"Where the HELL have you been all this time?" I almost screamed, instead trying to keep my voice down so as not to attract the attention of anyone who might still have been around that night. "I NEVER saw you at Maria's funeral! In fact, I haven't seen you since you came visiting us for Sunday dinner at the end of September."

"I might ask you the same question," Seppi answered, whilst taking another calm drag from his cigarette. "I didn't see you at Papa's funeral today."

"Was there one?" I asked, offering no reason for my own absence.

"Sure there was," answered Seppi, finally throwing his cigarette down on the charcoaled ground and rubbing it out with his shoe. "Except that there was hardly anyone there. Our family has suddenly become very unpopular, as you can see."

"WHY?" I demanded to know.

"Because we're all either Jewish or part-Jewish or otherwise tainted with Jewish blood," Seppi explained. "We're dangerous people to know. That's why I'm off on the first train to Innsbruck tomorrow. I'm off to join the Army to become a war hero like Papa. There's going to be another Great War, you know. I can feel it in my bones."

"But you'll be fighting for Nazi Germany," said Dani, immediately seeing the nonsense in Seppi's logic. "Your father fought for Austria and never believed in a Greater Germany. Now you'll be fighting for the very people who are persecuting us."

"Yes, but I'll still be a war hero," said Seppi. "That's what Papa always wanted me to be. In fact,

I´m sure that I could hear him telling me that through the lid of his coffin today."

I nearly laughed at the stupidity of Seppis imagination. With fools like him it was no wonder that the Nazis were able to make themselves so strong. However, I had better things to talk to him about.

"Where is Max?" I asked Seppi. "Do you happen to know where he might be?"

"Yes," answered Seppi, casually lighting up another cigarette. "He´s at the church, although he no longer looks too good. Only a couple of hours ago he was lying under all that burnt timber that used to be our house. They set it alight whilst he was still inside it."

"WHAT?" I cried out in anguish, almost ready to squeeze the living daylights out of the little weasel´s neck. "Are you trying to tell me that they burned him alive and that you did ABSOLUTELY NOTHING about it???"

"I couldn´t, could I?" Seppi answered, suddenly jumping out of the way as though he could read my thoughts. "I was on late duty at the railway station. I didn´t hear about this until the police told me."

"But what in the name of God made Slimey want to burn our chalet down with Uncle Max still in it???" I cried, whilst no doubt sounding for all the world as if I thought it were all Seppi´s fault.

"They said that he had been behaving suspiciously all week," Seppi explained, "and that they thought that he was a Resistance fighter."

"Do they usually burn down the homes of Resistance fighters whilst they´re still inside them?" Dani asked, his eyes agog.

"I guess so," Seppi replies, "although I´m damned if I know what a Resistance fighter is. Well, I´ve got to go now. I just came here to see if everything was really as bad as I was told. As to yourselves, I wouldn´t stick around for anyone to recognize you but head over the mountains to the South Tyrol for your own safety."

Seppi then turned around and began sauntering away without so much as a "Goodbye" or "Good Luck for the Future".

"Hey! Wait!" I cried, thinking in the moment more about my poor late uncle than myself and Dani. "Will there be ANYBODY at Max´s funeral?"

"Other than Father Gabriel and the grave-digger, I doubt it," said Seppi, before adding: "Our uncle was a traitor, Bulldog. A traitor. Traitors don´t deserve funerals – nor even gravestones."

Seppi then continued sauntering down the unlit road towards the center of the village, no doubt on his way back to his room over the railway station. Dani and I watched his dark figure slowly disappear amongst the other shadows of the village buildings beyond us before I finally commented:

"Gee-whizz: even though I´ve known Seppi all my life I still can´t say that I understand anything about him. Inside, he seemed to be genuinely upset by all that has happened to our family and yet, on the outside, he doesn't seem to care less."

"Do you think that he might have been making any of this up?" Dani asked me.

"I don't know," I replied, "although I wouldn't put it passed him. In fact, I now wish that I had also told him in no uncertain terms that he had better keep his trap shut about having seen us."

"Especially as we're both carrying a couple of rifles," Dani added. "In the meantime, we had better find our own place to sleep for what's left of the night. Does that farmer Mistkubel still have that lovely barn near the river?"

Although the Wipptal side of Gletschberg was not really my territory, Dani and I had stayed overnight at Mistkubel's barn more than a few times in summer whilst we were still young and liked to think of ourselves as an Alpine version of Tom Sawyer and Huckleberry Finn. Needless to say that Farmer Mistkubel, who was a sour gherkin if ever there was one, never knew about our escapades.

To get to our barn we had to avoid the chance of meeting people as much as possible. I mean, there was no knowing what drunken Nazis might be loafing about all over the place – even during the dead of night – and be ready to sound the alarm bell the moment that they saw two fellows wandering around with their rifles.

We therefore followed the darkness of the edge of the Holzbauer forest along the south of the village before walking some of the way down the steep grassy slope towards Gletschberg West below us. We then cut directly across both the Gletschberg Pass road and the Gletschberg Climb footpath to get to the edge of the Dinkelswald forest in the north, before climbing further down into the Wipptal Valley.

All this time Dani and I were pretty much quiet, not only because we had to concentrate on our footsteps in the darkness but also because the news of Max´s sudden and brutal death had shaken us both to the very core. It was only when we had finally crossed the Brenner road and the railway lines and had begun striding across the fields towards Mistkubel´s barn that we began to talk again.

"Well," I finally said, summing up my thoughts, "apart from the Retreat, Pete and each other, neither of us has anything or anyone left. We might therefore just as well do what we originally planned to do: namely to blow up that bastard Hofer´s car to smithereens, with or without Max to help us."

"And may his soul burn in Hell forever more," answered Dani.

"In fact," I continued, "It´s a pretty safe bet that Hofer will once again drive up for his usual weekend holiday on Friday afternoon, as regular as clockwork, which will give us the whole of tomorrow to prepare to barbeque him."

We at last came to the barn. Even though it was now well after midnight in the middle of November, the barn now felt like a favorite holiday hotel to us.

"I just hope that we don´t oversleep in the morning," I said, as Dani and I finally rolled up in some nice, prickly and smelly straw only a few minutes later.

"But even if we do oversleep we will still have the whole day to get things sorted out," Dani replied.

"Just think," I said, after a moment´s reflection. "When we wake up Seppi will have already got the train to Innsbruck. I wonder if we will ever see him again."

"I don´t know," Dani answered. "I often wonder if we´ll ever see anyone again. Ten Little Indians and all that."

With that morbid thought, we both tried to get some sleep. Indeed, I thought that, for my part at least, I would fall asleep instantly but didn´t. Eventually, I heard Dani fiddling about with something in the dark.

"Dani?" I said. "Is that you? Can´t you sleep either?"

Dani answered in the affirmative.

"I´ve been thinking," I continued. "If that dumb brother of mine wants to be a war hero then why shouldn´t I also want to? Maybe Papa wanted me to be the War Hero because I can´t imagine anything happening to Seppi except being shot for cowardice."

"That´s being very ungenerous, Bulldog," Dani replied. "People often change as they grow up. He may yet surprise us both."

"He´s always surprising me," I answered back. "No, if I were to be a War Hero it wouldn´t be of the Glorious Idiot German Nazi Army but of the Austrian Resistance. Does that sound pretty good to you? Papa would then definitely have something to be proud of in me."

"You may well become a Hero of the Resistance," Dani replied, trying to humor me. "Just make sure that you don´t first get captured!"

We both laughed at this before again trying to get some sleep. Once again, however, my train of thoughts kept me awake so that, when I heard Dani once more fiddling about in the dark, I asked him:

"Dani: what exactly did you mean by ´Ten Little Indians`?"

"That?" Dani answered. "Oh, yes: our sorry saga is rather like that American children´s song, ´**Ten Little Indians**`, where they all disappear one by one, except that this time we are ´Ten Little Tyroleans`. I mean there were ten of us altogether, with my family of three and your family of seven. Now there are just the two of us left: that is, if you count Seppi as being the eighth one to disappear."

"What happened to all the Indians?" I asked, vaguely remembering the song from my own childhood.

"Well, apart from toddling or tumbling off or getting drunk or simply falling asleep, one broke his neck, another shot the other and the other then kicked the bucket."

"Well, then, let´s just hope that you don´t end up being blown up and I captured," I remarked, jocularly.

"Oh," said Dani, "I forgot to say that the last one got married."

"Sooner you than me, Dani," I answered. "In fact I´d sooner take the capturing any day."

With that we both laughed and promptly fell fast asleep.

The next joke that I made was the following morning when Dani kept trying to find the explosives shed that was supposed to exist near the railway line.

"I knew that there was something else that I forgot to ask Seppi," I said, as we ran from one shed to another whilst again trying not to arouse attention with our rifles. "Where do the railways keep their bally explosives because our bloodhound has a cold nose?"

"Ha ha," said Dani, as we discovered that the next shed was full of canned food. "Look, **Iron Rations** for our din-dins!"

"Prime doggie food," I replied as we each began dropping several of the cans into our rucksacks. "Only the best for our explosives bloodhound."

The next shed turned out to be our explosives shed – and for the first time that week I saw Dani´s face suddenly light up with joy as if he were a child who had suddenly discovered a Santa Claus Grotto full of free toys. As I watched him now stuff not only his bags but also all his clothes with all the explosive goodies that he could manage to hustle into them, I must have myself looked like a child about to wet his pants. I was sure that he would also try to ram a couple of sticks of dynamite down those same pants of mine as well as in all of my pockets but, by the Grace of God, he didn´t.

"Don´t worry," he said, with a huge smirk all over his face as he now looked like a hamster that had just stuffed a whole load of food into its cheeks. "They won´t go off until I detonate them – or unless I suddenly trip up and fall over badly. In that case, you won´t see any more of me but you´ll have a great firework show."

Needless to say that I was very unhappy about spending our second night in the barn sleeping with those easily-excited buggers strewn all around us. At one point I was sure that I could hear Farmer Mistkubel wandering towards us in the dark outside and wondered if throwing one of those buggers at him might put him out of action if push came to shove. On the other hand, just switching on the electric flashlight torch gave me the willies in case it somehow sparked off all our Christmas presents to go "KA-BOOM!"

"Of course," said Dani, as we began running in and out of trees and bushes along the river shore the next morning, "we don´t want to blow up the bridge itself, just Franz Hofer´s car."

I felt like saying that if he detonated all his toys at once he would not only blow up the entire bridge as well as the car but also half the bally mountain to boot.

The road downhill sharply curved around a small cliff in the mountain so that one could only see both ends of the road bridge when one was almost upon it. I meanwhile took my position on top of the cliff above the bridge as it crossed over the river immediately below me. From that position I had an un-blocked view of each end of the bridge below on either side of me.

I had brought a smaller pair of binoculars with me that Max had kept as a spare pair at the Retreat because I found his massive hunting pair just too darn heavy and cumbersome to drag around if I needed to move quickly. However, even with this smaller pair I found that I could still see pretty far away.

I then began watching Dani laying out all the stuff that he had brought with him on the road below on my left side, so that, if all went well, Franz Hofer would be blown to Kingdom Come just moments after he had crossed the bridge. Of course I hadn´t a clue what Dani was doing, as he neatly set traps in the road before wiring them up and camouflaging them with fir leaves and other natural debris.

I was sure that someone would show up at any moment, so I kept turning my beady-eyes from one end of the road to the other, like a golden eagle that couldn´t decide which way the wind was blowing. I also kept wondering what would happen if the whole caboodle suddenly and unexpectedly went off there and then. Dani would be sprayed all over the place like tomato gulasch, whilst I might, if I were lucky, end up on top of a tree like a Christmas fairy.

As my mind kept wandering instead of concentrating on keeping a constant look-out on both sides of the road, I even began having doubts about the entire mission as I now also wondered if Max had been right all along. I already knew that Hofer was never accompanied by more than one other car instead of having the huge escort of bodyguards that someone in his high position was always entitled to have. Of course, this could have been because he was so arrogant that he didn´t think that anyone would dare assassinate him: as would also be the case with Reinhard **Heydrich** just a few years later.

However, what if Slimey had somehow got wind of my suggestion to blow up Franz Hofer through a leak in the cell? Would not Hofer then decide to travel with a huge escort for his protection, with bodyguards on motorbikes, as well as being armed with sub-machine guns? If we got into combat with those things, our rifles wouldn´t be much better than pop-guns, whilst we would also have zilch chance of getting away.

Worse still: what if Seppi had decided not to go to Innsbruck after all but to betray us instead by telling the village police first thing that morning?

And if all that weren´t bad enough, what if Franz Hofer didn´t come at all so that we were left staring like gold-fish at these explosives until some sharp-eyed Nazi weasel suddenly spotted them hidden under bits of trees and branches on the road?

Once Dani was finished with his meticulous preparations, we began the long wait for Franz Hofer to show up by lying down on my cliff-top directly above the Devil´s Bridge. From there we had a bird´s eye view of the Brenner Pass to our right below as it slowly serpentined its way upwards through the forests from the direction of Innsbruck and towards our bridge. As such, we would alternately take the binoculars to see if we could yet see the monster coming up any of the open stretches that we could occasionally see between the forest tops.

"This is exciting," Dani presently said, grinning like a schoolboy who was about to play his favorite prank on the schoolmaster. "In fact it reminds me of that **Luis Trenker** movie, ´The Rebel`."

"You know that I´ve never seen a movie, Dani," I replied. "Unlike Innsbruck, there aren´t any cinemas in Gletschberg."

"Then I must take you to the pictures sometime," said Dani, as if we were merely on a day out together and would be returning to our homes as soon as it were over. "Anyway, the movie is about these Tyrolean rebels who are fighting the French in 1809. In the end they wipe them out at a canyon like this by dropping huge boulders down onto them."

Dani then began making noises like a huge avalanche of rocks coming down onto the bridge and smashing it to smithereens.

"Hang on," I said, "I think I can see His Royal Highness the Arsehole of Tyrol slowing coming up towards us."

"It´s supposed to be one of Adolf Hitler´s favorite movies, although – here: give me those binos!"

It was indeed Franz Hofer, riding along in his gigantic, open-roofed Mercedes with, as per usual, just one other car as his usual escort. In fact, Franz Hofer couldn´t be mistaken as he sat in the front passenger suit whilst wearing his rich brown uniform and huge hat, complete with his bloody Nazi spider arm-band. Dani now ran down the side of the cliff to where he had hidden the detonator amongst the trees beside the road. I could no longer see him from my position so I just kept hoping that he was still there and that everything was still going as planned.

Slowly and surely, as if Hofer had all the time in the world to enjoy the brisk, wintry ride uphill, the two cars serpentined their way around the numerous bends in the road towards us. Indeed, as they seemingly bopped in and out of the tops of the forests as they leisurely cruised along, I could not help feeling that they were like a couple of dozy mice playing hide and seek in the trees.

Eventually they were so close that I had to get down so that I couldn´t be seen, whilst no longer using the binoculars in case they reflected the sunlight and so gave a tell-tale sign. I also made the sound of the cuckoo for Dani: something that we had previously arranged so that he would know when the cars were almost on the bridge. After that, my heart began racing as if it were itself doing the sprint – whilst my head spun all over the place so that it was a good thing that I was now lying down, otherwise I could have easily toppled off the cliff.

I closely watched Franz Hofer as he unwittingly crossed the bridge towards his final and justified Fate. Unfortunately, I couldn´t see his smug face because of the shade, as I thought of how he had destroyed my family, one by one. I watched intently as Hofer´s car crossed over the bridge, waiting for the bang.

Suddenly, the bomb went off – louder and sooner than I had expected. It was perfect marks for Dani as the front of Hofer´s car suddenly jumped up into the air with the explosion. For a moment it remained there like a dragon breathing fire before just as suddenly crashing down to the ground again as if it had just been slaughtered.

With mixed glee and horror I then saw Franz Hofer first slump towards the smashed windscreen in a pool of blood, before then sinking out of the open door and onto the road like a sack of dumb potatoes. The driver and the two Nazi goons sitting behind him were also apparently dead, being as motionless and as batty-eyed as a pair of Halloween dummies.

As all this was going on the second car swerved off the bridge and towards the forest on the right in order to avoid the exploding car ahead, before crashing against the trees and itself exploding. Just like the first car, its driver and passengers also then tumbled out of the car like stuffed rag dolls, whilst clearly also being as dead as dodos.

I guess that I must have been grinning with grim satisfaction as I now stood up to revel in Dani´s marvelous handiwork of Revenge, having taken out not just one of these Nazi swines but eight of the buggers. Stuff Ten Little Indians: this was a game of Eight Little Nazi Buggers, except that they all met their Maker at exactly the same moment.

It was also at the very next moment that I suddenly felt a huge WALLOP across the back of my head.

24: Truth and Torture

"You shouldn´t have stood up like that, you idiot!" the gorilla of a bully suddenly laughed at me, before suddenly punching my chin so hard that I´m sure one of my teeth fell out – whilst blood began pouring all over the inside of my mouth. "You were standing as proud as a peacock for all the world to see!"

"Or should he have said weather-cock?!" the other smarter-looking bully cried as he suddenly punched me in the groin. "COCK! COCK! COCK!"

For a moment I thought of my dear baby brother Pete and what they might have done to him. However, they wouldn´t be able to get anything out of him because he hadn´t a clue what was going on. I, on the other hand, had to make sure that I didn´t break. If I managed that, I had won, even if I were first driven through the Eleven Pits of Fiery Hell and died because of it. So I tried to forget Pete and all the others and draw a complete moronic blank over all of my memories.

"WHERE is your friend Dani?!" the gorilla bully shouted, smacking me across the mouth so that I immediately felt my blood swirling around inside it all over again.

"We´re NOT stupid!" cried the smarter bully. "We saw that other kid running away from the detonator after the explosion! And we know that Dani from Innsbruck is still your best mate and that his Jewish father used to be a demolition expert!"

"So WHERE the hell is he?!" demanded the gorilla, whilst giving me a punch that nearly knocked my brains out of my skull.

"WHERE is he hiding?!" shouted the smart bully, whilst the gorilla suddenly grabbed me under the pelvis and began spinning me until I was hanging upside down from his huge hands. "Where is his SAFE-HOUSE?!"

I was glad when he asked that, even though I was still trying to turn my memories into a blank of forgetfulness that I hoped would not be permanently damaging. If they thought that Dani was in a Safe-House then that meant that they didn´t suspect us of having a Retreat on the mountain, in spite of all the tracks that we had left in the snow. But did that mean that they also suspected the butcher, the baker and the furniture maker or, more likely, dear Father Gabriel, as they had already suspected Max?

However, when I replied nothing, the gorilla simply swung me so hard that my head seemed to crash against the prison wall. I was only beginning to come to again when I realized that the two godless bullies were stripping me stark-bollocks naked. I suddenly felt as if I were freezing cold even though my warm sweat – or blood – was now pouring all over my body.

I then had both my wrists and my ankles tied together with belts and in such a way that their sharp-edged buckles would cut into me every time that I moved. Two desks were then pulled apart before I was thrown face down between them like a human suspension bridge. I was scared shitless that the smart bully would start kicking me in the bollocks as they hung in the air below me and was therefore gladdened when he "only" started whipping me like a savage. So much for his smart and upper-crust appearance.

When all that I did was to shout, scream, swear like hell and bleed whilst repeatedly saying that I didn´t have a goddamned idea what they were crapping on about, they untied me from the desks and began rolling me up in a ball on one of them, as if they were about to change my diapers. Smartie-pants then pulled out his pistol and, for a moment, I thought he had rectal ideas about what he could do with it before he suddenly thrust it into my mouth, threatening to blow my brains out if I didn´t talk soon. How, I wondered, the dummy expected me to talk to him with a pistol stuck in my mouth was beyond me.

When it finally dawned on these two idiots that all this was a waste of time, they tied my arms and legs to an old wicker chair that was so incredibly spikey and painful that I felt I was sitting on a porcupine. They then started punching me constantly in the face, so that I not only began to spit my own blood at their faces but also the very teeth that they had managed to knock out.

All this time they kept asking me questions about where Dani was and who I was working with – and all this time I still kept repeatedly answering that I didn´t have a goddamned idea what they were crapping on about. All this time I kept trying to remind myself that they were trying to break me so that I would grass on my mates – and that, as long as I didn´t break and reveal everything, I still had a chance of staying alive. Or as Father Gabriel sometimes put it: "Sometimes you have to travel through Hell in order to get to Paradise."

Eventually, I started to feel so sick and dizzy from the constant batterings that I didn´t know if I were being hit or not. The stupid bullies then seemed to finally give up on me, even though I still kept feeling the searing pains all over my body as if they were still torturing me.

I presently realized that I had been left all alone in my dark cell, even though I was still tied to the porcupine wicker chair by my arms and legs. I suddenly had the urge to urinate and simply let it go instead of trying to hold it in, although it was probably just a little trickle. I also began to smell what seemed like faeces, as if I had defecated on my own chair – but I really didn´t know for sure.

After that, time really seemed to drag on, as if the hours were now slowly passing by whilst I kept dropping in and out of consciousness, with bouts of what seemed to be my talking to myself. I meanwhile noticed that a small shaft of light was shining through one of the tiny windows high above me but that soon disappeared altogether, as if night had finally arrived so that I was now left in complete darkness.

As well as all this, I not only began to feel as if I were slowly freezing to death in my nakedness but also that my back couldn´t stand the agony of sitting crouched up and tied to my prickly chair for much longer. Eventually I therefore decided to try and roll the damned wicker chair over so that I might get into some kind of sleeping position on the floor. However, when I did finally manage to turn the wicker chair over with myself still tied to it, I also knocked myself out for what seemed a long while.

When I eventually woke up again I was still lying in utter darkness, just as I still had my agonizing back pain. Worse still, the floor that I had made myself fall onto was made of stone and as cold as the highest and iciest mountains. I therefore spent a night of shivering in what felt like a lifetime of frozen purgatory.

As if any kind of change were a welcome break, I was actually glad when the two bullies showed up again in what I assumed to be the next morning. Even better was when they untied me from the chair so that, for a brief and whimsical moment, I actually thought that they were going to let me off scot-free. Some chance as all that they did was to kick the bottom out of the wicker chair before tying me back onto it by my arms and legs.

Indeed, with a whole night to refresh their pea-sized brains, the bullies now had a new trick up their sleeves, even though it was actually just a classic text-book means of torture. Sitting as I now was with my naked bollocks hanging out of where the seat of my chair had just been, the smartie bully was now able to whip me with his buckled belt exactly where it hurt whenever the sadistic desire took a hold of his deformed half-brain.

The pain in my back seemed to miraculously disappear when the new agony of my slaughtered testicles suddenly took center stage. More than even before I now tried to shut down my mind whilst all the time being whipped back into Reality by the searing buckle.

"Really, Bulldog, such profane language," said the smartie bully before I realized that I had been swearing profanely away the whole time. "I doubt if your friend Father Gabriel would approve."

"Nor would your dead Fatherland Papi have also likely approved!" cried the gorilla just as the smartie-arse suddenly whipped my bollocks with the buckle yet again.

The pain of my father´s death was nothing compared to the pain in my testicles right now. In fact, I was already wondering if they might now be hanging loosely out of my torn scrotum sack, ready to drop off whatever they were hanging onto at the next sling of the buckle.

The two bullies then began going on about Father Gabriel, as if they not only suspected that he was part of the Resistance cell but were trying to find a good reason for arresting him without half the village being enraged about it.

My bollocks must have been on absolute fire – as if a horde of fire-ants had suddenly taken to nesting in them – when I heard a third voice suddenly snap at the two bullies:

"That's enough of that, you two shit-for-brains bullies! Now get the harry hell out of here – and at the double march!"

The two bullies hurriedly obeyed their Lord and Master without a word and a tall, dark and ugly figure then lumbered towards me, before drawing up a nearby stool just before me and sitting calmly down on it. He then tried to look into my eyes but found that difficult because my face was so swollen around them, especially the right eye, that I could hardly see out of them.

"You do know who I am, don't you?" said the tall, dark and ugly figure as he lay each of his hands on my naked knees.

For a brief moment I thought that I had become delirious and that this was in fact Father Gabriel, who had come to comfort me. Perhaps the Nazis had decided that they would hang me for being a Resistance fighter and that the dear priest should at least be given a chance to administer the last Rites for me. At least I would be dying as a Hero of the Resistance and that my final wish of becoming one had indeed come true.

However, I then managed to make out Slimey's maniac face grinning at me before turning into a condescending look of mock pity, as if he were milking the role of the psychopath with fake compassion for all that it was worth.

"OF COURSE I BALLY DO!!!" I suddenly tried to cry out with full, venomous rage, although it was probably no more than a whimper because I could hardly speak with my swollen mouth. I also realized that my arms were still tied around the back of my porcupine wicker chair, just as my legs were tied to its own front legs.

"Temper, temper," Slimey said softly, almost sarcastically, whilst slowly and sensually beginning to stroke my naked thighs up and down with the palms of his hands and ever closer towards my groin. "We can do this either the soft way or the HARD way. Which way do you want, BULLDOG?!"

Slimey put a particular emphasis on my name as if my earning it at the end of that fatal boxing tournament had been the source of all our trouble.

"What do you want, Stefan?" I demanded. "Are you still mad about that boxing match of ours? That´s all Ancient History now. Besides, you were already tired after so many fights whilst I was fresh and mad at you for beating up Seppi more than he actually deserved! It was just one of those stupid things in life – but hardly a life-changer!"

"Oh, no?" Slimey asked, whilst now looking at me as if he were also about to take a slug at my face like the two bullies. "You REALLY humiliated me that day. In fact, it took me years to recover my reputation."

"What reputation?" I again tried to shout, whilst at least managing to spit some of the blood still in my mouth at him. "The only reputation that you ever had was for being the Worst Bully in the Village."

This time I really felt that Slimey was going to belt me one, whilst I wondered why I kept behaving so antagonistically towards him in spite of his conciliatory tone. Years later I realized that it was because I had already decided in my sub-conscience that they were going to kill me anyway and so wanted to give them a piece of my mind before I finally departed their wicked world, instead of being sold for a cowering fool.

However, instead of paying me back for my piece of mind with a fist in my mouth or a kick in the bollocks, Slimey then said to me:

"You know, Bulldog, it REALLY is me who should be mad at you, even today, and not you at me. You do realize that the guy who you killed yesterday was not Franz Hofer but my father? Obviously you can´t tell the difference between Mercedes cabriolets any more than you can between the uniform of a Gauleiter and that of a retired army major."

"Crikey!" I suddenly thought to myself: I really had messed up this assassination Big Time, especially as I was used to seeing both Hofer and Kratzkopf in their very different-looking uniforms. I had just assumed that Hofer had other different-looking uniforms of his own, even if they weren´t so grandiose as his usual Gauleiter uniform. There would, of course, be no posthumous accolades by the Resistance for Yours Truly for screwing this brainwave of mine up royally, just as Papa would hardly be glad to see me if I now entered the Kingdom of Heaven as a direct result of my wally-ish attempt to make the world a better place.

"But don´t worry," Slimey went on, this time with clear amusement at my sudden realization that I had just made a supreme dickhead of myself. "Apart from also killing seven other poor sods who would as likely as not ever have laid a finger on you, you actually did me a favor."

"WHAT??" I asked, thinking that the only silver lining for Slimey in any of this was that he now got to inherit his father´s hotel.

"HA HA!" Slimey shouted back. "I can now actually see your eye-balls goggling out of your bashed-up face with wonder! I don´t know what people have been telling you but I never ever loved my father."

"I bet that you never ever loved anyone," I muttered under my breath.

"In fact I hated him," Slimey continued, ignoring my answer. "I hated the way that he was always trying to control me as if I had only been born to be a mere duplicate of himself."

"I sort of know your feeling there," I also muttered, thinking that my own Papa had also wanted me to be another himself – and had actually begun to succeed. "But that´s hardly a reason for hating someone, especially your own Papa."

"But I tell you who I did love," Slimey went on, again ignoring my answer, "and that was my Mama. I absolutely adored her to pieces, so it was a damned brutal thing for her to have to go the way that she did. That's another reason why I hate you bastards, Bulldog: you've no idea of how much grief you have caused."

"I could also say the same of you and your gang," I now clearly said, thinking of how many Little Indians Dani and I had already lost.

"But I'll tell you what was so funny," said Slimey, yet again ignoring me whilst beginning to talk in his psychopathic way. "That was the fact that, as much as my father loved my Mama and myself, my Mama also couldn't stand my father, even though she often pretended to. I never found out exactly why she had married my father but I often thought that her own father had made her do it – as an opening for starting an elite Nazi enclave in the Austrian Alps. How wacky is that?"

"Not as wacky as you are," I almost said in reply before managing to stop myself.

"But that's not where it ends," said Slimey, suddenly folding his arms and grinning at me like a Cheshire Cat as if he had come to the juicy part of the tale that would really interest me. "My father wasn't only in love with my Mama but also had another bit on the side. And guess who that was? Correct: it was your own Mama: Lilly Schilling."

As soon as I heard that I felt like kicking Slimey in his own goolies but, of course, couldn't.

"Of course, your Mama wasn´t yet Frau Schilling when my father kept having his way with her," said Slimey, beginning to laugh at the way that I was starting to squirm at everything that he was now telling me about my Mama´s history. "She was still just an unmarried virgin chamber-maid at the newly renovated Berghof when all this was going on. I was eight years old at the time and I can remember clearly when he finally got round to actually screwing her when he thought everyone else was out of our apartment."

Slimey now paused to observe my face to see if his story were sufficiently upsetting me. He was pleased to see that it certainly was, so he continued:

"That was because Mama had returned to Germany for a short while but I was hiding in the bedroom wardrobe. God, my old man would have given me Hell on Earth if he had found me in there: but he didn´t, so I got to have the time of my life peeping through the wardrobe key-hole and watching him giving your Mama the business."

This time I really tried to tear myself away from my wicker chair so that I could give Slimey another sort of business for enjoying telling me this hideous story.

"Anyway," Slimey nevertheless continued, whilst practically laughing his head off as he delightedly recalled what was evidently one of his favorite memories from his life. "Do you know what the result of all this fucking business was? It was Seppi!"

"Don´t be ridiculous," I said, suddenly calming down and trying to talk reason. "Seppi was my Papa´s child. My Papa even married my Mama before Seppi was born."

"Oh, he married your Mama alright," said Slimey, "but that was AFTER Seppi had been conceived with my father´s ejaculation."

"You´re disgusting," I said. "You´re way over the limits of anyone´s decency."

"Oh, but we haven´t finished yet – not by a long stretch," said Slimey, reveling in his amusement. "The joke is – "

"Joke?" I said, wondering what on Earth could be funny about any of this.

"The joke is that Max was at that time engaged to be married to your Mama but when he found out that she was pregnant with Kratzkopf´s spawn, he broke the engagement off. He literally dumped her and would have left her on the streets had it not been for your Papa."

"What do you mean?" I asked, although I could immediately guess the answer.

"Why, your Papa offered to marry her instead and raise my own Papa´s child – that is, my half-brother – as if it were his own," Slimey answered with a cruel laugh.

"Why do you laugh?" I asked. "That was a pretty chivalrous and noble thing to do."

"Like heck it was!" Slimey ejaculated. "He fancied your Mama just as much as Max did when he returned home from the War and found that she was already engaged to Max."

"You´re a cynic," was all that I answered.

"A cynic is just a posh name for a realist," Slimey answered back. "Max was never the marrying type if it meant having the responsibility of having to raise a family. He just wanted to remain a dreamer and continue enjoying his life of freedom in the mountains. Meanwhile: your Papa no doubt thought that he could pull one over my Papa and hold him in his power by threatening to tell the whole village that my Papa was Seppi´s real father – but your Papa miscalculated because it was the other way round, as it was my Papa who now held your Papa in his power. The villagers might well have forgiven their only hotel owner and wannabe Buergermeister for spawning illegitimate children all over the place but they would have just laughed a policeman out of office if they had known that he was raising another guy´s kid free of charge."

"That maybe so," I said, regretfully having to admit to my late Papa´s short-comings but without also saying that he had been a pretty rotten father to Seppi. "But whatever weaknesses my Papa may have had you can´t say that Max wasn´t a family man. He taught me everything that I know about these mountains."

"Ha ha! And that was an even BIGGER joke!" Slimey roared out laughing, whilst I wondered what the Hell he meant by that. "What you never knew was that you were no more Josef Schilling's kid than Seppi was."

"Surely to goodness," I said, aghast, "you're not saying that I'm also your half-brother?"

Of course I thought that what Slimey was really inferring to was that Kratzkopf must have therefore still been raping my Mama, even though she was now married to my Papa (that is, my supposed Papa).

"No, no!" Slimey cried back, still finding everything absolutely hilarious. "You ARE Max's kid! Your Mama must have soon got bored of trying to have marital sex with Josef and therefore decided to get back with Max, at least on the quiet. And if you don't believe me then, just as Seppi and I are both tall and skinny, you and Max are both short and stumpy."

It was at that terrible moment that the Entire Truth suddenly dawned on me. As I mentioned when I described how my Mama had helped Dani and I prepare for our flight to the Retreat just over a week earlier, I had never known her to have visited the Retreat during my own life-time and yet she had seemed to have had an intimate knowledge of what it was like up there. Had Max therefore actually managed to woo my now-married Mama into bedding with him at the Retreat whilst my Papa had been busy at work?

"I know that brothers are often bitter rivals," Slimey added, "with princes often even killing their older brothers to become King but this was way off the charts! These two gherkins certainly had plenty to have beef with each other about – especially as Josef must have noticed that Max was your real Papa! Now he had two cuckoos in his nest but still hadn´t managed to spawn any young of his own!"

"He did so with Maria and Pete," I immediately answered: "or are you also going to tell me that they were also cuckoos?"

"Well, if anyone were cuckoo than it was definitely your idiot younger brother!" Slimey cried whilst bursting out laughing even louder than before, so that I yet again wanted to punch the living crap out of his cruel mind.

Meanwhile, Slimey seemed to have such a detailed grasp of our family´s history that I certainly found it hard to believe that he was making any of this up. As well as my own close relationship with Max, it also convincingly explained why Seppi was like Slimey in that he seemed to be pretty dim most of the time even though he in fact wasn´t – although Seppi was certainly not as vicious as Slimey and most definitely not a psychopath.

"Well it certainly explains why you and Seppi are BOTH a couple of MORONS," I foolishly said whilst thinking aloud.

This time Slimey really did kick me in the balls from under the chair and it was frigging painful.

"Now will you behave as I tell you your family story?" Slimey asked me as I finally came to again.

"Is there more to come?" I asked, with the tears of agony still flowing down my cheeks.

"Oh, yes: lots. You of course know that Seppi really hated your guts. He also knew that he was a cuckoo in the nest, although no one ever seemed to have told him whose, just as he wasn´t smart enough to have figured it out for himself. In fact, he was so daft that he actually thought that he was Josef´s son but not your mother´s, although how that could have even been possible if she was the one who actually gave birth to him never ever seemed to have crossed his idiot mind."

Of course that was a part of the story that I could certainly believe, knowing just how more and more dim-witted Seppi had gradually become over the years, due to, as I have said before, his sheer laziness.

"In fact," Slimey continued without my interrupting him again, "although it can hardly be said that he had loved what he thought was his father, he did admire him in a strange sort of way. On the other hand, he absolutely hated your family and especially the way that your Papa was always encouraging you and Maria to be smarter than he was. Oh, yes, your Papa may have treated Seppi a lot less stricter than yourselves and allowed him to get away with a lot more mischief and rudeness, but he resented being treated as a fool like your dumb Pete all of the time."

It was only now that I saw a snag in Slimey´s story of my family history:

"But if Max had been my real Papa why did my supposed Papa – Josef, that is – treat me better than Seppi and more like Maria?"

"Because, unlike Seppi, you were still part of his flesh-and-blood family, being his nephew!" Slimey briskly answered.

This seemed to make perfect sense – but then Slimey said something about Seppi that certainly shook me to the core:

"But of all of you, Seppi hated your Mama most of all, especially when he found out that she was a Jew."

"But that must have been YOUR doing!" I quickly shouted back. "The only way that he could have found out that secret of hers was if you or your father had told him – and I doubt if your father would have been so dumb to have done that."

"Temper, temper, Bulldog!" said Slimey, looking as if he were about to kick me in the bollocks again. "Now I´ve already told you about misbehaving like this!"

"Well, it´s true," I said. "Look at all the hurt that it has caused. You should have just let things be, as your father had wanted to."

"After all the times that Josef had had me locked up in that jail-cage of his for just speaking my mind?!" Slimey cried angrily, as he seemed to finally reach the end of his tether with me. "It was always the same with that damned self-righteous family of yours, with one humiliation after another. So I decided to have a bit of fun of my own – and that dumb half-brother of both of us was a willing tool of mine!"

Slimey began to smirk at me as if he suddenly realized just how much power he now had over my mind and that he was able to reap all the revenge that he wanted with it.

"When I remembered how easily I got him to paint that Star of David and the word ´Jew` on your Mama´s hut," Slimey continued in a perverse and grotesque manner, "I knew that I could get him to do even more when the time was ripe. And this autumn it was more than ripe. It was a synch getting Seppi to do exactly what I told him all the time whilst all the while making out that it was his own master-plan! And so it was Seppi who slashed your pig as a distraction when he knew that you were alone with your sister at your house. Likewise, it was he who then went into your house through the front-door when you had disappeared into the stall house and pig-sty – and promptly and quietly disappeared up the stairs to Maria´s room."

I could now see it all happening in my mind, as plain as if it were actually happening before my very eyes. Maria was trying to get some rest in my parents´ bed when she heard Seppi calling from her room.

"Seppi, what are you doing in my room?" she asked, getting up to see what he was up to whilst expecting that it was only something trivial.

"I´ve got some flowers for Mama," Seppi might well have answered. "I thought that I might hide them in your room until we are ready to give them to her."

"But I can´t see any flowers," said Maria, coming through her own bedroom door and seeing Seppi standing empty-handed in her room.

"No, they´re outside," Seppi could have said, pointing out of the window. "You can see them from here."

Maria would have then looked out of her bedroom window – a thing that she had safely done a million times before – whilst expecting to see a pot of flowers in the front garden. Only she saw nothing. Instead she just felt a pair of hands suddenly grab her by the throat and then slowly squeeze all the life and breath out of her: Seppi´s hands.

"He then hung her up from her bedroom ceiling," Slimey said, continuing the awful story for me, "in order to make it look like a suicide."

I was devastated. In fact, I was so devastated that I couldn´t even say a word for a long while, as I simply continued to sit bollock naked on my porcupine wicker chair. If telling the Truth was psychological torture, then it was certainly working better than the physical version as it was totally breaking me up. After letting all this horror sink deep into my wretched soul while obviously relishing watching it happen in real time, Slimey then added:

"And then there was just this week when I persuaded Seppi to even burn down your entire chalet – with the prize of your dear, soppy uncle being trapped inside and burned alive in the bargain! Of course we needed several men to get the fire going properly but Seppi was the one who started it."

"It wasn´t just Max that you murderers burned alive!" I immediately tried to roar back through my swollen mouth and bloodied teeth. "You also set all our animals alight!"

Slimey now laughed as if our family misfortunes were the funniest thing in the whole, wide world. He then carried on as if half in jest and half in earnest:

"Of course we can talk about these things now that we are both orphans. After all, both of us no longer have any parents left to look after us."

"What do you mean?" I asked.

"Surely you know that your Mama was taken to the Rossau concentration camp just outside Innsbruck?" Slimey asked me. "She was supposed to have been deported with others to a place in the East but she tried to escape by scaling over the perimeter fence. You can´t imagine the absurd risks that some of these degenerates take instead of waiting to see what else is in store for them. So she was machine-gunned down dead from the fence. Still, she was lucky: she could have been torn apart by the guard dogs whilst she was still alive."

With that Slimey now left me to stew in my own sufferings of grief and sorrow. I must have sat there for even more hours than the day before, still tied bollocks naked to my porcupine wicker chair, whilst starting to shiver with the cold all over again. As far as I was concerned, I might just as well not have existed as the two bullies finally came to untie my limp and useless body and tossed me onto a wooden bed nearby with just one itchy blanket and no pillow.

I´ve no idea how long I lay on that wooden bed or what Slimey Stefan might have had in store for me for the following day. All that I know is that at some time of that night there was a sudden explosion and the entire roof above myself seemed to fly off its rafters. Looking up I saw the faces of not only Dani but also Max grinning down at me like a couple of mischievous schoolboys who had just rescued me from the headmaster´s study.

25: Don't Look Behind

I was so stunned that I didn't know if I were in a dream or if the Ghost of Max really had come to wish me Farewell. Before I knew it, however, both he and Dani had jumped down from where the roof had just been and were lifting me from my bed. They then quickly bundled me up in some clothes and stuck a pair of warm, fur-lined boots onto my feet.

"There," said the Ghost of Max, "how's that for size?"

"But I thought you were dead," I weakly said, still wondering if I were only dreaming.

Max, however, didn't answer as he and Dani began helping me up a narrow flight of stairs and into the open.

I was bowled over with surprise when I realized that I hadn't been incarcerated in the cellars of the Gestapo Headquarters in the Herrengasse in Innsbruck, as I had believed all along. Instead I now found myself standing on the outside of a modest castle, which seemed to have been partially rebuilt as a mini-palace during the Baroque Age, whilst the dungeons that I had been in had been part of a medieval keep.

There were no views from the castle, however, as it was surrounded on all sides by forests, although the trees might have been a lot shorter when the castle had first been built in the long-distant past.

"There," said Max after he had virtually carried me down a whole series of steep and narrow footpaths through the forests and finally sat me down on a flat, mossy boulder. "I bet you've no idea where you are, have you?"

I shook my head in agreement.

"Castle Jitter," said Max, with a warm smile as he offered me a hip-flask of brandy, whilst Dani broke off some chocolate for me to try to eat. "It's not exactly our neck of the woods, being on the other side of the Brenner Pass from our Gletschberg. Also: you can hardly see the castle from the road because of the trees, which is why it always been such a darn good hide-out for the Nazis in the past."

"God, you look a bloody mess, Bulldog," said Dani, being more interested in my present condition than the geography of where we were. "Are you managing with that chocolate?"

"Just about," I replied. "It's easiest to just let it melt in my mouth. I think they've knocked my back teeth out."

"Then don't try to talk too much or even laugh," said Max, suddenly looking serious. "We'll have to get you to a doctor sometime soon. For all that we know those swines may have also dislocated your jaw."

"But where the hell did you spring up from, Max?" I demanded to know whilst ignoring his sage advice of staying quiet. "I thought that you were dead. Seppi told us that you had been burnt alive inside the chalet when the Nazis burnt it down."

"Fake body, I'm afraid," said Max, starting to grin as if escaping had been as easy as pie. "Before they set fire to the house, they sent one of their gorilla henchmen to reconnoiter around the back of the chalet. I knew what they wanted to do with me inside the house, so I gave him the commando treatment by creeping up on him as he came through the kitchen door – and broke his neck. I then crept out of the house just as they began torching it. The stupid fools never knew that they had set fire to one of their own instead of me. Although I will say he was already dead so that he wasn't burned alive."

"But that makes you a MURDERER!" I cried, not knowing whether to congratulate Max for his resourcefulness or be disgusted by the callous approach that he seemed to have employed.

"So are you two," said Max, still grinning. "You killed eight men with that explosion of yours. That's four each. The only snag is that you got Kratzkopf instead of Hofer, whilst Hofer is absolutely hopping mad about it. You'll be lucky if that Hofer doesn't start arresting – "

"Yes, I heard all about Kratzkopf," I said, interrupting Max because I didn't want to hear about what the Nazis might now start doing to some of the villagers, in spite of claiming that Austrians were also their own countrymen. "Slimey told me all about him."

"Yes," Max said, looking unsurprised. "We wanted to get that bastard as well until we found out that he´s disappeared again. At least he must be pretty pissed off about his Papikins suddenly biting the dust."

I wanted to answer Max but my mouth was now swelling up so badly that I could hardly speak. I therefore made a sign for some more brandy and Max thankfully obliged.

"Not in the least," I finally answered but with a lot of strain. "Slimey couldn´t stand his old man. In fact, he said we had done him – "

I began coughing up some blood: so Max told me to shut up and go to sleep. Go to sleep I certainly did for even the small amount of brandy that I now managed to drink knocked me completely out for the rest of the night and most of the next day. By that time, however, we were all safely tucked up in our Retreat again and as snug as three peas in a pod.

How Max managed to get me "home" was a miracle, although he said that it was simply because he was as fit as a mountain goat. Well if he was, he was one hell of a mountain goat. The man literally carried me not only down to the Brenner Pass below the castle but then all the way up the Holzbauer Ridge on the other side, which was almost covered from top to bottom in forests.

With there hardly being any tracks through the forest, Max and Dani had to clamber their way up through all kinds of forest debris – and all in the dark too, especially as what precious little moonlight that there was wasn´t able to penetrate through the tops of the trees. Yes, they did have a torch but you can only point a torch at one place at a time whilst almost blinding yourself to everything else, so that it becomes useless when tramping over erratic ground.

As such, it was long past daybreak and almost noon when Max and Dani finally made it back with me to the Retreat in the Messner Valley on the other side of the forested Holzbauer Ridge. That meant that it was already dark again by the time that they also woke up after taking their own well-deserved sleep. We didn´t have much to say that evening as we were all still damned exhausted but I do remember Max telling me that I wasn´t very heavy. I may have been short and stumpy like a kobold, he said, but I wasn´t podgy.

"Snap!" I thought: because he was also short and stumpy like a kobold. As my thoughts then began rambling all over the place, I then wondered if my Mama had realized that she was still in love with Max after she had married my (supposed) Papa and in spite of his having dumped her?

Of course, if I had been conceived out of an extra-marital love affair then it had at least it been out of love, whereas Seppi was simply and vilely the crass result of rape.

Whatever may have happened, though, Mama´s love for Papa had clearly grown stronger as I was growing up, although there was always that feeling that Papa preferred it when Max was nowhere near our house.

We were all much more alive the following day, which was a Monday. Max then told me what he had obviously already told Dani after managing to find him shortly after our bombing on the Friday. After he had faked his own pyrolytic death in the chalet he had managed to whip round to our neighbors and hide in their chalet.

At some time he decided to return up to the mountain to our Retreat, never having expected us to have seen the fire from so far away and therefore try to find out what was going on so soon. Indeed, with Max not checking his watch to see when he set off back up the mountain for the Retreat from our neighbor´s house, for all that we knew Dani and I might have been talking to Seppi just one house away at the very same time that he took off, with none of us being any wiser.

When Max got back to our Retreat before daybreak on that Thursday and found that we had gone, he immediately guessed that I would come on the mad-cap idea of blowing up Franz Hofer at the Devil´s Bridge the very next day without proper "intelligence". Max therefore decided to try and rendezvous with Dani and me on the Devil´s Bridge and so decided to start walking there that same Thursday night.

However, fearing that the Nazis might have meanwhile realized that he had duped them with a fake body and have men snooping all over and around the meadows of Gletschberg on the look-out for him, he decided to go straight up through the forests of the Holzbauer Ridge directly to the west of our Retreat and get to the Brenner Pass on the other side that way.

It was then that I pointed out that, judging by what Slimey had told me, the Nazis still believed Max was dead – even though that could change any day now depending on if a sufficient autopsy was made on the dead, burnt body.

"Well, it´s a pity that I didn´t know that at the time," said Max, "because, as it turned out, the Army was busy practicing all sorts of maneuver exercises that day on that part of the Brenner Pass. As such, I didn´t dare try to go anywhere near it in case I was stopped and asked questions. It seems incredible: the Army is already beginning to behave as if they are expecting another Great War."

"That´s what Seppi also told us," Dani said in such a way that it was obvious that he had also already told Max our side of the story. "It seems as if he´s not as dim as some people keep saying he is, hey Bulldog?"

"Anyway," Max continued, "it may not have been such an unlucky detour after all as it did help remind me exactly which way to go over the Holzbauer on our return from the castle."

"Although," Dani added, "had you not been detoured then you might have been able to save Bulldog from being captured in the first place just after I had detonated the bomb."

"Oh yes: that was a performance," Max continued. "I managed to almost get to the Devil´s Bridge just as your bomb went off – and was lucky enough to see Dani fleeing through the woods and so be able to catch up with him."

"Unfortunately," Dani again added, "the moment that I saw your being captured I ran like hell out of eyesight without thinking for a moment what might then happen to you."

"It´s only to be expected in this game of survival," said Max, as if he were somehow already used to it in spite of supposedly only having been an air cadet at the end of the War. As they say: ´Don´t look behind when running`. Anyway, knowing that all the dumb Nazis would be rushing off to the Devil´s Bridge to find out what the hell the explosion was all about, Dani and I sneaked up the hill and through the trees and then into the village and through the back-door of Kabinett´s furniture shop."

As if trying to elicit a moment of suspension, Max now called Dani for another mug of coffee, got it, took a sip from it and continued his story:

"Well, you can say that old Kabinett was rum surprised to see me still alive, as well as thinking that Dani had already fled to the South Tyrol. Unfortunately, he was unable to get any intelligence from his mysterious contact: so we finished up spending the night in his secret room. However, the next afternoon he told us that he had finally been told that Slimey had gone to Castle Jitter, so off we went, only to find out when we arrived that Slimey had already gone back to Gletschberg, although you were still there in what used to be the dungeon."

"Whilst we were armed with a couple of explosives that I still had left," added Dani, looking as pleased as Punch that he hadn´t literally blown them all on what should have been Franz Hofer´s car.

We spent the entirety of the following week in hiding at the Retreat whilst I was convalescing. Fortunately, I seemed to still be in good shape, with no lasting signs of possible broken bones or even a broken jaw, although I still found it difficult to talk for long because of my swollen mouth and missing teeth.

"We Schillings are a pretty robust species," Max told me as he began rubbing Bepanthen all over my bruises for the first time. "We´re strong and sturdy and built like miniature tanks."

Once again this reminded me of how Slimey had claimed I was Max´s child. However, now that I had had some proper rest as well as having some food back inside me, I found it impossible to believe that Max could be my father. Somehow that theory no longer seemed to fit as well as before: although I couldn´t tell whether Slimey had deliberately lied to me so as to upset me or genuinely believed that he had got his facts right.

In the meantime, not only were our supplies of canned and salted foods beginning to get dangerously low but so too was our fire-wood, which was of course much needed to keep us warm. Whilst Max was loathe to start firing his rifle even once for attracting attention, he and Dani were able to chop some trees down during the day whilst I kept look-out from the tinted windows.

I could see that much of the snow had by then disappeared altogether from Gletschberg and its lower meadows, whereas there was still plenty of snow up here on the mountain. This was in fact a bit of a nuisance because, if any of the Nazis had decided to come snooping around our secret territory, then they would have easily noticed that there had been an awful lot of activity around our Retreat – in spite of the number of times that we kept trying to cover our tracks.

As I have said before, at any other time it might have been nice and jolly and Christmasy to be in the Retreat with all the snow around us – but not at this hour of our family nightmares. As the week wore on and we had little to do except read books, talk, play chess and repair odds and sods, our personal griefs began turning into irritation with each other. The original camaraderie and relief that all three of us had experienced when we had found each of ourselves still alive soon began evaporating into despair, fear and anger, especially when I began asking about what our next move would be when I began to feel physically better at the end of the week.

"WHAT?!" I roared at Max, in much the same way as Papa had so often done when he was also having altercations with Max. "Do you mean to say that you just want us to pussy over the mountains and to safety in the **South Tyrol**? Good luck to that because the whole place is also swarming with Nazis over there."

"Not as much as here, Bulldog," said Dani. "From Italy we might be able to get to New York. I have family relations there who might be able to help us out."

"What about our Resistance Plans?" I shouted back. "Franz Hofer is still at large. We've still got to bring that bastard down!"

"How?" Max demanded. "By trying to bomb his car a second time round? It's because he's 'still at large' that he's now more dangerous than ever. You scared the beejeezus out of him, Bulldog. He won't take very kindly to that. The entire valley will now be better guarded than Berchtesgaden. Our only chance of getting out here alive and without first starving to death is by going over the Messner Glacier – and the sooner the better."

"Alright, alright!" I answered, still shouting. "I get all that – but what about Pete? We can't just leave him in that clinic in Hall without trying to first break him out. At least we could try doing that!"

"Are you completely DEVOID of Reality?!" Max shouted back at me. "We would first have to try and find a way of getting to Innsbruck. After our last escapade not only will the Brenner Pass be covered with road blocks but all the guards on the railways will also be on red alert."

"Then we´ll go over the mountains and through the forests, just as Andreas Hofer did in 1809," I suggested, beginning to grab at straws.

"Andreas Hofer had friends everywhere," Max immediately answered. "It was the whole of Austria against the French."

"And the Bavarians," said Dani. "Don´t forget that the **white-blue men** of Bavaria were also fighting with the French: the traitors."

"Whereas half of Austria today are already Nazis," Max continued, ignoring Dani´s pedantic note. "And even if we could get to Hall whilst not knowing who we could and could not trust, do you really think that we could just take Pete out of the hospital without anyone noticing? You know how he starts to wildly carry on whenever he gets the least excited."

"Max is right," Dani said mournfully. "It was hard enough for your Mama and Maria to look after Pete inside your own home but we would never manage to get him all the way back here to the Retreat without his kicking up a fuss at every turn of the journey, with or without Nazis swarming everywhere."

Without admitting it, I knew that my plans were straight out of cuckoo-land, being the sort of thing that one merely dreams or are the stuff of fiction.

"It will all be for the best, Bulldog," Dani said softly whilst holding my arm as Father Gabriel might have done. "Pete will be safer inside the clinic than if he were trying to tag along with us."

I only hoped that it were true.

Max told us that it would be best if we set off for the Messner Glacier at the crack of dawn on the Sunday.

"With any luck we'll be over the mountains by midday," he added. "And if anyone then sees us they might think that we're just three weekend climbers having fun."

It was difficult choosing what to take with us. It would have been easy to have packed everything but the kitchen sink in our rucksacks but we needed to be nimble on our feet once we were over the mountains. Besides, the extra weight would have only weighed us down as we made the difficult climb up the glacier, whilst I was still in no condition to carry anything but the bare minimum.

As such we just packed a change of clothes, essential toiletries and enough light food for two days – and just one book each for Dani and I. However, we still had to carry ropes and pick-ices, as well as crampons and skis, not to mention wearing enough clothing to keep ourselves warm. It was all the more pity because we knew that we would have to dump all this stuff when we no longer needed them, although Dani thought that we might be able to sell them for cash.

As to identity papers, Max had managed to save the family's passports and certificates before the fire had properly taken hold of the chalet, whereas Dani had barely managed to escape from his parents' apartment with just his life. However, since Max had Seppi´s passport (but not his identity papers) Dani would just have to start getting used to be called Seppi.

Of course we couldn´t take our rifles with us if we were to look like mountaineers instead of partisans. Dani suggested that we at least take the skinning knife with us but Max replied that we only had to be stopped and searched and we would be in deep trouble trying to explain why we were carrying a hunting knife over a glacier.

I used to love getting up early in the morning for my wanders in the mountains but this time everything was inside-out and upside-down. At least that was the way that my stomach felt as my gut now began churning on itself in agony as we stepped out of our Retreat for the last time for what might be years, decades or even forever. These roller-coasting emotions became even worse when we took a last long look at the still-sleeping village of Gletschberg far, far below us.

"It´s best that we don´t keep looking behind us like this," said Max as he turned to begin the long climb up the mountain, "but concentrate on what´s ahead of us."

"And the Future," said Dani, joining Max.

I found that this was easier said than done as I still kept staring down the valley towards the village that, up till that month, had been my life-long home. I knew that I was kissing goodbye to all my youthful dreams whilst ironically now doing what I loved best: namely, wandering over the mountains.

However, when I saw that Max and Dani were soon way ahead of me, I quickly decided to follow them.

I soon realized, however, that I wasn't anywhere near as recovered as I had felt in the Retreat – although my complete lack of exercise during that week certainly wouldn't have helped. The walk up the mountain was steeper than I could ever remember but then it was the first time that I had ever been so far up in the snow! In spite of what he had just said, Max kept looking back to see if I were okay, whilst Dani also kept telling me that it wasn't necessary for me to try to prove myself by not slowing down whenever I needed to.

The first hour of any climb, hike or walk is often the most gruelling as one's condition tries to kick itself into gear. However, this hour was particularly treacherous for me now as I kept seeing spots before my eyes, felt as if my skull were in a giant iron clamp and began sliding more and more often back downhill again, even though I already had my crampons on. I was also sure that Max and Dani kept quietly saying to each other, "He doesn't look at all well" and "I'm not sure if he can make it." However, I was blown if I would let them get away with these remarks so I just kept going.

Things nonetheless seemed to get worse when I began hallucinating. Feeling my bones and muscles aching all over, I began to imagine the blood starting to seep out of them, through my clothes and then all over the snow below me, until it became a river of blood and finally a frozen glacier of gleaming, glinting rubies.

They also say that you must never rest when struggling through the ice because the cold will suddenly freeze you and kill you outright. As it happened, I must have blacked out and fallen asleep at some point because I was woken up by Max cheerfully offering me a flask of hot tea.

"Here drink this – and have a sausage as well," he said. "It seems as if we should have given you some breakfast before we set off. Still, you fell asleep exactly on the right spot."

It was to my amazement that I now found myself sitting right on the edge of the glacier, with the sun brightly shining right across the white-glazed mountains, so that their peaks glinted whilst the glacier shone like a billion jagged diamonds. Dani meanwhile seemed to have perked up and be having the time of his life as he explored the furrows and fissures of the cracked glacier whilst popping up and going down all over the place as if he were a rabbit exploring an exciting new warren.

Indeed, I kept imagining that all our recent sorrows had just been one ghastly nightmare and that we were indeed just enjoying an early winter's break on the tops of the mountains. Better still, when we returned to Gletschberg everything would have returned to normal, with the entire family back in the chalet and all Mama's animals still alive in their stall house.

"Wow!" said Dani, returning to his own ration of the hot tea after he had had his fill of glacier bopping. "This is just like that Luis Trenker movie, ´The Son of the White Mountain` from 1930, before everyone thinks he´s gotten lost in the glacier."

I smiled, whilst wondering if we could really turn back Time to the way things used to be if we really wanted. As if to test if our mountain world were real and that we could indeed enjoy ourselves just for the moment, I picked up some of the snow and sprinkled it through the sunlight, as if magically turning sugar crystals into sparkling flakes of diamonds.

"Nobody here – nobody for miles to go," I said, as if mesmerized. "Life can be absolute Heaven."

"All the more´s the pity that not everyone wants it to be," Dani sagely replied.

It was at this very moment, however, that I suddenly heard the noise of what sounded for all the world to be a ginormous bumble-bee coming out of absolutely nowhere.

"What in thundering Hell´s name is that?" I suddenly gasped as I looked up and saw the most hideous man-made contraption suddenly coming straight for us out of the sky, as if we were now part of an **H.G. Wells** dystopian novel . . .

26: Ghosts on the Mountain

"Shut up and get the f*** out of here!" Max suddenly cried as he threw everything that we had and himself down one of the glacier´s rivulets. "Hide and don´t look up or they´ll see our faces!"

As if I still couldn´t believe what was really happening, Max just as suddenly grabbed me by the scruff of my neck and also threw me down the glacier, whilst tea went flying in all directions.

Although I knew I shouldn´t, I couldn´t resist the urge to look up through the crack in the glacier above us as I heard the monster machine hovering above whilst seemingly making a devil of a crashing noise with its flapping wings. Wings, however, they were not: but two sets of propellers that were whirling around at the speed of sound.

"What the hell is that damned thing?" I asked, looking aghast at Max.

"It´s Germany´s latest magic machine," Max replied, with clear amusement that I hadn´t yet seen such an invention. "They call it a ´**hubschrauber**`, with this being the most successful version: the Focker-Wulf Fw 61."

"How do you know this stuff ?" I asked Max in wonder.

"Because I only read things that matter," Max answered puckishly, having only ever read newspapers and magazines. "And as you can see, it can even fly over mountains."

"But what´s it doing all the way up our bally mountain?" I then asked. "Surely they can´t have sent it all the way up here just to search for us?"

The answer came quicker than I had expected as a shower of bullets suddenly came pouring into our glacier from above us.

"Crikey, Moses!" I cried, "how does he even know we´re down here?"

"Probably because you keep looking up at him!" Max cried back, as he grabbed hold of my shoulder and pushed me down a chute within the glacier.

As the two of us then hid within a tiny ice-cove within the glacier, the hubschrauber-thingy might have been out of sight but it certainly wasn´t out of mind. I could hear it constantly coming and going immediately above us, like a fox searching for rabbits in their warren.

"Where the hell has Dani got to?" I soon asked, noticing that he was missing.

"Keep your mouth shut," Max suddenly said as he put his hand over my mouth without saying why.

The way that Max now held up his head to listen intently to the roar of the propellers near us, he might just as well have been a rabbit listening for trouble, even if his ears weren´t pricked up like a pair of soup spoons. All that I heard was the engine gradually becoming quieter until it almost stopped.

"The bugger´s gone and landed," Max whispered to me.

"They can land an air plane on a mountain without an air strip?" I almost cried, feeling sure that I must be dreaming all this nonsense.

"For the last time," Max said impatiently. "It's not an air plane. A hubschrauber can land and take off vertically just about anywhere on the planet."

I was now too stunned for words whilst, at that moment, Dani suddenly popped up in the entrance to our cove.

"I'm going out to finish off this Nazi bastard for once and for all," he said, holding something that looked awfully like a stick of dynamite that he still had left over.

"Don't be stupid, Dani!" Max almost shouted. "Just stay down here with us and be quiet. The pilot will soon give up looking for us because he can't afford to keep his engine running for too long or he risks the chance of running too low on fuel. And in this cold, if he switches the engine off, he might not be able to switch it on again."

"Couldn't we just bump him off?" I suggested to Max. "Then we could fly off in this hubschrauber-wotsit of his with you as the pilot."

Max then looked at me as if this were the most stupid thing I had said in a long, long while, before replying with a growl:

"There is only ONE seat in that hubschrauber, Bulldog."

If Max looked as if he were angry with me, then it was nothing compared to the way that Dani was now looking at Max.

"Listen, old airman," Dani told Max in a rare moment of zero respect, "those bastards killed my parents right in front of my eyes, so if this bastard wants to see more blood then he can watch it spurting out of his own evil body!"

"No, Dani! Don´t be a fool!" was all that Max had time to cry as Dani then shot up the glacier fissure towards his quarry.

Of course, all that Max and I could do was to try and follow Dani and hopefully stop him before he carried out his madcap plan, having finally snapped under the strain of his parents´ cruel deaths.

Dani soon came to a crest inside the glacier, before suddenly popping over its edge and into the wide open. Max and I were just in time to peep over the crest of the glacier ourselves and see Dani running towards the pilot, who was snooping around the edge of another crevice in the glacier whilst having his back towards us. What happened next is all a fuzzle in my memory.

Either I shouted out something like "Stop Dani!" or Dani tripped up, or the pilot had darned good hearing in spite of his ear muffs. The fact is that Dani hadn´t even got close to the pilot when the pilot turned round and saw Dani running at full pelt towards him. Without a second thought the pilot let Dani have a belly-full of bullets from the sub-machine gun that he was carrying.

In an almost grotesquely comic way Dani suddenly let out his arms like a bird that had just been shot in mid-air, whilst his legs splayed out beneath him. The next moment Dani lay flat on his back and, even from where we were, I could now see a pool of bright-red blood sleeping across the ice around him.

I have no idea if I wanted to cry and scream or throw up all over the glacier or even kick the entire mountain down: but I now felt worse than I had ever yet felt as all my insides suddenly melted into a putrid jelly. Gone was the best and probably only ever friend I had had outside of my family: a lad who was only just younger than myself and yet who was infinitely so much smarter and braver than I was and who had so much to offer in his life: all gone in just a matter of seconds.

For all my grief, horror and sheer anger I knew better than to go charging over the ridge of the glacier in a fit of mad revenge. It was therefore all the more surprising when Max suddenly jumped up and did just that – but not before first pulling out a **Luger PO8** pistol from his pocket: a gun which I had had no idea that he even had.

"Take this you Nazi bully!" I heard Max cry, whilst I saw his own life of adventures with me suddenly flash before my eyes.

However, all that now came out of the pilot´s sub-machine gun was a series of futile clicks. I then saw the pilot´s face turn into various contortions of mingled surprise, frustration and finally horror as he tried to speedily figure out why his trusty death machine had suddenly seized up before he was himself shot to pieces.

The next thing that I heard and saw was a single bullet firing from Max´s Luger PO8 and hitting the pilot bang in the middle of his voluptuous leather jacket, as if it were about to go straight through the middle of his heart. However, for all that I knew, the pilot did not have a heart but was just a stupid Nazi robot as no blood came pouring out of him. The horrid creature simply slumped to the ground like a sack of dumb potatoes in exactly the same way that Kratzkopf had done from his car.

Max and I certainly couldn´t care less for the dead Nazi swine as we both instead now ran towards Dani´s blood-soaked body, whilst I first jumped out of the glacier like a jack rabbit. There was of course nothing that we could do for my poor friend except offer his God Yahweh a prayer of death. It was, however, as I was holding Dani´s hand for the first and last time ever whilst I began muttering some words to his dead soul that I suddenly realized that his other hand was still holding his stick of dynamite and that it was still lit.

As quick as lightning, I therefore grabbed hold of the dynamite with the intention of throwing it well out of the way and before it blew us all up to Merry Kingdom Come. I was going to throw it down the glacier when I saw the Nazi hubshrauber contraption thing standing about ten meters beyond us. Now landed and without its pilot, it looked more like a ridiculous **Heath Robinson** invention than an H.G. Wells monster. However, with the Nazi swastika emblazoned across its tail it was the perfect target for my apoplectic anger.

"TAKE THAT YOU BASTARDS!!!" I roared as I hurled the dynamite at the hubschrauber, so that the next moment the entire bally machine blew up with a massive, fiery explosion straight out of the Devil´s deepest pit of Hell. Bits and bats of God-knew-what suddenly went flying in all directions – including at us – whilst flames roared every which way but loose.

"That was a bally stupid thing to do!" Max suddenly yelled at me, almost as angrily as I now was. "They´ll be able to see this explosion from all over the valley now. They are bound to send a force up straight away to see what the hell has happened."

"Then we had better get over the glacier pretty sharpish," I grimly answered, as if I were now in charge.

"Not bally likely," Max shouted back. "They´ll suspect that we´re at the bottom of all this and will have patrols also looking for us on the other side. No, we had better bolt like rabbits back into our Retreat – but first we must get rid of the bodies pretty sharpish. We don´t want the Nazis to know their pilot was shot dead by what could only be us, just as we don´t want them to know that Dani is now – you know what I mean."

Throwing the Nazi pilot´s body down one of the many deep chasms in the glacier so that it wouldn´t be found for another hundred years as the **ice slowly moved forward** was an easy enough experience.

However, throwing Dani's fresh body down the glacier was an altogether different kettle of fish. It was not only completely un-dignifying and ungracious but we didn't even have a large bag to put the poor fellow in.

We did, however, make sure that Dani's body never had the misfortune in death to meet up with the Nazi's whilst the glacier ice slowly shifted along through the decades: by choosing a completely different chasm for him far, far away from the Nazi's. And although we had to be pretty quick if we were to get back to the Retreat before the Nazis had even set foot on the mountain, this still didn't stop us completing our Jewish prayer for Dani before we sent him hurtling down and on his journey into the frozen under-world.

Having brought our skis with us, we were pretty nifty in getting back down to the Retreat on them, as well as having plenty of time to clear our tracks before hiding in our refuge yet again. It was almost midday before the first of the Nazi scouts inevitably came struggling up the mountain below us, whilst making a hell of a commotion doing so.

However, if I thought I had been slow earlier that morning, they were even slower, being completely unfit. I didn't know where they got their boys from but it certainly didn't seem to be from the usual round of local ski and mountain patrols.

As I looked through the tinted look-out windows at the top of the Retreat whilst the Nazis obviously had no idea we were there, I couldn't help thinking that, had it not been for that damned Nazi hubschrauber, we would now have been over the glacier and climbing down into South Tyrol. However, I didn't have much chance of daydreaming at the windows because the Nazis were so damned loud that I could often hear every word that they shouted at one another.

"They've somehow completely vanished from the face of the mountain," I heard some self-important buffoon yelling as he marched straight back down from where he had just been standing right beside our hidden Retreat. "Like ghosts on a mountain!"

With this final admission of defeat the Nazis also immediately vanished from the mountain, although I wished that they had just been mere ghosts themselves and were no longer a danger to ourselves.

"We're caught in a trap with nowhere else to go," I sharply said to Max when he came rolling up the stairs one afternoon to join me at the look-out windows. "We've got Nazis waiting for us not only in the village but also the whole of both the North and the South of Tyrol. Our food is meanwhile running out and we daren't shoot any animals for arousing suspicion, just as we dare not go out to chop any more wood for fear of being either seen or heard. At this rate we'll be reduced to stealing food from the village at night even though there are probably guards posted everywhere."

Max, however, simply looked back at me with a huge smile of admiration whilst energetically rubbing my shoulder with sympathy.

"It´s good to see that you are getting better, Bulldog!" he enthusiastically told me. "At this rate you´ll soon be fighting fit again!"

I looked back at Max as though he were already starting to crack up in what was now our prison – but was at least glad to see that he was beginning to take a lot more interest in what was going on outside. Indeed, it was on the morning of Saturday the Third of December that things suddenly took an unexpected turn. We had now been cooked up in our refuge for almost an entire week, having tried to escape the previous Sunday, which had been the First Advent. The next day would be the Second Advent and only three weeks later it would be Christmas Day. As such, I could not help thinking how, until now, we had all been together at this time of year and preparing for Christmas.

Max´s thoughts, however, were clearly focused on the here and now instead of the past and what-might-have-been as he now began to scan the valley and the village with his giant binoculars. It certainly was a glorious day – almost spring-like, in fact, with the snow around the Retreat now also rapidly melting. As I again began day-dreaming Max suddenly shouted out with joy as he eyes caught sight of something glinting in the far, far distance.

"I do believe that I have just found the perfect answer to all of our problems," he slowly said with a huge grin.

27: The Spirit of Adventure

"What is it, Max?" I asked, wondering what on Earth he had seen that could mean an escape for us.

"It must have landed early this morning: before we were even awake," answered Max, giving me the binoculars so that I could see what he meant. "There: a little birdie, standing in the meadows before the Berghof."

As I took the binoculars from Max I wondered if he had indeed already gone full-blown cuckoo or just re-kindled his old interest in ornithology in order to calm his nerves. However, as I now scanned the meadows before the Berghof it wasn´t a golden eagle that I saw but a two-seater reconnaissance bi-plane with the markings of the German Luftwaffe.

"That´s an Austrian **Phoenix C.I.** that you are now looking at," Max now told me with evident admiration for the contraption. "It was in one of those beauties that I learnt how to fly right at the end of the War. In fact, now that I´ve come to think of it, I wouldn´t be at all surprised if that exact aircraft that you now see standing there before your very eyes was the very same baby that I used to fly in. Hofer must have managed to get hold of it so as to avoid also getting blown up in his car on the Brenner Pass."

It was of course obvious what Max was now thinking and it wasn´t a nostalgic aviation trip down Memory Lane.

"You must be crazy!" I told Max. "Do you really think that we can just hop in that thing and fly it away like a little birdie without being first machine-gunned down to pieces?"

"Why not?" Max almost roared back at me as if he were seized by his own passions. "I´ve done it before so I can do it again."

"But suppose the plane doesn´t properly work after all these years," I suggested. "Or suppose its fuel tank is empty."

"If it didn´t work properly it couldn´t have flown here," Max almost shouted back, although he didn´t add "dummy" as Maria would have done. "And these babies always have their fuel tanks re-filled the moment that they land. Can´t you see, Bulldog? This is a golden opportunity that has been literally sent to us from the Heavens!"

I now had to agree with Max, even though I was still very wary of the chances that we had of simply tumbling into the aircraft without anyone noticing and raising the alarm. Indeed, there is a mountain climbing joke about a priest who once got stuck up a mountain just before a thunderstorm. A solo climber, a helicopter and even a golden eagle all came to rescue him in turn but each time he told them that he didn´t need their help because he knew that God would save him. However, when he suddenly got struck by lightning and got sent to Heaven he had plenty to say to Saint Peter at its Gates.

"Why didn´t the Good Lord come to save me as I believed he would?" the priest demanded of the apostle.

"He did," Saint Peter quickly replied. "In fact he offered you help on three different occasions and each time you said naff off."

I expected that Max would try to fly away with the plane during the night when there was a lot less of a chance of our being seen. However, Max wanted us to be as bold as brass, rather like the guy who no one thought of stopping whilst he kept constantly stealing furniture out of a shop by simply carrying it out through its front door in broad daylight: because they all thought that no one would be dumb enough to try something that obvious. As such, we not only took our rifles with us this time but also dressed ourselves up like soldiers on patrol. Max even brought his old flying cap with him, being a keepsake that he had treasured with other memorabilia at the Retreat all these years.

When we arrived at the meadows before the Berghof early that afternoon, the hotel terrace was in full swing. The oompah-oompah band was blasting out its usual repertoire of jolly pieces and no doubt Franz Hofer was sitting gleefully in the middle of all the merriment and madness.

"But surely the old basket will get wise the moment he hears the plane´s engine revving up?" I asked Max.

"With all that horrid music in his ears?" Max asked me in return. "Neither is he likely to see anything with all his cronies fawning all over him, whilst the few guards who see us will merely think that we are just a couple of servicemen come to make a routine check-over."

As bold as brass, as cool as cucumbers and as sassy as mint-sauce were just three of the many similes that kept whizzing through my head as Max and I walked briskly up to the aircraft like two mice about to throw a dozing cat´s saucer of milk slap bang into its face. As we kept looking straight in front of our selves so as not to look at all suspicious, I saw that the bi-plane was in fact parked in a long, flat field that was unfortunately still full of puddles from the recently melted snow.

I just hoped that after all these years Max would still be able to take the plane off on the bumpy ground. Worst still, as we were almost upon the plane, I began wondering if Max were really still capable of remembering all the necessary actions for takeoff from what had in fact still been his youth twenty years before. My heart was therefore beating faster than a machine gun as we finally arrived at the plane and we both climbed up the side of the plane and jumped into our appropriate seats, even though I had never done such a thing before. I fully expected to hear a round of real machine gun fire ringing in my ears as Max began fiddling about with all sorts of controls that I couldn´t see in front of himself.

Suddenly the engine began roaring – and, by Golly, it made a hell of a clatter. I was therefore sure at this point that all the World and his brother would suddenly wake up and, like the small child who refuses to look at a scolding grown-up in the hope that they might somehow vanish into thin air, I too refused to look left or right of myself to see what might now be going on around us. Indeed, I even tried to actually drop so deep down into my seat that I could neither be seen nor shot at.

It was therefore with a mighty sigh of relief – even though my heart must have now been racing faster than the speed of sound – that I then felt the great bird moving forward under us, whilst wondering if it would ever, ever be able to lift itself off the ground and up into the air, let alone over the mountains. However, no sooner had we begun rumbling across the bumpy meadow then I heard shouts from all around – more out of surprise than actual anger.

There was certainly no sound of firing pistols or rifles, let alone any machine gun fire as we began travelling faster and faster, so that we suddenly lifted off and left the godforsaken village that had been our home all our lives behind us. Indeed, I almost wet myself once we were soon out of any kind of fire, whilst knowing that it would be ages before any craft that the Nazis sent after us from Innsbruck would be able to catch up with us.

"Is there anything that you CAN'T do?" I therefore asked Max with elation, now that we were airborne and finally out of the reach of the Nazi swines.

"You know me," Max replied, pulling a little more on the throttle. "I´m the Spirit of Adventure."

Flying higher and higher in circles above the huge arena of the Gletschberg Watzkessel, we passed from the thrill of danger and into the thrill of exhilaration. Up here we were truly as free as eagles as we swept pass the massive, craggy, snow-filled walls of the Kricklhorn and Mammut mountains. I especially took time to look carefully down at the Messner Valley whilst wondering if we would ever see our secret Retreat again.

I had never been out of Gletschberg or its immediate valleys during the sixteen years of my life so far. Neither had I ever seen a movie, let alone one that showed an aerial view of the world. You can therefore imagine my overwhelming surprise and sheer wonder once we had risen above our own familiar peaks and saw a thousand other peaks and intertwining valleys sprawling in all directions below and beyond us. Lordy may, I thought: if it had taken me sixteen years just to explore Gletschberg, how many life-times would I need for the entire Alps?!

Once we had flown over the Holzbauer Ridge I naturally expected Max to turn due south and up the Wipptal Valley to the top of the Brenner Pass and into Italy. As it was, he just kept flying due west towards what seemed to be even larger mountains.

"Where are we going?" I shouted, with the wind bellowing so hard around us that even that sounded like a whisper. "Italy´s to our left!"

"To Switzerland!" Max answered with a laugh.

"WHAT?" I tried to roar back, yet sounding no louder than a squeaking mouse. "If we land there they´ll just **send us back to Austria as German citizens**! Even I know that!"

"Nonsense, Bulldog!" Max actually managed to roar back at me through the wind. "We´re not seeking asylum in Switzerland. Instead I have the address of Dani´s relatives in New York with me. We can get a train to Normandy in France and then a ship to America."

"I just hope that we have enough money for all that," I said.

However, after all that Max had achieved so far I could not help thinking that Max would somehow manage all of this as well. Meanwhile, the exhilaration of flying high up in the Alps was so intoxicating that I couldn´t but help feeling as happy as a sandboy at Christmas, as I seemed to forget all about our family tragedies and instead dreamed of a bright, new future in New York.

In fact, I was so happy that I was now literally living on Cloud Nine, whilst I failed to notice the sweep of clouds that kept steadily creeping towards us from the south. It was therefore not until Max told me, "Watch out, Bulldog, things are about going to get turbulent for us!" that I began looking directly ahead of ourselves.

We were soon covered on all sides by misty cloud, as if not only the very mountains below us but also the very skies around us had both suddenly ceased to exist. Likewise, I soon also discovered exactly what "turbulent" meant as the bottom suddenly seemed to drop out of the plane and we began tumbling around like a bird being swung about in a net. I was also damned sure that we were about to be smashed into a mountain peak and so began saying my prayers as quickly as I could, whilst wishing I had a rosary with me.

Needless to say that Heaven above Earth had suddenly turned into Hell, although it wasn´t the dark and fiery place of medieval lore and pictures but of the blindingly white and freezing kind. Worse still, with no way of knowing where anything was other than that there were solid mountains all around us, it took me all my energy and iron discipline not to suddenly un-belt myself in panic and jump out of the plane in terror.

None of this prepared me for the massive dive to the bottom that we suddenly took when the engine suddenly cut off. If planes and machines have souls then this little birdie was clearly terrified as it soon nose-dived faster than a rock towards Earth whilst screaming away in agony.

"Don´t worry!" Max suddenly cried when the engine began coughing and splattering back into action. "I think I´ve got her now!"

Sure enough our bird found her wings and spirit again so that we began flying once more in a vertical straight line through the cloud. I thought that we had got over the worst but Max now seemed to be wildly agitated about something as he kept mumbling a phrase over and over again.

I began to wonder with real fear if Max had suddenly lost his mind, whilst the body of the aircraft began to shake all over as if it were about to fall apart at any moment. It was only when I was able to make out the words "Oh-Five", "Mayday" and what seemed like a couple of code-names that I realized that Max was trying to send a message by radio.

These were the last words that Max ever spoke as we suddenly plummeted into a huge bank of snow. As our plane continued to plough through the snow at a devastating speed, I prayed that we weren´t about to tear over a cliff when we suddenly seemed to hit a ton and a half of rock and ice.

The whole world as well as the aircraft suddenly seemed to spin around me like a gigantic Catherine wheel, whilst debris and shrapnel went whirling in all directions like splinters off shattered glass. I wondered for a fleeting moment if my time really had also come or if I would just black out for several hours, when I suddenly landed with a savage thump on the ground and somehow remained conscious.

Goodness only knows how long I then lay there as if it were a sleepy new morning in my working life and I kept endlessly mulling over in my confused mind if I should yet get up or not. Rise I presently did as I was forced to accept that this were no horrid dream of mine but hard and unescapable Reality, unbelievable though it seemed to be.

The first thing that I did was to crawl through the freezing snow to see if Max were okay, with there being just enough light to see the smashed up wreckage of the precious Phoenix C.I. aircraft around me. It was therefore to my utter and devastating horror that I now found him lying stretched out like a lifeless ragdoll that had just been thrown out with the rest of the garbage.

"MAX! MAX!" I kept crying over and over again, trying to bring his life back into him whilst pumping his chest as if there were no tomorrow. However, as Max´s eyes remained staring into space as a life now spent, I finally had to realize that my poor beloved friend and uncle was now also just as dead as my parents, my sister and Dani.

Indeed, it was now that I finally realized that Max had been the only true guide and mentor in my entire life, even when I was growing towards my Papa during my spell as a police cadet. He had indeed been the Spirit of Adventure: from ski instructor to mountain guide to hunter, airman and possibly even (considering everything that he knew about guerilla combat) a secret commando towards the end of the Great War – whereas I was just a nobody trying but hopelessly failing to be a Hero.

I therefore now remained beside my poor, dear Max like a faithful dog who refuses to leave its deceased master, holding his hand as it steadily grew colder and stiffer whilst the cloud continued to whirl around us. For all that I cared, I could have remained like this for an eternity, had it not been for the freezing cold also slowly starting to bite deeply into my own body and bones.

It had been Max who had taught me how to survive in the wilderness mountains and it was with his thoughts in mind that I finally decided to focus and "keep marching on" through the snow and the ice and the cold and to not allow myself to fall asleep.

But "keep marching on"? Where on Earth was I suppose to go except to start climbing downhill through the knee-deep snow, hoping that I would eventually find a warm and cozy hut and perhaps also a warm and friendly farmer or even a climber? Yet, slim as the chances of any of this happening were, the only alternative was to wait to fall unconscious whilst slowly freezing to death. As such, I picked up Max´s rucksack with mine and began the long and possibly futile trek downhill.

I, of course, had to leave Max´s body as it was. Although I managed to close his eyes and draw his broken goggles back over them, I couldn´t cross his arms over his chest in a saintly position because they were already too stiff. As to covering him with a blanket, that was laughable because there wasn´t one anywhere and it would have blown away anyway the moment that the wind had whipped itself up again.

Without even a glacier to hide Max away in as with Dani, I therefore had to leave Max where he was. For the first time I hoped that we had crashed sufficiently high up the mountain for his body to be preserved throughout the winter, if not for seeming eternity until some unfortunate climber stumbled upon it in perhaps the long, long future.

On the other hand, I also hoped that we had crashed sufficiently low down on the mountain for me to be able to at least find that warm hut with the farmer or climber before I froze to death. So or so, I had no choice but to start putting one foot in front of the other as I began the long struggle back to humanity.

However, although Max had trained me to survive in the freezing mountains as a fully-equipped and properly clothed mountaineer, I had never expected to do so dressed as just an air serviceman without even wooly mittens and bobble hat, never mind about crampons, an ice-pick and a good, warm jacket.

Just as bad was the fact that the cloud around the mountain wouldn´t clear, so that I was constantly having to look for possible crevices and sudden drops that might be hidden just a few feet before myself in the knee-deep snow. And, if all that wasn´t enough, I found my legs constantly buckling whilst my trail of deep foot-steps behind me looked as if they were colored with tomato-colored nail-varnish.

Eventually, however, I found myself clambering down a steep slope that was free of jagged rocks poking out all over the place, so that it might have been a hanging valley like our own Messner Valley.

This gave me more confidence, so that I now began to find it easier to "keep marching on", even though I also felt as if I were now more exhausted than even totally exhausted. Meanwhile, as I kept scrambling downwards like an ever-more frozen snowman, I began to count my blessings one by one: or at least the blessings that I had enjoyed in life before this terrible year of Naziism.

It was as I was doing so that I began to feel as if someone were walking beside me. Was it my soul, my future heavenly spirit, my guardian angel, a protecting saint or even God himself?

28: Living with God

I must have passed out without even first knowing that I might do so: for when I finally came to it was in intensive care in a hospital. My first reaction was that the Nazis had got me but I began noticing that an awful lot of nuns and monks and priests kept wandering up and down the corridor outside my room. I then thought that I was in Heaven – but it was a funny sort of Heaven where I was still bandaged up like an Egyptian mummy, whilst those parts of my hands and arms that I could see were blacky-blue.

My thighs were also in intense pain – but not my legs: which I could no longer feel. In fact, as I later found out, I hadn´t any legs to feel because they had both been amputated. Unknown to me in the freezing cold, both my legs had been slashed open with shrapnel. My climb through the snow down the mountain had meant that they had both then turned gangrenous and had to go.

Max´s call to "Oh-Five" had had its effect as it had reached Father Gabriel: who, believe it or not, had a radio in the belfry of the church! He had immediately alarmed the Kloster of Saint Jerome in the Inn Valley and they had sent out a team of climbers to find me. They found me huddled up and almost lifeless, like a curled-up frozen prawn, and immediately set to work bringing me back to life, before taking me to the Kloster to be looked after.

By co-incidence – or perhaps by Fate or even a Higher Command – this was the very same Kloster where my Mama had been born and brought up. It was in fact a "Doppel Kloster": that is, a "double monastery", with one Kloster for the monks and another for the nuns, whilst the hospital was shared between them as needs required.

As soon as I was well enough to sit in a wheelchair, I was hurried out of the hospital to live a life of seclusion and secrecy in the cellars of the monks´ Kloster, whilst only occasionally being allowed to be driven out in the wheelchair in an enclosed garden.

I did, however, have a small window through which I could look out of and at that garden, so that I took immense joy at watching the flowers bloom the following spring, the trees blossom and then turn into a blaze of Thanksgiving that autumn, as well as the snow return for another winter at the monastery, as it began to slowly fill the garden and cover its trees with silent snowflakes.

The lightly falling snow was all very simple and yet extremely beautiful, as well as peaceful and tranquil, but I knew that this heavenliness would not last long. World War Two had begun that September and soon enough such Christmasy winter scenes would be blotched all over by the blood of fighting soldiers.

I often wondered what would happen if the Nazis ever tried to "invade" the Kloster and break its sanctity whilst trying to hunt down hidden

"Enemies of the People" like myself. I also wondered what would happen if push eventually came to shove and that, for some reason, the Allies began bombing the Inn Valley. However, I was assured that the foundations of the two Klosters were not only solid enough to withstand bombings but that they were a veritable labyrinth of warrens so that we were as safe as rabbits from the Nazi foxes down there.

It was during this first year of my new life in secret seclusion that I was given my "new legs" and taught how to walk by an energetic young monk called Brother Sebastian. He also gave me a Bible, as well as many bible lessons, teaching me about the endless treasures that were to be discovered inside this "library of books" without ever sounding preachy or condescending. As it was, he turned out to be the younger brother of Father Gabriel.

Needless to say that I was almost in ecstasy when he told me that his older brother would soon be visiting the monks´ Kloster and would certainly want to look me up. After all, Father Gabriel was the only friend or relative that I still had left from my Gletschberg years. When he did finally arrive, however, Father Gabriel didn´t seem so pleased to see me again.

"You killed eight human beings just because they were Nazis," he told me. "What was the point of that, other than making the Nazis even more mad and keener to find other victims? Besides, you didn´t even manage to get your target but killed

Kranzkopf instead: the very man who been trying to protect you from the lunacies of Hofer and Slimey."

I felt like answering that on that score alone Kratzkopf hadn´t been much use to us, so what the heck? However, I owed my entire life to Father Gabriel, so I certainly wasn´t going to show any ingratitude by refusing to eat humble pie.

As it was, I didn´t need to answer anything for, having made his point, Father Gabriel now simply put his arms around me like a father who hadn´t seen his prodigal son in a long, long time.

"I forgive you, Bulldog," he said. "This mad, mad world is trying to turn us all into wicked beings and to seek vengeance all over the place."

Another year passed before Father Gabriel gave me another visit after he had apparently been active in other parts of Austria.

"I want to become a monk," I told him, trying to rise from my wheelchair with my false legs when he arrived. "I´ve now read the Bible all the way through and think that I´m ready to commit the rest of my life to the Service of God."

"Sit down, my son," Father Gabriel answered, as he then also sat down on a stool before me and, as he so often did, laid his hands down upon my own – even though they were no longer on my real knees. "I have no doubt that you have put your heart and soul into learning the Lord´s Good Book by heart but I´m afraid that the ancient rules of the Kloster mean that only the physically fit are allowed to become monks and nuns of the Order."

I nearly replied that I could at least walk – but even that wasn´t quite true. In spite of Brother Sebastian´s constant lessons and never-ending encouragement I still had a lot of trouble in walking alone on my two new pins. This was because, secluded as I was beneath the Kloster with very few opportunities to get out into the garden and have some proper exercise, I was not beginning to shape up very well. The Kloster´s powers-that-be were very aware of the need for tight security and the fact that the Nazis could spring up on them at any moment and tear the place apart.

"They could change the rules," I said. "´New Times, New Rules` and all that. The Nazis would never think of looking for ex-Resistance fighters amongst the monks."

"No, I´m afraid the clergy won´t buy that. The technologies and life-styles might change but people stay essentially the same, with the same sins and avarices, as well as the same chivalries and virtues."

"Then does mean that I will be kicked out into the wide world again?" I asked, suddenly becoming fearful of my future. "I would have to go to somewhere where nobody knows me – but, if they don´t know me, why should they look after me?"

Indeed, the idea of starting out a fresh, new life just now with total strangers whilst also constantly trying to avoid the Nazis, remembering especially how they had already tortured me, was not exactly inducing. Besides, I felt at home in the basement of the Kloster, even if it was a bit dark and mangy. For one, I was as safe as safe could be and, for two, I felt that I was living with God. Yes, it was true that I wasn't allowed to visit any of the church services but I was often visited by various priests and monks so that they could attend to my spiritual needs.

"No, no: you're a special case – a very special case, Bulldog," I was glad to hear Father Gabriel answer. "We will keep you here for as long as this insane war goes on. In the meantime, you could become a teacher. The younger monks need a teacher and you might fill the position perfectly as I hear that you love reading books. In fact, my brother tells you that you've as good as devoured every book that he has so far lent you."

This was indeed true as Brother Sebastian seemed to have a never-ending supply of books about history, the mountains, far-away places and even novels. I only wished that Dani had been there to have enjoyed them with me.

"But you must make sure that you don't make the same mistake that others do in teaching and that is to pre-judge the abilities of others," Father Gabriel warned. "You can't go around putting people in pre-ordained boxes of smart and stupid without expecting things to go disastrously wrong. Always encourage your scholars to discover and fulfil their potential, as well as to make their own choices in life – and tell them that they can only improve, not get worse."

"Or, as Plutarch said, 'The mind is not a vessel to be filled but a fire to be kindled`."

"Very good, Bulldog!" Father Gabriel said before adding: "And don´t forget that there are many different types of intelligence, with apparent dim-wits being blessed with rare intuition, just as there are brilliant scientists and doctors who have zero common sense and are incapable of doing the simplest tasks."

So it was decided that I would teach the younger monks various bits of what I already knew of the outside world, whilst they were sworn to secrecy of my existence. My third winter at the monastery meanwhile passed into spring again – and then into summer and later autumn before becoming winter all over again. It was then, at the beginning of 1942, that I heard upsetting news from Russia – although I´m not sure if I was so much upset by the news as by my envying his suddenly becoming a War Hero.

Seppi, it was reported in military circles, had been killed in the snow on the Russian Front whilst leading a force of men to do a demolition job on a bridge in a desperate bid to try to stop the Russian counter offensive after the Battle of Moscow. When it seemed that their bomb couldn´t be detonated without one of the troops remaining to do it, Seppi had been the one who volunteered to let himself be blown up in the name of the Glorious German Reich. I could just see him telling his comrades before they left him to his Fate that his father would have been proud of him, little knowing that his real father may well instead have been little better than a draught dodger.

Achieving his wish by at least dying as a War Hero, Seppi was posthumously awarded the Iron Cross First Class. Normally that was only awarded for repeated acts of bravery but this one act of suicidal bravery seemed to be good enough, rather like a cat that had just used up all of its nine lives at once. Who exactly got the medal I do not know, as all his relatives were now supposed to be dead, mental or simply missing, presumed dead. And for all that I knew, Seppi might have actually made some real friends by then.

After that, every time that I looked out of my tiny window and saw the snow, I saw Seppi shivering in the freezing cold as he waited for the final moment to blow both himself and the bridge and possibly also a convoy to High Heavens. I also couldn't help imagining his blood and guts being thrown all over the snow and right across my window. At least he wouldn't have felt a thing.

It was with some conceit that I also wondered if Seppi had got his idea from Dani and I on the Devil's Bridge, as he may well have heard of the incident afterwards. He might even have regarded us two as being Heroes of the Resistance and wanted to go one better on us, all in the name of our Papa and in spite of the fact that we had a made a complete hash of the entire mission by getting the wrong man. On the other hand, we didn't finish up paying with our lives for this supposed glory – or, at least, not directly.

If the news of Seppi´s sudden death had been shocking it was nothing compared to the news that I soon got afterwards through Father Gabriel´s network of Resistance agents: namely, of Pete´s own sudden death. Indeed, if Seppi´s death had been suicide in the name of the supposedly Glorious German Reich, then Pete´s had been wanton murder in the name of that very same Reich. In fact, Pete´s death was just one in a genocide of 300,000 patients who were selected for mass murder by physicians in Germany, Austria, Poland and the Czech Protectorate.

The program lasted throughout the entire War and would come to be known as "Aktion T4" in court cases afterwards. The worst of it was that, although it was officially ended in 1941 due to protests and adverse publicity, some doctors (including some in Catholic asylums) continued to implement it, not only because of eugenics and "racial hygiene" but also simply to save money. Even the name of Pete´s hospital had been a typically sick Nazi euphemism: the Heil and Pflege Klinik: that is, "The Cure and Care Clinic". They might just as well have called it the "Kill and be Killed Clinic".

In the meantime, if Seppi´s becoming a war hero had re-kindled my notion in the barn that I should also be one, albeit for the Resistance, then my rage at hearing what the damned Nazis had done to my little baby brother Pete finally set it completely ablaze.

"I need to become a Resistance agent," was the first thing that I said to Father Gabriel when he next visited me. "I´ve got it all worked out. You could set me up with one of your agents to work as a radio intelligence operator whilst giving me a new identity, backed up with documents. If nothing else, I could be made out to be a war hero who has lost his legs in battle. The Nazis would be very averse to snooping around someone like that. Besides, I would be in the mountains again. The only time that I ever get to see the mountains these days is on the few occasions that I get to exercise my legs in the garden – and even then I can only see the peaks peeping over the Kloster roof-tops."

"I see that your spirit for adventure is catching up with you again," said Father Gabriel, little knowing that he was quoting my dear, old Uncle Max. "It is certainly a most commendable idea and one that I have also often thought about for you. However, it is simply too impractical to work. As you well know, everyone knows everybody else in these villages, so that a stranger popping up from nowhere and pretending to be somebody´s relation that nobody has ever seen – disabled war hero or not – would immediately arouse the Gestapo´s suspicion. Of course, Innsbruck is much more anonymous so that you and another agent could always pretend to be a couple of merchantmen looking for new work but that is hardly likely to fly under the Gestapo´s radar for long. And if anyone outside Gletschberg is aware of who has gone missing in the Tyrol then it is the Innsbruck Gestapo."

As if my Life had been cursed by having all my family and friends killed off one by one in Ten Little Indians style, Father Gabriel then also suddenly died. I say "suddenly" because, at least for me, his death was unexpected: since I saw him so rarely and the last time that I did so was three months before he breathed his last breath.

At that time, unknown to myself and many others, he had advanced leukemia: but he made such a pretense that he was just feeling a bit off-color that I kept telling him to get some proper sleep before he ended up being on sick leave for a couple of weeks.

Father Gabriel´s sad and untimely departure made the fact that I was destined to spend the entire War stuck like a prisoner in the cellar of a monastery all the more terrible. I know that I should be eternally grateful to its rather aloof Abbot for at least having had the heart to continue Father Gabriel´s wish that I remain a refuge from the Nazis in the Kloster but the fact was that I would one day look as if I had completely chickened out of the War. The irony was, of course, that I had probably been one of the first of the Resistance to actually kill a Nazi – and eight of them at that.

It was also Resistance agents who would later go onto helping the American forces considerably shorten the so-called "War of the Alpine Rebound". They would relay crucial intelligence to these forces so that they could bomb strategic targets instead of blowing everything up willy-nilly (as the British liked to do at night). The Tyrolean Resistance movement was particularly strong, no doubt because of the deep roots of Catholicism in Tyrolean culture and thinking.

It wasn´t until the 1970s that I also heard of "Operation Greenup": one of the most sensational and successful operations in the late War.

29: The Edelweiss Blooms Again

Its key players were Fred Mayer, Hans Wijnberg and Franz Weber. Mayer and Wijnberg were both Jews who had fled Germany and the Netherlands as teenagers just before the War, before becoming American citizens and joining the U.S. army. Franz Weber was an Austrian who had deserted the Germany Army after he became disgusted by the increasing war atrocities of the Nazis.

They were recruited for American spy work because of their German language and sheer nerves and, in February, 1945, all three of them were flown over the Stubai Glacier near where I had grown up, before parachuting onto its ridge. They then made their way down to the valley of Innsbruck. Weber was a Tyrolean who came from the nearby village of Oberperfuss, where his girlfriend´s family were involved with the Resistance.

As such, Wijnberg was able to quietly sit with a radio in seclusion whilst relaying messages to American intelligence that he had got through a complex network of Resistance agents. The messages came from Mayer, who was using his uncanny ability to get unwary officers, simple soldiers and staff to casually talk to him and unwittingly reveal war secrets, in much the same way that I had quietly listened to the Nazis whilst I had been working at the Berghof all those years ago.

Yet Mayer didn't stop there. He had no problem in dressing up and changing his identity, such as when he pretended to be a French electrician so that he could case an entire underground Messerschmidt factory. With his skills and daring, he was able to tell the Americans exactly what to hit and when, which was especially useful regarding the railways. Mayer's biggest coup was undoubtedly when he discovered that twenty-six different goods trains, each made up of between thirty and forty cars, would be running up the Brenner Pass one night.

Unfortunately, after three months, Mayer was finally captured and tortured in the Herrengasse much the same way that I had been by the two bullies in Castle Jitter. His life was no doubt saved when another American spy claimed that Mayer was a super-spy and that only the highest authority had the right to interrogate him. In typically bizarre and grotesque fashion, Mayer was then sent to Franz Hofer's villa to dine with him and other fine guests, even though Mayer had just been thoroughly beaten up black and blue and should have been in hospital.

I could, of course, not help envying them. It was Max, Dani and I who should come have down that glacier, with Dani as our radio operator. However, whilst Max could have been our contacts man I found it difficult imagining myself as the ultimate hero, Fred Mayer, who had simply over-flowed with sheer audacity and chutzpah. He had not only seized with both hands the fake claim that he was some kind of super-spy but even had the gall to make out that he was a lieutenant, whereas he was just a sergeant. Being an officer meant that he would have the authority to negotiate Franz Hofer´s surrender of Innsbruck to the Americans after first persuading the vicious Gauleiter to declare it an "open city".

It was a stroke of genius because it therefore meant that Innsbruck became the only city in the entire German Reich to surrender without a single fight – and all because Franz Hofer fell hook, line and sinker for Mayer´s B.S. that he was some kind of bigwig who could guarantee that nothing would happen to him afterwards. Of course this wasn´t the case.

Hofer was arrested three days after the capitulation and put in an internment camp. However, he managed to escape (as he had before in 1933) in 1948 to Germany. A year later the Germans sentenced him to three and a half years in a labor camp whilst he remained an unrepentant Nazi.

This was infinitely better for him than the sentence that a People´s Court in Innsbruck passed in his absence at the same time: namely, that he should be executed for all the grief that he had caused. Hofer then continued living in West Germany whilst working in his original trade as a salesman. He finally died of natural causes in 1975, aged 72, just one year before the second Winter Olympics of Innsbruck.

In the meantime, I only wish I knew what had happened to Slimey Stefan. The only thing that I knew about him is that he had disappeared from the Berghof at some point during the War and never returned.

As to myself, I moved out of the Kloster basement as soon as the Surrender was announced. I cannot, of course, begin to describe the sudden exhilaration of Freedom that I now felt as I walked out of the Kloster and into the village around it for the first time, even though I was now walking on pin-legs and would never be able to climb the mountains all around me.

I took a room in a small guest-house next to the Kloster and which was also run by the Order. I also continued to teach the monks at the monastery for another two years whilst studying for some proper pedagogic exams so that I could teach at secondary school level. I then had the luck to be offered such a teaching job in the village of Ehrwald, which is just under the Zugspitz mountain on the border with Germany.

It was there that I met my later wife, a local hotel accountant called Elsa, with whom we had a child whom she let me call Max. I remembered what Father Gabriel had told me about letting people discover their own choices in life but little Max turned out to be just like his name-sake, becoming both a ski instructor and a mountain guide when he eventually grew up.

As to myself, I had come to accept that I could never be like my dear mountain man Uncle Max or even young Max again. However, I also remembered what one old man had once told me when I met him sitting on a bench below the Kricklhorn whilst enjoying the panorama of Gletschberg spread out below us: "Young man: these tired, old eyes of mine see more of this valley in five minutes than most people see in eight hours of hiking."

Occasionally, we would make a long family trip with the car all the way to Innsbruck and then up the Brenner Pass to Gletschberg: mainly so that we could visit my family's grave there. I had been visiting the graveyard occasionally ever since the War had ended. In fact, getting on the train at Sachs before changing trains in Innsbruck for Gletschberg had been one of the very first things I had done after the Surrender.

To my surprise I discovered on this first visit that Father Gabriel had also been buried in Gletschberg's cemetery. What's more, even though his grave was now three years old and its headstone already two, it was still decked from top to bottom with fresh, bright flowers. I therefore had no doubt that the faithful of the village put in a tidy fortune to have that grave kept spic and span for their popular priest, even though he had only served them for the four years from 1938 to 1942.

It was an even greater surprise to me when I discovered that my family's grave now had a headstone on it and was also decorated with flowers. When Maria became the first to be buried there in 1938, it was just an empty plot in a far corner of the cemetery that Papa had reserved for what he had thought would be the far, far future. Just two weeks later, Papa would be buried there as well.

I had forgotten to mention earlier that the ever conscientious Father Gabriel managed to get some local climbers to search for Uncle Max's body in the mountains during the summer of 1940. Max's body was then duly brought back to Gletschberg, where it was supposed to be quietly buried. As things turned out, however, almost half the village attended Max's funeral.

When Father Gabriel told me about this I thought Herr Zeller and the Gestapo would kick up a stink about how he had managed to obtain the body. Father Gabriel, however, replied with much amusement that they hadn't dared to say anything in case they might look foolish. After all, Max had pulled a fast one by stealing Franz Hofer's private plane right in front of his nose!

Two years later Father Gabriel also told me all about his fight with the Hall clinic of Death in getting my baby brother's euthanized body back from it. He ultimately triumphed, saving it from an ignominious burial in the clinic's back garden without even any kind of marker.

However, whilst Father Gabriel had told me all this he never mentioned the gravestone, which I now assumed he must have also arranged for us. As such, I had instead expected to see four wooden crosses on the grave, as are used whilst the grave is still settling in its first year.

My heart, however, nearly broke open when I finally read the four names of my family upon the grave, as if a catatonic bell were telling me that they really were all dead:

JOSEF RUDOLF LEOPOLD SCHILLING 1895-1938

MAXIMILIAN FRANZ SCHILLING 1900-1938

MARIA THERESA SCHILLING 1923-1938

PETER LEOPOLD SCHILLING 1924-1942

Whilst it was also a surprise to see that someone else in the village still cared sufficiently about at least one of us to have laid flowers on the grave as I now did, I wasn´t in any mood for telling anyone in the village – let alone the entire village – that I was back in town, even if it were for just for the afternoon.

Simply put, I still had so many traumatic memories of my last half year in the village that, apart from the churchyard, I wanted to avoid it like the plague. I was therefore also glad that no one recognized me since I now had a completely different walking gait because of my tin legs, as well as having meanwhile grown a modest moustache and also wearing bookish glasses.

Over the years, however, I would come to see more and more of Gletschberg on what gradually became almost annual events, especially when young Max started growing up. At the same time, Gletschberg would almost completely change so that it was only a few of the original houses in the center that still stood as much as they had used to, instead of being renovated or completely re-built, as was the case with just about every other building. The Berghof would also eventually be completely pulled down and replaced by a large sport and tourist complex around the miniature lake, with one guy even selling Gluehwein as Mama and I had once done.

However, there were two places that I never dared to visit again. One was where our chalet had once stood and Maria had so grotesquely died. I have no doubt that another more jolly chalet with proper stone walls was later built where ours had been and that other children were already playing where we Schilling kids had once played: but the thought of seeing it for real always filled me with dread.

The other place was the Retreat, which would have flooded me with painful memories of Max and Dani if I had ever dared to have even approach it again, let alone tried to get inside. No doubt you will be saying that I couldn´t have gone there even if I had wanted to because of my phony legs. As it turned out, a long chair-lift has was later built up the Messner Valley, which apparently made a great red ski-run – and I have a sneaky feeling that its middle station is about where our Retreat lies hidden. However, I still have my iron key, which I shall leave for my son Max in my Will, along with a covering letter and this manuscript, for when I die.

In the meantime, there was another reason for my visiting my family´s grave every so regularly. It began during the autumn after my first visit to Gletschberg immediately after the War. I got a telephone call from the Mother Superior of the Nun´s Kloster in which she announced that I had a very, very special visitor and that she was waiting for me in the congress hall in the mixed reception building of the Doppel Kloster.

When I hobbled into the darkened room where my unexpected visitor was standing all alone I didn´t recognize her, for she looked old and frail as if she could have been my grandmother. But then she said just one word to me whilst I saw her eyes suddenly light up like diamonds:

"Edelweiss!"

"Mama!" was the very next thing that I suddenly cried, whilst I strained on my tin legs to rush towards my poor, frail mother before wrapping my arms tenderly around her. "Mama."

It was all so surreal that I thought that I was now having a wonderful dream and that it would shatter if I said anything else. Yet here she was. In Reality she would now be forty-five years old but the torture and cruelties that she had endured through those seven wicked years of man-made Hell had made her age another thirty years. Yet in spite of the fact that her face was long and thin and tired, as was the rest of her now withered and scrawny skeleton-like body, there was still the same old sparkle of life in her eyes that I had seen every day for the first sixteen years of my life.

"It was only the memory of you and the hope that you might still be alive that kept me going these last few months," Mama finally told me.

Mama would later also tell me how the first thing that she had done that spring when she was finally released from her concentration camp was to go straight back home to Gletschberg and look up her family. You can therefore imagine her horror of horrors when she found that our chalet had long been burned to the ground and was now just an open field. Fortunately one of the neighbors saw her sitting on the charcoaled rubble of what had once been her animal farm, crying in the rain, and took her in.

Naturally, they eventually had to tell her the story of how Papa had died because he refused to divorce her and how Pete was later euthanized. They also told her about Max and that here had been a lot of relief amongst many of the villagers, including a sense of victory against the injustice of what had quickly turned out to be mere tyrants, when it was discovered that Max had not been burned alive in the chalet after all but had actually escaped in Franz Hofer´s very own plane, along with myself.

On the other hand, Father Gabriel´s returning Max´s body to Gletschberg for burial a couple of years later put a dampener on the spirits of the village faithful. Whilst the good father admitted to our plane having crashed in the mountains whilst killing Max outright, he remained totally silent about what might have happened to me, whilst then also taking my little "secret" about living in the monastery to the grave with him.

Had he known that Mama might still be alive and not believed what I thought myself to be true, he might have left a message for her, as I too would have done. Indeed, it was only now that I suddenly realized that Slimey must have heard me talking in my sleep in Castle Jitter – as Dani had already told me I did – and so gaslighted me into believing that my nightmare of my Mama being machine-gunned down were really true.

Without any such leads, Mama went to Reichenau in Innsbruck to visit the **Displaced Persons Camp**. When she pulled a blank there she began having wild hopes that I might have even managed to get to America before the War had broken out and that one day – one wonderful day – a letter might arrive at the church for Father Gabriel. She therefore told the young and kind new replacement priest her story. However, as the weeks passed by and turned into months she became less and less hopeful: for even a letter from America to the newly liberated Austria didn´t take that long to arrive.

Finally, however, as she was waking up one morning with the early sun tenderly stroking her face, Mama suddenly had a flash of inspiration.

"Why not," she asked herself, "visit the indefatigable Mother Superior of the Nuns' Kloster in Sachs and ask her?" After all, the Mother Superior seemed to have a knack for pulling miracles out of her habit.

Mother Superior was of course able to tell my Mama the good news that I was still alive but the bad news that I now had tin legs. She also warned Mama that I might not recognize her after all that she had suffered in the concentration camp: something that fortunately soon proved to be unnecessary.

I decided to later tell her that Seppi had died a hero's death whilst fighting on the Russian Front, although I'm not sure that she was so impressed when I also told her how – and that he had done it because he wanted to be like Papa.

Meanwhile, in spite of her concentration camp injuries Mama managed to live for another ten years whilst later coming to live with me and Elsa in Ehrwald. In fact, she fell in love with Elsa's natural empathy and perkiness as much as I did.

Mama then died peacefully in her sleep early in the night of the Twenty-fifth of October, 1955, aged only fifty-five. The very next day the Second Republic of Austria officially became a **sovereign state** again, this time a neutral one like Switzerland.

Mama had always called Austria her Edelweiss Republic, even during the Anschluss of 1938, just as she had always called me her "Edelweiss" because, as a kid, I had always been bringing her Edelweiss from high up in the mountains.

THE END

Timeline of National Events

May 20th, 1932: Engelbert Dollfuss becomes Chancellor of Austria

January 30th, 1933: Hitler becomes Chancellor of Germany

March 7th, 1933: Engelbert Dollfuss claims that the Nationalrat had "self-eliminated" itself and uses an emergency decree to make himself de facto fascist dictator of Austria

March 31st, 1933: Dollfuss bans the "Republican Schutzbund" (the paramilitary wing of the Social Democrats)

May 20th, 1933: Dollfuss founds the Fatherland Front, which will gradually absorb the Landbund (Rural Union) as well as various right-wing "Heimwehr" paramilitary forces, whilst also strongly supporting the Catholic Church

May 26th, 1933: Dollfuss bans the Communists in Austria

June 19th, 1933: Dollfuss bans the Nazis in Austria

July 1st, 1933: Beginning of Hitler´s "1000 Mark Barrier"

October 3rd, 1933: first assassination attempt on Dollfuss´ life by a Nazi. Dollfuss then declares martial law and re-introduces capital punishment

February 12th-15th, 1934: "Civil War" with the fascist "Fatherland Front" government fighting with the Social Democrats, who are now also banned

May 1st, 1934: beginning of Dollfuss´ new "May" Constitution

July 25th, 1934: second but this time successful attempt by the Nazis to assassinate Dollfuss as part of an unsuccessful "July Coup" to topple the government

July 29th, 1934: Kurt Schuschnigg becomes Chancellor of Austria in a continuation of the "Fatherland Front" fascist dictatorship

August 1st-16th, 1936: Eleventh Summer Olympics in Berlin

August 31st, 1936: the "1000 Mark Barrier" comes to an end

February 12th, 1938: Berchtesgaden Agreement in which Schuschnigg submits to many of Hitler´s demands for allowing more Nazi influence in the Austrian government

Wednesday, March 9th, 1938: Schuschnigg announces referendum to decide on an Anschluss with Germany for the following Sunday the 13th.

Friday, March 11th, 1938: De facto Nazi coup of Austria throughout all the cities and many of the towns and villages

Saturday, March 12th, 1938: De facto invasion of Austria by the German Army even though there is no resistance and many Austrians actively support it

Sunday, April 10th, 1938: mock referendum for the Anschluss organized by the Nazis themselves whilst already being in power

May, 1938: the Nuremberg Race Laws are extended to Austria

May 24th, 1938: Franz Hofer officially becomes Gauleiter of Tyrol and Vorarlberg

Wednesday, November 9th, 1938: a pre-organized Pogrom or "Crystal Night" of rioting, destruction, murder, beatings and plundering against entire Jewish communities throughout the entire German Reich (including Austria) is carried out by the Nazis. The pretext that they give for this is that a German diplomat in Paris, vom Rath, was assassinated in Paris by a Jew just two days before.

September 3rd, 1939: Britain and France declare war on Britain so that the Second World War now begins

June 22nd, 1941: beginning of Germany´s invasion of Russia

December 7th, 1941: Japans attacks the U.S. naval base at Pearl Harbor so that the U.S.A. declares war on Japan the following day

December 11th, 1941: Hitler declares war on the U.S.A.

February to April, 1945: Operation Green-up in the Tyrol

April 27th, 1945: the Austrian Second Republic is declared, although it is not until the autumn that the western allies formally recognize it

May 3rd, 1945: Franz Hofer surrenders Innsbruck as a "free city" to the Americans after negotiations initiated through the U.S.-German spy Fred Mayer

May 4th, 7th and 8th, 1945: Germany surrenders unconditionally to the Allies in three separate "instruments"

May 15th, 1955: the Austrian State Treaty is signed by Austria after being occupied by the Allied forces for ten years. In return for the Allied forces leaving that October Austria will then become "permanently neutral"

October 25th, 1955: the last of the Allied forces leaves Austria

October 26th, 1955: the Austrian Second Republic is now a sovereign state in accordance with the Austrian State Treaty of the previous May and which demands that Austria remains "permanently neutral"

Glossary with Editorial Notes

The **380 Mercedes-Benz Cabriolet "A"** was a brand-new model of car when the Kratzkopfs drove it in April, 1933, having just been first produced a couple of months before, although it would already cease production the following year. It came on the market as a four-door limousine and as a touring wagon, as well as a two-door sport roadster and three types of cabriolet, with a total of 150 such cars being built.

All Saints´ Day is a Catholic religious holiday on the first day of November and in which the faithful are obliged to attend mass and then the graves of their deceased relatives. Some Protestant dominions also observe this practice whilst others simply regard it as a day for commemorating all Christians, as well as all the saints. The Orthodox Church commemorates All Saints´ Day on the first Sunday after Whit Sunday.

The planned **Autobahn along the Brenner Pass** was never begun by the Nazis because of the intervention of the Second World War. Because of the exorbitant costs involved it was not until the 1960s that its building began and not until 1971 that it was fully opened. Over two million lorry crossings are estimated to be made every year.

Reaching 620 feet above the valley floor the "Europa Bridge" is its highest bridge whilst having a length of 2,500 feet. The bridge also offers the fifth highest bungee jump in the world.

Meanwhile, the railway line along the pass from Innsbruck in the North Tyrol to Bolzano in the **South Tyrol** had already been completed in 1867 after three years of construction.

Berghof as a holiday home: Only two years later Adolf Hitler would begin refurbishing and extending his own holiday home in Berchtesgaden in the Bavarian Alps (on the western side of the mountain border from Austria's Salzburg) whilst also re-naming it the "Berghof", which is a popular chalet and hotel name. However, although "Berghof" literally translates as "Mountain Court", a "hof" or "court" is not necessarily a royal palace but can also be a small yard.

Hitler's Berghof not only became both his holiday headquarters and guest-house to top-ranking Nazis and their families but was also visited by national leaders and diplomats, including Neville Chamberlain and Mussolini. Likewise, other leading party members also began purchasing chalets around the village.

Indeed, the Nazis systematically took over the village, pressurizing unwilling locals to sell their land to them whenever they wanted. They then built a surrogate municipality of national government offices and amenities, as well as defensive military barracks and an underground labyrinth of service tunnels.

the **cappello romano** (Italian for "roman hat") used to be the typical outdoor hat of Catholic priests when not performing services. Although Erich Schilling doesn't say so, Father Murrsea and Father Gabriel would have most likely also worn cassocks during the 1930s. Just as "roman hats" are less common today, priests often wear black shirts with a tab collar and black trousers instead of a cassock today.

The "roman hat" is also sometimes called a "Saturn" because its wide brim and rounded crown are similar in shape to the planet of that name.

chamois are small mountain antelopes that are native to the Alps, the Balkans and the Turkish and Caucasus mountains. Both the males and females have small horns.

The **Christkind** was "invented" by Martin Luther of the Reformation in the sixteenth century because he didn't like the tradition of an old man (ie. Saint Nicholas) bringing gifts to the children. Martin Luther intended that the Christkind be a baby-like incarnation of Jesus but it later morphed into an angel-like child.

Ironically, the Christkind didn't catch on with the Protestants but with the Catholics, with it secretly bringing gifts to the children on Christmas Eve in

Catholic countries. The Catholics also hung onto their Saint Nicholas tradition of his also bringing presents directly to the children on his Saint´s Day, which is the Sixth of December, with the Christkind often accompanying him on these visits.

After the Saint Nicholas tradition had survived with some of the Protestants, especially in the Netherlands, he made a major come-back when he was re-generated as the non-religious Santa Claus in America. (see also the **"Christmas Man"**)

The **"Christmas Man"** or "Weihnachtsman" is the German name for the Santa Claus tradition which is today also kept in many parts of northern, Protestant Germany. The idea of Santa Claus being an elf who jumps down chimneys was first inspired by New York Dutch colonists based on their own version of St Nicholas or "Sinter Klaas" from the Netherlands. He is also known as "Father Christmas" in Britain. (see also **Christkind**)

the **Citroen Traction Avant** was a range of saloon and executive cars built by the French company between 1934 and 1956. Its saloon car was a particular favorite with the Gestapo, and is therefore often seen in vintage and historic movies featuring them.

Civil War: this occurred between the 12th and the 15th of February of 1934 when government forces demanded the right to search a Social

Democrat building in Vienna for concealed weapons. The paramilitary wing of the Social Democrats, the Republican Schutzbund, had already been banned by **Dollfuss** a year before in March. When their now illegal members began defending the building, Dollfuss then banned the entire party of Social Democrats.

The fighting against government forces quickly spread to other cities and industrial centers so that it became known as the "Civil War" of Austria. Supported by the federal army, the government was able to defeat the Social Democrats after four days of fighting, with 350 people dying because of it.

code name for Austria, which is Oh-Five: Austria is called "Österreich" in German, with its first letter being an "ö". This is pronounced as a flat "o-eah" as if one doesn´t like something, instead of as a joyous "oh!" as in the much simpler "o".

Since "ö" can also be written as "oe", "Österreich" can also be written as "Oesterreich". Instead of simply using the first two letters "Oe" as an abbreviation of "Oesterreich", the Resistance cryptically wrote the "e" as "5" because it is the fifth letter of the alphabet: hence "O5". Erich Schilling, however, writes "O5" as "Oh-Five" in order to make the pronunciation more recognizable during reading.

Confirmation or "chrismation" is a **sacrament** that follows baptism. In the Catholic and Protestant churches this is usually done in groups when the children are old enough to make decisions for themselves, which is often when they are fourteen. In the eastern Orthodox churches, people are confirmed at the same time that they are baptized, such as when they are still babies.

Czech hedgehogs are large three-dimensional metal crosses that serve as effective barriers against all except the largest tanks, as well as all other vehicles and even infantry. They were invented by the Czechs to re-inforce their borders during the mid-1930s – hence the name – although the first versions were made of concrete, which can easily be shot apart with machine-gun fire. They are often featured in war movies, especially when sea defenses are shown.

desert rats: the Nazis are supposed to have got their brown uniforms when they were looking for surplus uniforms to dress their paramilitary wing, the S.A., with and stumbled across a depot of unused brown desert outfits, thus giving them the appearance of being desert soldiers. As a result of this the Nazis came to be known as the "Brown Party".

Displaced Persons Camp: a displaced person is a person who has been forced to leave their home, be it in their own country or as refugees. Camps were therefore established immediately after the

Second World War for previous inmates of Nazi concentration and extermination camps and other refugees, many of who came from Eastern Europe. By 1947 there were nearly a million people living in such camps.

Engelbert **Dollfuss** was born in 1892 and made his way into politics whilst administrating for farmers and agriculture. He was chosen in May, 1932 to be Chancellor of Austria by the then president in a coalition government that included the Christian Socialists.

The **Edelweiss** is a rare white flower that grows at altitudes between six and eleven thousand feet in the Alps, the Italian Apennines and the Pyrenees. Its name is German for "fine white" or "noble white" and it has become the national flower of several European countries, as well as a symbol of many alpine clubs, mountain corps and numerous other bodies.

Fasching is the Carnival period immediately before Ash Wednesday, which is the first day of Lent. Whilst Lent is a religious period of solemnity, fasting and abstinence, Fasching (Carnival) is a folk holiday that is marked by partying, organized games and shows, masquerading with carved wooden masks or wearing fancy dress, playing the fool and eating pancakes or doughnuts.

Festive activities often occur during the four days before Ash Wednesday, although the main celebrations are either on the "Rose Monday" or "Shrove Tuesday". Whilst Fasching (Carnival) is very much an annual highlight like Christmas and Easter in Europe, with many people getting dressed up for it, even if it is only for work, it tends to be only sporadically celebrated in Britain and America.

The **Fatherland Front** was founded by Engelbert **Dollfuss** in May, 1933. It was essentially a new version of the Christian Socialist party and would gradually also absorb the Landbund (Rural Union) and various right-wing "Heimwehr" paramilitary forces, as well as being a strong supporter of the Catholic Church.

It claimed to represent all the "People" of Austria and, within a year, had become the only legal major party of a de facto dictatorship. Although the Fatherland Front was a fascist party based on Mussolini's Italian model, it did not propagate racial ideologies.

"Feierabend" literally means "Celebration Eve" in English and was originally used to denote the end of a work-day before a Festival Day when the first drinks were already poured out. In time it became such a much-loved expression for finishing work on any day that it is now universally used as a standard word by virtually everyone in Germany, Austria and even Switzerland.

Although most people do not regularly finish their working day with an alcoholic beverage, a "Feierabend Bier" is particularly common with heavy manual laborers and chefs, with some firms and hotels even offering them a free daily beer after work.

the **First of May** was first commemorated as a "Day of Work" with demonstrations for workers´ rights by the Australians in 1856. In commemoration of the first day of a General Strike in the U.S.A. in 1886, many socialist groups and particularly the International Workers´ Congress also chose to hold further demonstrations for workers´ rights on the First of May of each year. Whilst this soon became known as International Workers´ Day in many countries, in the U.S.A. it became known as Labor Day and is instead held on the first Monday of each September.

"May Day", as it is also commonly known as, has meanwhile become a public holiday in many countries in tribute to workers and their rights. The Fatherland Front, however, instead tried to turn the First of May into a celebration of their new Constitution of 1934, whilst the Nazis tried to Germanize it as the "Day of National Work".

May Day is also traditionally a folk festival to celebrate the arrival of Spring, with flowers, dancing around a maypole and the coronation of a "May Queen" being almost universal practices in villages in many countries. In nineteenth century

Tyrol they also used to scare off witches and other evil spirits by making as much noise as they could by ringing bells and banging pots and anything else that clanged, as well as with the leaves of divine herbs.

The **Fokker-Leimberger machine-gun** was designed in Germany in 1916. It was a twelve barrel rotary machine-gun that could be set up on a tripod or other pivot and reached a speed of up to 7,000 r.p.m.

Gauleiter: the Nazis very efficiently re-organized the administration of Germany, with its system of federal states being instead replaced by "Gaus" or counties, each with its own "Gauleiter" at the top and directly answerable to Hitler. After the Anschluss of 1938, Austria was similarly organized as an extension of Germany. The two states of (North) Tyrol and Vorarlberg were joined together as one Gau with Franz Hofer in charge, whilst East Tyrol was now made a part of Kaernten (Carinthia) instead of (North) Tyrol.

A **Gemeinde** is a local borough. Many rural Gemeinde are centered around a village or market town whilst sometimes encompassing huge areas, such as entire valleys and even mountains.

the **Gemeinderat** is the borough council, with the suffix "rat" meaning "advice". A Gemeinderat may instead be called a Gemeindetag, with the suffix "tag" meaning "day" as in a day´s meeting.

The **German Reich** was proclaimed in 1871 after Prussia had won the Franco-Prussian war the previous year and its chancellor Otto von Bismarck had managed to persuade other German kingdoms to unite as a proper federation, with the Prussian king as their emperor or Kaiser.

Although Germany lost the First World War and subsequently became a republic whilst being unofficially known as the "Weimar Republic", the state of Germany continued to be officially called the "German Reich". This continued under Nazi dictatorship, with the country´s name being partly-officially changed to the "Greater Germanic Reich" as new territories were annexed. The German Reich juristically ceased to be on June the Fifth, 1945.

The Nazis helped coin the phrase "Third Reich" for their era of government, with the "Second Reich" being regarded as the Imperial Reich of the German Kaisership between 1871 and 1918. The original empire of Charlemagne in the eighth and ninth centuries was regarded as the "First Reich". This would then develop into the loose confederation of mainly German kingdoms and territories that were later called the "Holy Roman Empire" and which lasted right through until 1806, when Napoleon officially dissolved it.

As a result, calls for a united Germany grew in the nineteenth century whilst Austria meanwhile now had its own Austrian Empire of multi-national territories. When Austria lost this Empire by losing the First World War and instead became a republic like Germany, the calls for annexation or "Anschluss" to Germany increased. However, whilst these calls further increased in various quarters when Hitler came to power in 1933, it also decreased in other quarters, as the Nazis both excited many Austrian voters whilst repelling others. Austria´s chancellor of the time, Engelbert **Dollfuss**, only favoured annexation to a non-Nazi Germany.

Gluehwein is a punch-like hot winter´s drink made from red wine and spices and is served at Christkindl markets throughout Germany and Austria and many other European countries during the Advent period. Its name literally means "glow wine": probably because it used to be kept warm over the glowing embers of fires.

the **golden eagle** is native to Europe, Asia and North America. Whilst they are most famous for living in mountains and nesting in cliffs with literally a "bird´s eye" view of their hunting territory, they also live in forests and on desolate lowlands. They may nest in any high place, including man-made structures, such as windmills and observation towers. Those that live in the mountains usually nest around the so-called "tree line" where trees stop growing. The German name for the golden eagle is "Steinadler" or "stone eagle".

The **Great War** was the name given to the First World War before the Second World War began. Since Erich Schilling is writing about this period between the two wars he uses the name that he would have heard at that time.

The **guillotine** was used in a number of German states after the French Revolution and was one of the three forms of capital punishment during the German Reich – the other two being beheading by axe and a firing squad. The Nazis primarily used the guillotine, as well as hanging and the firing squad. Most of the 16,500 guillotine executions that were performed occurred during the last two years of the War. Additionally, the Nazis are estimated to have carried out as many as 400,000 unofficial executions during the War.
Although the Allies continued to execute war criminals until 1951, the newly formed Federal Republic of Germany immediately abolished capital punishment in 1949. Some historians have since claimed that this was so that ex-Nazis could not be executed. The communist-controlled German Democratic Republic didn´t abolish capital punishment until 1987, whilst using the guillotine and shooting as its methods of execution. Most of their executions, however, occurred in the 1950s.

The Austrians abolished capital punishment in 1918 but the Fatherland Front re-introduced it in 1933, with a total of 45 people being hanged between 1934 and 1938. This included 10 Socialists and 15 Nazis (including four assassins) for political terrorism, 19 civil murderers and one arsonist. Hanging was replaced by the guillotine during the Nazi era. Capital punishment for murder was abolished in Austria in 1950 and completely abolished in 1968. However, the Allies continued to hang war criminals in Austria into the early 1950s.

The French held its last public guillotining in 1939 and abolished capital punishment altogether in 1981, with the last two executions occurring in 1977.

steep hanging Messner Valley: a hanging valley is a side valley that drops into a lower main valley, having been formed by a tributary glacier feeding into a main glacier. Whilst some hanging valleys gradually drop all the way into the main valley, as is the case with the Messner Valley and the Watzkessel meadows below it, other hanging valleys end with steep, cliff-like drops into the main valley. These would have been caused when the tributary glacier melted before the main glacier.

William **Heath Robinson** (1872-1944) was a British illustrator and cartoonist who produced hilarious books of full-page cartoons of highly-complicated contraptions that people had invented for the most menial tasks. They were basically a parody of a world gone mad with the "need for progress".

Reinhard **Heydrich** (1904-42) was a young, high-ranking Nazi security officer whose many posts included being deputy leader of the **S.S.** under Heinrich Himmler. He was renowned for being one of the most ruthless of the Nazis, with even Adolf Hitler calling him "The Man with an Iron Heart".

It was in his capacity as Deputy Protector of Bohemia and Moravia (today´s Czech Republic) that Heydrich was assassinated at the end of May, 1942 by the Czech Resistance and with the support and training of the Special Operations Executive of the British Secret Service.

This was made easier in that Heydrich was so confident that he had scared all the Czechs into submission that he used to ride to work in an opened convertible and without an escort. An assassin tried to shoot him down with a sub-machine gun but, when the gun jammed, a second assassin threw a tank grenade at Heydrich´s car.

Heydrich received severe multiple wounds in his abdomen and spent a week in agony before dying in June. The Nazis were meanwhile able to trace the conspirators to a church and shoot them down. The Nazi reprisals were extreme: with the village of Lidice (population 500) being razed to the ground and almost all of its men and older boys being shot, whilst everyone else was sent to the concentration and extermination camps.

All 33 adults of the smaller village of Lezacky were also shot, with eleven of their thirteen children being sent to an extermination camp and the remaining two being adopted for Germanization.

Another 13,000 Czechs were also arrested and up to 5,000 of them executed. A number of films have been made of the assassination but the violence in them is too graphic for most people to want to watch.

H.G. Wells: (1866-1946) was a prolific and highly popular writer of science-fiction, social drama and non-fiction. Whilst his novellas "The Time Machine", "The War of the Worlds" and "The Invisible Man" soon became iconic classics that were very relatable for the time, his dark cynicism about human nature and un-empathetic views have meant that his many other books have become outdated.

the **"Horst Wessel Lied"** ("Horst Wesel Song": otherwise known as "Die Fahne Hoch" or "Hoist the Flag") was written by Horst Wessel (a then twenty-one year old Storm Leader in the S.A.) for the Nazis in 1929. After the murder of Horst Wessel a year later by two communists it was then chosen as the Nazi Anthem. It also became the second national anthem of Germany after the "Deutschlandlied" when the Nazis came to power in

1933. Although the Nazis claimed that Horst Wessel had also composed the music, it was clearly based on a troops´ marching song from the First World War.

Hubschrauber: pronounced "hoob-schrauber" and literally meaning "hub-screws", this is the German name for "helicopter". The first practical rotor-craft were developed in the 1920s but the Focke-Wulf Fw 61 was the first helicopter to be successfully commercialized.

Developed by the German airplane designer Heinrich Focke in 1936, it looked like an ordinary plane that had had each wing replaced with a diagonal shaft with a set of rotary blades at the end. It could reach an altitude of 11,000 feet, had a range of 140 miles and a speed of 77 m.p.h. The Flettner Fl 282 Kolibri and the Focke-Achgelis Fa 223 Drache were then introduced in 1940 and 1941 respectively and looked much more like helicopters.

Although helicopters were useful to the Germans during the Second World War for observation and transportation, the Allies managed to bomb their production before they managed to play a significant part in the War. The Americans meanwhile developed the Sikorsky R4 in the early 1940s and this soon became the world´s first large-scale mass-produced helicopter.

"Hunter´s Tea" (German: "Jaegertee") is a spiced hot drink that is made with black tea and rum and which is often served as an alternative to **Gluehwein**. It was originally popular with hunters and foresters throughout the Austrian Empire in the nineteenth century.

ibex mountain goat: ibex goats are native to Europe, Asia and Africa, with this particular sort being the alpine ibex. The curved and ridged horns of the males are so large that they reach half way across their backs. The German for ibex is "Steinbock" or "stone ram".

ice slowly moved forward: little did Erich Schilling know that glaciers would begin melting with "global warming" towards the end of the century. As such, the bodies of many lost climbers and tourists have since been found on the edges of glaciers this century as they continue to retreat.

in-built ceramic bench: in many small and modest-sized houses the oven and stove also served as the main source of heating instead of an open fire-hearth. Consequently, the kitchen was often part of a larger room that was also used as a dining- and living-room. Some ovens were also covered with decorative ceramic tiles, with some of these also having an in-built bench on the side for sitting on and staying especially warm.

Iron Rations or "Halbesierne" were 300 gram cans of dried beef that were issued to German troops during especially the First World War. Being dried, the meat could last for several weeks and were therefore used as emergency rations. The Allies also had their own versions of Iron Rations.

Kaiser (Emperor) **Franz-Josef** (1830-1916) became the Emperor of Austria and the King of Hungary in 1848 when he was just eighteen after a revolution had forced his epileptic uncle to abdicate. Following pressure for more autonomy from the Hungarians, the "Austrian Empire" was later re-formed as "Austria-Hungary" in 1867, before it collapsed in 1918 as a result of Austria losing the First World War.

At this time, Franz-Josef´s nephew Karl was the "dual monarch" of the two joint countries, with Franz-Josef having died in 1916 at the then grand age of eighty-six. Austria and Hungary then became two separate republics whilst the rest of the Empire became parts of other countries.

The Austrian-Hungarian monarchy was also officially known as the "Kaiser and King" monarchy, so that this period of history has since come to be nostalgically remembered by this name in a similar way to the Victorian Age of Britain.

Kirchtag is a religious holiday that falls on either the third or fourth Sunday of October whilst also being a traditional folk festival. In north-west Germany it is also known as "Kirmes". Kirchtag unofficially marks the end of the summer season in alpine tourism, with hotels often remaining closed for nearly two months as they then open again just before Christmas to begin the winter season.

A **Kloster** can either be a monastery or a nunnery. A Doppelkloster is a twinned monastery and nunnery that share certain facilities while remaining otherwise separate in their functions, although they are often physically proximate to each other. A religious Order may have charitable institutions (such as a school and a hospital) that are attached to a Kloster without actually being part of it.

Krampus and the Perchten during Advent: the Krampus is a mischievous demon who appears on the night of the Fifth of December: that is, on the eve of Saint Nicholas´ Saint´s Day. The Krampus often carries a birch rod for hitting the children (or adults) who have misbehaved. Some villages have "Krampus runs" in which young men and boys who are dressed up as Krampuses basically run amok. This is similar to the much older Perchten tradition in which such groups of young men and boys dress up as wild animals with horns and claws and try to frighten everyone, including young children.

Numerous authorities and the Church tried to ban the Krampus and Perchten in both the nineteenth and early twentieth centuries. However, these traditions were difficult to keep in check in villages, especially as some of the villagers actually enjoyed and treasured them.

The Fatherland Front banned the Krampus for being un-Christian and the early coalition governments of Austria after the Second World War also had reservations about the practice. As such, especially in larger towns, the Krampus is sometimes accompanied by Saint Nicholas in order to make the tradition more respectful and less wild.

The **Lourdes pilgrim sanctum** is a holy grotto just outside the village of Lourdes in the French Pyrenees. It was here that the peasant girl Bernadette Soubirous claimed to have seen eighteen separate apparitions of the Virgin Mary in 1858. The grotto has since become a world-renowned shrine for pilgrimage whilst its waters are supposed to have healing properties.

The **Luger PO8** pistol was a self-automatic that was also known as the "Pistol Parabellum", which is Latin for "prepare for war". Designed by the Austrian Georg Luger in 1898 it soon became popular with the Imperial German Army, as well as many other armies around the world. Indeed, three million such pistols were produced in several countries and in several models between 1900 and the 1970s, including Germany up till 1953.

Luis Trenker was a highly successful producer, director and actor of some fifty so-called "Heimat" or "Homeland" movies between 1924 until 1982. Many of them were filmed in the Alps with spectacular photography of the mountains and winter sports, with his black-and-white movies of the 1930s being amongst his most iconic and popular.

Hitler was particularly fascinated by Trenker´s 1932 adventure drama "The Rebel", which had been inspired by the Tyrolean rebellions of 1809 against the French. Joseph Goebbels as Propaganda Minister was also particularly keen for Trenker to make Nazi-inspired movies. However, not only did Trenker want to stick to his own formulas but he also found all the rules that the Nazis imposed on movie-making to be artistically stifling. As such, Trenker was only able to make a couple of movies during the War years, although he was able to achieve a major come-back during the 1950s.

"mentally handicapped": taking that Erich Schilling most likely wrote this memoir in the late 1970s this would have been the correct expression for what is now often called "intellectually disabled".

The expression "mentally handicapped" was first used in the late nineteenth century for what had previously been scientifically classified as morons, imbeciles, idiots and cretins according to the degree of disability. The word "retarded" was also used for a while at the beginning of the twentieth century but as it quickly became a popular term of abuse it was soon discarded.

Mussolini´s fascism was based on the ideal of a corporate state where the various guilds, economic, scientific and cultural groups selected delegates to help run the national and local governments. Although this was essentially a one-party authoritarian dictatorship that was copied by **Dollfuss**, it was not as totalitarian as Hitler´s Nazi dictatorship, which attempted to control all walks of life with its ideologies. (see also **Staendestaat**)

Napoleon kept invading Austria: Max is clearly referring to the Napoleonic Wars here, with Austria having been a part of all but one of the Seven Coalitions against Napoleon between 1792 and 1815. Napoleon, however, only actually invaded Austria and its capital of Vienna twice – in 1805 and 1809 – before forcing treaties on its Kaiser.

Napoleon also had a separate army, supported by the Bavarians, successfully invade the Tyrol in 1805, so that Tyrol was occupied by these forces until 1814. The Tyroleans did, however, stage a series of mostly unsuccessful rebellions and battles during 1809. This uprising, however, has remained a central bulwark of the Tyrolean historic identity, rather like Britain´s "Finest Hour" of 1940 and the American War of Independence.

negroes would have been the accepted word used to describe "blacks" in the 1930s, not only in Austria and Germany but also America and Britain. It was still being used during the 1970s when Erich Schilling probably wrote this memoir, although the word "blacks" was rapidly replacing it as a result of the Black Power movement of the time.

"Blacks" had already been an alternate but lesser used word for negroes in America since the beginnings of its colonization. Today many American blacks prefer to call themselves "African Americans".

the **Northkette** is the chain of mountains to the immediate north of Innsbruck. Its colloquial German name is "Nordkette", which means "North Chain" in English, with both locals and tourists sometimes compounding the two languages to form "North Kette". Its proper name is the "Inntalkette", which means "Inn Valley Chain".

The Nordkette has several peaks, the highest of which is 8,650 feet, with Innsbruck having an elevation of 2,000 feet directly below it. A cable-car way reaches the Hafelekar peak at 7,500 feet, with a mid-station platform, the "Seegrube", at 6,250 feet. The cable-car way was first opened in 1928.

October that that Nazi assassin: this was Rudolf Dertill, a twenty-two year old who had joined the Nazi party a year before. He was given a five year prison sentence for attempted murder. It was because of this assassination attempt that **Dollfuss** re-introduced the death penalty.

one night: the news that Erich Schilling had heard was actually misleading because the Roehm Purge, which had been planned as "Operation Hummingbird" by the Nazis, actually took place over three days (from Saturday the 30th of June till Monday, the 2nd of July, 1934) with Roehm being executed on the Sunday after he refused to shoot himself.

Many past political rivals, including Kurt von **Schleicher**, were also arrested and executed. It was because most of the arrests had been planned for the early morning of the Saturday that the English-speaking press coined the infamous name "The Night of the Long Knives." (see also Ernst **Roehm**)

Franz von **Papen** (1879-1969) would later become the German ambassador to Austria whilst resigning a month before the Anschluss, as well as ambassador to Turkey. He was one of the twenty-one defendants to appear at the first of the Nuremberg Trials but was acquitted. However, he still had to do two years´ hard labor for enabling Nazism before living to the grand age of eighty-nine when he died in 1969.

the **Phoenix C.I.** was the first plane that the Austrian-Hungarian company "Phoenix Flugzeugwerke" built. Although it wasn´t introduced until the last year of the First World War in 1918 it was so successful that nearly a hundred such models were built. The Swedish army would then build another thirty of them under license.

The rather stumpy two-seater bi-plane could fly at a speed of 110 m.p.h. and climb a thousand feet within one and a half minutes.

A **Pietà** is a statue of the Virgin Mary holding the dead body of Christ after his crucifixion. The most famous Pietà was carved by Michelangelo Buonarroti (1475-1564) for a French cardinal and ambassador in Rome. It was originally shown in the old Saint Peter´s Basilica but this was demolished a few years later for the building of the new basilica of Saint Peter´s, in which it now stands.

a **Rathaus** is the German word for "town hall": that is, the seat of local government and administration. Although it literally translates as the "advice" or "council house" many English-speaking tourists think that it has something to do with the legend of the Pied Piper of Hamelin.

reconcile themselves with the split: the relationship between the two Tyrols became even closer when Austria joined the European Union in 1995, of which Italy had been a founding member. In 2011 they and the Italian region of Trentino formed a European (Union) Group of Territorial Cooperation which brought them further together.

red-white-red republic: the triband red-white-red flag of Austria dates back to the coat of arms of the House of Babenberg in the twelfth century, which preceded the House of Habsburg, who during the following century became the rulers of what is today Austria. Whilst the Babenburg colors were used to represent the country of Austria, the Habsburg´s own black and yellow flag from its dual-colored coat of arms was often flown instead on state occasions until the monarchy was abolished in 1918.

In spite of Austria later being officially known as the Republic of German Austria, the Federal State of Austria and (twice, including today) the Republic of Austria, it has kept the same Babenberg flag, making it one of the oldest flags in the world that is still in use. It was only during the Nazi era that Austria ceased to have a flag because it was now a part of the (Greater) German Reich. (see also the **white-blue men**)

Ernst **Roehm** (1887-1934) clearly had his own more leftist agenda to Hitler´s, with many of his S.A. men being from the working class. Indeed, although Hitler had originally conceived the Nazis as being a national and quasi-socialist party, he began leaning more and more to the right as he began courting the big business and industrial concerns for their donations.

Roehm also wanted to replace the much more effective and professional Wehrmacht with the S.A. for when War eventually came, which Hitler was completely against. After the Roehm Purge the S.A. was therefore down-sized into a much smaller organization, with many of its parts then being included in other Nazi organizations. (see also **one night**).

a **sacrament** is a personal holy pact with God. In the Catholic, Orthodox and Anglo-Catholic churches, as well as the Church of the Latter-Day Saints, these include baptism, confirmation, Holy Communion, penance, marriage, holy orders and the anointing of the sick. Other Dominions also often regard some or many of these rites to be sacraments, as well as sometimes others as well.

For example, the Church of the East doesn't regard marriage or the anointing of the sick to be sacraments but instead regards Leaven and the Sign of the Cross to be sacraments. The Catholic Church argues that divorce should only be permissible under special circumstances because marriage is a sacrament that should not be broken.

Saint Jerome was a fourth and fifth century Christian priest and academic who translated the Bible. He is the patron saint of Bible scholars, librarians, translators, students and also school children. In short, a learned man.

Saturnalia was in fact held just before when we now celebrate Christmas. Originally just a Roman feast day on the Seventeenth of December in honor of their god Saturn, Saturnalia gradually became a whole week of celebrations that finished on the Twenty-third. Saturn was the God of wealth and abundance, as well as agriculture and renewal, and his children included Jupiter, Neptune and Pluto.

school-free Saturday afternoon: before the late 1990s Austrian school children also had to attend lessons on Saturday mornings, although they usually got Wednesday afternoons off in lieu. After the 1990s more and more schools closed for the entire weekend, with only a handful of schools still having Saturday morning lessons today.

The **Schilling** was the currency of Austria between 1925 and 2002, with the exception of the Nazi era when it was replaced by the German Reichsmark. 100 Groschen made up a Schilling. At the time that Austria changed to the Euro in 2002 an Austria Schilling had the same value as five new pence in Britain, which was the equivalent of the old shilling that the British had used in their pre-decimal "L.S.D." system of pounds, shillings and pence until 1971.

This was the exact same system that Charlemagne had introduced into the Holy Roman Empire at the end of the eighth century, with twelve pennies in a shilling and twenty shillings in a pound. The German word for penny was "Pfennig", with 100 Pfennigs being in the Deutsche Mark until Germany also switched to the Euro in 2002.

Kurt von **Schleicher** (1882-1834) was a friend of the leader of the S.A., Ernst **Roehm**, and, like Roehm, was one of the many murdered victims of the so-called "Night of the Long Knives" of 1934. (see also **one night**)

a **schmaltzy Berlin movie** means a "soppy" or a "cheesy" Berlin movie in English. Berlin already had a large and very successful film industry before the Nazis under their Propaganda Minister Joseph Goebbels tried to control and use it. However, about 800 leading film personnel fled Nazi Germany for America, with the most famous of all probably being the singer-actress Marlene Dietrich. (see also **Luis Trenker**)

Kurt **Schuschnigg** was at first put under house arrest in a hotel in Vienna before being sent to various concentration camps as a political prisoner with prominent status. After spending two years in Italy after the War, he and his family then moved to Missouri in the U.S.A., where he worked as a professor of political science.

Although he became an American citizen in 1956 he and his wife returned to the Tyrol in 1967, where he died ten years later. Schuschnigg wasn´t allowed to join the new Austrian conservative party (the Ö.V.P. or Austrian People´s Party) because of his Austro-Fascist history and the fact that he had been jointly responsible for the execution of ten Social Democrats.

the **S.D.** was a daughter organization of the notorious **S.S.**, with its full name being the "Sicherheitsdienst des Reichsfuehrers S.S." or the "Security Service of the Reichfuehrer S.S." The Reichfuehrer S.S. was the boss of the S.S., and was none other than the psychopathic Heinrich Himmler, who organized the Holocaust and the Nuremberg Race Laws.

send us back to Austria as German citizens: Switzerland became officially neutral after the Napoleonic Wars in 1815 whilst becoming a refugee-friendly country. However, the rise of Nazi Germany put Switzerland in a difficult position as a huge exodus of refugees from that country and its later conquered territories began.

Switzerland had had its own share of severe economic difficulties in the 1930s whilst also feeling that it had to appease the Third Reich in many respects if it were to avoid the real threat of invasion by it. As such Switzerland´s refugee laws kept becoming increasingly stricter, with tens of thousands of refugees being turned back at its borders.

A **sovereign state** is a country that has total control over its own laws without, theoretically, outside influence from other countries. Like Germany, Austria had been occupied and divided into four zones by the four Allied forces – the U.S.A., Britain, France and Russia – even though Russia had claimed that the Austrians had been victims of Naziism and not perpetuators of it.

After ten years of Occupation the Austrian State Treaty was signed by Austria and the Allies on May 15th, 1955. It was agreed that, in return for the Allied forces leaving before the 26th of October, Austria would promise to be "permanently neutral" and not try to re-unite with Germany. Because being "permanently neutral" was meant only in the military sense, Austria was able to join the European Union in 1995.

Of course, countries that join economic unions like the European Union naturally give up a certain amount of their sovereignty in return for tangible benefits. This is the same as an individual joining a club with certain obligations so that he can enjoy amenities that only the club can offer.

South Tyrol: Following the so-called Hitler-Mussolini Agreement of 1939 all German South Tyroleans were given the choice of deciding whether they were German or Italian citizens. It was in fact a lose-lose situation because the first choice meant that they would have to move to (North) Tyrol and the second south of the River Po in Italy.

Either way they were losing their traditional homeland and identity.

The **S.S.** is short for "Schutzstaffel", which means "Protection Squadron". Beginning as a simple group of volunteers to protect Nazi members at party meetings during the 1920s, it soon became an elite paramilitary organization that was superior to the much larger S.A. of the Nazi Party.

Once the Nazis came to power in 1933, the S.S. quickly developed into a large security and intelligence organization of its own. Run by two of the most ruthless of the Nazis, Heinrich Himmler and Reinhard **Heydrich**, its name was as much feared as the Gestapo whilst also carrying out the Crystal Night.

a **Staendestaat** or "corporate state" is a state that is governed by its various corporate and state interest groups, especially those that represent trade, commerce and industry, as well as culture and the sciences. All citizens are categorized according to their professional groups and should be able to vote for representatives accordingly.

When the new Constitution came into force in May, 1934, Austria officially changed its name from the Republic of Austria to the Federal State of Austria whilst being colloquially known as the "Staendestaat". (see also **Mussolini´s fascism**)

"**Stille Nacht**" or "Silent Night" was composed in 1818 in the Austrian village of Oberndorf in Salzburg Land when the organ broke down on Christmas Eve. The impromptu piece was therefore written for the guitar by Franz Xaver Gruber, with the lyrics by Joseph Mohr. It has since become one of the most recognizable and perhaps the most loved Christmas carol of all in the entire world.

Ten Little Indians: the song that Dani remembers is not the original version (which is just a counting rhyme) but an 1868 minstrel version, in which the destinies of each Indian are accounted for. Whilst the 1868 version was called "Ten Little Injuns" the original song used the extremely derogatory and racist name of "niggers".

In fact, Agatha Christie even called her 1939 mystery novel "Ten Little Niggers", even though its plot was based on the 1868 "Ten Little Injuns" song. It was not until 1985, nine years after her death, that her British publishers changed the title of her book to "Ten Little Indians".

The Americans, meanwhile, had always instead used the title "And then there were None", being the last half-line of the minstrel song. When the book was made into a movie in 1945 under this same name a new and darker version of the minstrels' song was written for it.

twenty-four of them: fifteen of them were later pardoned so that nine were in fact executed.

The **W150 version of the 770 Mercedes-Benz** was the second series of this 770 model, being produced between 1938 and 1944, whereas the first series (the W07) had been produced between 1933 and 1938. The 770 Mercedes-Benz was also known as the "Large Mercedes" because of its huge size, with 205 cars being produced as four- or six-seat limousines, six-seat touring cars and also as cabriolets. The W150 was a literal big favorite of top Nazis and other Axis leaders.

the **white-blue men:** whereas the colors of the Austrian flag are three horizontal red-white-red stripes (whilst the Habsburg flag had two horizontal black-yellow stripes) the Bavarian flag was and still is either two horizontal white-blue stripes or the much more loved version of alternating white and blue diamonds. (see also **red-white-red republic**)

The **Wipptal** (or Wipp Valley) is the name of both of the two valleys along which the Brenner Pass road and railway today run. Spanning a total length of forty-three miles, the northern valley runs through the (North) Tyrol from Innsbruck to the top of the Brenner Pass, whilst the southern valley runs through the South Tyrol before joining up with the Eisack valley. Whilst the main river of the northern Wipptal is the Sill, the main river of the southern Wipptal is the Eisack.

Bibliography

I used the following books for the research for this story. Most of them are published only in German.

Michael Forcher "Kleine Geschichte Tirols" (Haymon Taschenbücher)

Michael Forcher "Geschichte der Stadt Innsbruck" (Haymon Verlag)

Michael Forcher "Tirols Geschichte in Wort und Bild" (Haymon Verlag)

Sabine Pitscheider "Seefeld in Tirol in der NS-Zeit" (Studien Verlag)

Lukas Morscher "Innsbrucker Alltagsleben 1930-80" (Haymon Verlag)

Horst Schreiber "1938: Der Anschluss in den Bezirken Tirols" (Studien Verlag)

Thomas Albrich "Luftkrieg über der Alpenfestung 1943-1945 Wort und Bild" (Universitäts Verlag Wagner)

Johannes Breit "Das Gestapo-Lager Innsbruck-Reichenau" (Tyrolia Verlag)

Peter Pirker and Matthias Breit "Schnappschüss der Befreiung" (Tyrolia Verlag)

Peter Pirker "Codename Brooklyn" (Tyrolia Verlag)

"Timeline" also has an excellent video in "YouTube" about Fred Mayer and his part in "Operation Greenup" and which is called "The Real Inglorious Basterds"

About the Author

Rabbit Warren is the author of two historic novels about the Nazis and two books of short stories of the supernatural and sinister, as well as a pair of light-hearted autobiographies of his life´s dreams and travels and eight children´s fantasies.

Born and raised in England, Rabbit Warren has lived most of his adult life living in the Swiss, German and Austrian Alps, whilst both training and working as a chef, pastry chef, children´s entertainer and magic clown. He is now a naturalized Austrian and lives in Innsbruck.

Also by Rabbit Warren

Let Sleeping Nazis Lie

The psycho-spy thriller of a man during the fall of the Iron Curtain in 1989 who confronts his memories of the ghastly Dresden bombings of 1945 before discovering an awful secret about his Nazi youth – with a time machine.

The Madman and other Tales with a Chilling Twist

Ranging from gruesome shockers to tragic mistakes to black humor, this is a cornucopia of richly assorted shockers of ghosts, murderers, aliens, pirates and time-travel that each end with a chilling twist.

Tragic and Twisted Tales of Unexpected Death

Including heart-breaking tragedies, ghastly experiments and cold-blooded revenge, these assorted tales are so peppered with surprises and twists that the reader will be kept busy guessing what each cruel ending might be.

My Dreams and Travels

In this prequel to "My Dreams in the Alps", Rabbit Warren describes, with many amusing anecdotes, how he discovered his first dreams whilst at school in England of being a writer and working with children, before then also realizing his dream of travelling and living in the Alps, as well as returning shortly to Britain.

My Dreams in the Alps

In this sequel to "My Dreams and Travels", Rabbit Warren describes with even more amusing anecdotes how he finally fulfilled his "Alpine Dream" by training as both a chef and a pastry chef in the Bavarian Alps, as well as then also becoming a children´s entertainer and a magic clown in the Austrian Tyrol.

Children's Fantasies by Rabbit Warren

THE FANTASTIC WORLD OF BOZ, a time-travel fantasy with Charles Dickens (10 years up)

THE CURSE OF GRIFFIN GEORGE, a comic horror fantasy (9 years up)

BIG BLOKE AND THE NIGHTMARE ALIENS, a sci-fi fantasy (9 years up)

CHARMING STINKERS, an historic fantasy (9 years up)

GOGONUTS, a comic fantasy (8 years up)

THE GREMLIN OF NOGOLAND, an adventure fantasy (8 years up)

THE PIXIE´S MAGIC CHRISTMAS, a toy fantasy (7 years up)

ESCAPE TO THE DREAM KING, a fairytale fantasy (7 years up)

All books are available at Amazon on Kindle and as both paperbacks and hardbacks.

www.rogerhase.com

Printed in Great Britain
by Amazon